UNSOLVED, COLD-CASE
HOMICIDES

UNSOLVED, COLD-CASE HOMICIDES OF LAW ENFORCEMENT OFFICERS

JAMES BULTEMA

ALSO BY JAMES BULTEMA

The Protectors: A Photographic History of Police Departments in the United States

Guardians of Angels: A History of the Los Angeles Police Department

Documentary: Behind the Badge: An Insiders History of the Los Angeles Police Department

ABOUT THE AUTHOR

Historian and former cop James Bultema knows about policing in America. He is the author of the acclaimed books, *Guardians of Angels: A History of the Los Angeles Police Department* and *The Protectors: A Photographic History of Police Departments in the United States*. Current LAPD Chief of Police Charlie Beck and former New York City Police Commissioner William Bratton thought so much of what Bultema had accomplished that they each wrote a foreword for these histories. For his new book, *Unsolved: Cold-Case Homicides of Law Enforcement Officers*, Bultema has compiled the first comprehensive national compendium of unsolved cases, including information on each fallen officer and, in many cases, an informed account of the officer's murder. *Unsolved* is a touching tribute to these courageous law enforcement officers. Bultema is retired from the Los Angeles Police Department and lives in Arizona with his wife of 46 years.

COPYRIGHT

Copyright © 2018 by James Bultema All rights reserved.

ISBN-13 (trade softcover): 978-0997425-11-6
ISBN-13 (Ebook): 978-09974251-12-3

In accordance with the U.S. Copyright Act of 1976, the scanning, uploading, and electronic sharing of any part of this book without permission of the publisher constitute unlawful piracy and theft of the author's intellectual property. No part of this book may be reproduced or transmitted in any form or by any means, electronic or mechanical, including photocopying, recording, or by any information storage and retrieval system, except for excerpts used for reviews, without permission in writing from the publisher.

Edited by Craig Young.
Published by P.D. Publishing
Printed by IngramSpark
Cover and Interior Design WSDG Design

Library of Congress Control Number:
2018930651

www.policehistorybyjamesbultema.com.
policehistoryjamesbultema@gmail.com.

(928) 607.1210.

DEDICATION

To all the law enforcement officers who have laid down their lives and whose murders remain unsolved.

and

To the surviving family members who must continue with their lives without the loved ones whom they cherish.

One heartfelt note exemplifies this point, written publicly by the still grieving daughter of Detective Raymond Gonser, 38 years after her dad's unsolved murder:

> *I am very proud of my dad. We all know about the ultimate sacrifice a police officer makes; his family, in a way, makes the same sacrifice because we no longer have our loved one. I wish he could have seen his children grow up and, now, see his grandchildren and great-grandchildren. How proud he would be to see how his family has flourished. To know that his murderer is walking free is gut wrenching. His murderer has had to live with himself/herself for all their living days with his death on their conscience. I live with it as a reality. There will always be a hole in my heart for my dad no matter how long it has been since he's been gone. He will never be forgotten. He is always in my thoughts. Thanks for keeping us in your prayers. I love you Dad!!!!*

ACKNOWLEDGMENTS

I want to recognize the Officer Down Memorial Page for their stellar work in documenting America's fallen law enforcement heroes since 1791. A truly commendable undertaking. And likewise to the National Law Enforcement Officers Memorial Fund (and soon the National Law Enforcement Museum), for the very thorough records of officers killed in the line of duty. Both of these institutions records were a significant aid in my research for Unsolved.

I want to mention those individuals who helped in bringing this book to fruition. A special thank you to Debi Libonati who was the secretary to numerous police chiefs while serving on the Denver Police Department. Also thank you to retired Denver police Lt. Bill Finch, for his insight in the Kathleen Garcia murder (chapter 74).

A thank you to retired Detective Tom Lange of the Los Angeles Police Department for taking time to read my manuscript and writing a review—a great friend and a great detective. To Tobi Wallingford, the daughter of slain LAPD Officer Michael Edwards, (chapter 68) for providing me her valuable knowledge on the case—my heart goes out to you for your loss.

Lastly, a sincere thank you to my editor, Craig Young who has toiled over all three of my books. As always he continues to do a fabulous job. And to my sister, Judy Styburski, who I discovered at the last moment has a sharp eye in spotting those errors that sneak into what you think is a finished book. Thanks Sis! And to the woman of my life for not only putting up with my endless hours in my office, but taking the time out of her busy life to proof read the manuscript. Thank you Carole. And I would be remiss if I did not point out that any errors belong to me—I have no excuses.

TABLE OF CONTENTS

INTRODUCTION XV

CHAPTER 1 1
The First

CHAPTER 2 4
"I am going to kill you"

CHAPTER 3 6
Hobos

CHAPTER 4 9
"I told you I'd get the son of a bitch"

CHAPTER 5 13
The Frontier Sheriff

CHAPTER 6 16
"Oh, Paul, help me, I'm hurt"

CHAPTER 7 20
Victim of a Strike

CHAPTER 8 23
An Unsolved Homicide That Time Forgot

CHAPTER 9 26
The Truant Officer

CHAPTER 10 28
"Blackie"

CHAPTER 11 31
An Assassin on the Loose

CHAPTER 12 34
The Jungle

CHAPTER 13 36
"Tell all the boys goodbye. I had bad luck"

CHAPTER 14 40

"Don't get excited; we're officers of the law"

CHAPTER 15 43
"If I had only been a little quicker"

CHAPTER 16 47
"There was another report and a spurt of flame from the revolver"

CHAPTER 17 50
"Walk in the paths of righteousness"

CHAPTER 18 53
"Beware! The last notice!"

CHAPTER 19 57
"He got what was coming to him"

CHAPTER 20 59
"Killed on a footbridge over English Ditch"

CHAPTER 21 64
"The other fellow shot me from behind"

CHAPTER 22 69
A Long Death

CHAPTER 23 72
The Second Deadliest Day in Law Enforcement History

CHAPTER 24 76
"Ma"

CHAPTER 25 79
"Negro cop shot by white man"

CHAPTER 26 81
The Colorado Rangers

CHAPTER 27 83
"Killed by thugs"

CHAPTER 28 86
"Iowa City cop is killed in chase"

CHAPTER 29 89
A Casual Drive Turned Deadly

CHAPTER 30 92
"I'm afraid the bootleggers are going to get me."

CHAPTER 31 95
"My God, I'm shot"

CHAPTER 32 98
The Secret Boarder

CHAPTER 33 102
Prohibition Party Takes Life of Town Marshal

CHAPTER 34 105
"The Skipper"

CHAPTER 35 109
The Bootlegger's Car

CHAPTER 36 112
Rumrunners

CHAPTER 37 115
A Small City Marshal

CHAPTER 38 118
Killed By One of His Own?

CHAPTER 39 125
The Man With the Keys

CHAPTER 40 128
"Two men in black Ford. Shot sheriff, myself"

CHAPTER 41 133
The Traveling Tent Show

CHAPTER 42 136
The Bomb Squad

CHAPTER 43 .... **140**
"Look out Charlie! He looks bad"

CHAPTER 44 .... **142**
More Than Deposits and Withdrawals

CHAPTER 45 .... **146**
A Day Off

CHAPTER 46 .... **148**
A Thanksgiving Day Robbery

CHAPTER 47 .... **151**
The Unassuming Sheriff

CHAPTER 48 .... **155**
An Alibi for Murder

CHAPTER 49 .... **161**
The Politically Motivated Killings of Two Deputies

CHAPTER 50 .... **164**
"Just give me a minute"

CHAPTER 51 .... **167**
"Beat No. 2"

CHAPTER 52 .... **169**
The Killing of a Small-Town Marshal

CHAPTER 53 .... **172**
The Fight for Integration

CHAPTER 54 .... **176**
The Prowler

CHAPTER 55 .... **179**
A Department That Refuses to Forget

CHAPTER 56 .... **182**
The TSU Riot

CHAPTER 57 .... **185**
The Recreation Building

CHAPTER 58 189
    The Black Panthers

CHAPTER 59 193
    The Chief Who Fought a Town Gang

CHAPTER 60 197
    "We will never give up"

CHAPTER 61 201
    A Case for the President

CHAPTER 62 206
    Ambush

CHAPTER 63 210
    Tragedy Inspires Success for Daughter

CHAPTER 64 213
    Ambushed at Home

CHAPTER 65 215
    "Fred"

CHAPTER 66 219
    The Black Liberation Army

CHAPTER 67 224
    Kidnapped

CHAPTER 68 227
    "Who executed Mike?"

CHAPTER 69 233
    An Off-Duty Barbecue Turns Tragic

CHAPTER 70 236
    Three Paths to the Killing of a Police Officer

CHAPTER 71 240
    The Off-Duty Job

CHAPTER 72 243
    A Mysterious Death

CHAPTER 73 246
  An Unsolved Homicide Solved?

CHAPTER 74 250
  The Neighbor

CHAPTER 75 254
  Protecting Our Nation's Buildings

CHAPTER 76 256
  "I've always wanted the death penalty. He needs to die"

CHAPTER 77 259
  Ambush of a Park Police Officer

CHAPTER 78 261
  Suicide or Murder

CHAPTER 79 266
  Double Jeopardy

CHAPTER 80 271
  Airport Police Killing Left Few Clues

CHAPTER 81 273
  Burglary or Setup?

CHAPTER 82 276
  "Inconclusive"

CHAPTER 83 281
  One That Got Away

CHAPTER 84 285
  "Don't move or I'll bust a cap in you"

CHAPTER 85 288
  The Sniper Shooting of a Chief of Police

CHAPTER 86 292
  "Show me out with three"

CHAPTER 87 297
  Always on Duty

CHAPTER 88 300
   The Case of the White Van

CHAPTER 89 303
   Sacred Ground

CHAPTER 90 308
   "If I get stopped, I'm gonna kill the cop"

CHAPTER 91 316
   Murder or Suicide—Which Was It?

CHAPTER 92 321
   "Daddy is not coming back"

APPENDIX I 325

   Unsolved Homicides of Law Enforcement Officers (Confirmed)
      Research Notes
      Research Suggestions
      Key Facts And Data

APPENDIX II 348

   Year-by-Year Breakdown of U.S. Law Enforcement Deaths Compared to Unsolved Law Enforcement Homicides

INDEX 351

INTRODUCTION

Law enforcement officers make their living fighting crime. They have taken an oath to protect the citizens of their community, county and state, and they will do whatever it takes to fulfill their sworn duty. Yet for many of these brave men and women, the battle of good versus evil means the ultimate sacrifice—laying down their lives in the unconditional fulfillment of their duty.

The death of an officer killed while on duty presents the most heartfelt crisis an agency can face. When an officer is struck down, the death sends shock waves reverberating throughout the department and the community he or she served. Law enforcement agencies make it the highest priority to solve the case and bring the murderers to justice. But it is not a perfect world, and sometimes, but not many, they are not successful.

What was first an unbearable loss of a brother or sister officer swells into a mountain of guilt and remorse when a killer avoids capture. Many in the law enforcement community experience survivor guilt, believing they had done something wrong or they could have done more. Some officers cry out, "This just couldn't happen!" Many will suffer nightmares and flashbacks to the tragic event. The loss of a brother or sister officer is something that never leaves your soul.

Investigations of homicides of law enforcement officers are not unlike a roaring river, which can become a trickle as it passes through a dam. Clues in the murder of a police officer come thundering in by the hundreds the first few weeks and then become a dribble the following month. Front-page stories fade to the back of the paper and then are gone altogether. Rewards are posted, government officials cry out for justice and television stations run the story—for a time. Soon weeks turn to months, and before you know it, years have melted away. But there is one given that is the same in virtually all unsolved police cases—no matter how stale things get, the detectives investigating the case will never give up. Never. Even though many will promote, retire and die, there are others coming up through the ranks who will take over the reins of the investigation and keep fighting to identify the perpetrators.

These dedicated and savvy detectives handling cold-case files become very creative in generating new interest in cases that are long forgotten by most. Decades after the 1967 murder of Officer Walter Franklin Stathers (chapter 54), detectives from the Miami-Dade Police Department conducted a detailed reenactment of the murder, going so far as to finding an old Plymouth police cruiser like the one Stathers was driving the night he was murdered. Consequently, the story was run on all the local stations offering investigators hope that someone might come forward and turn the tide in the case.

New investigators look at long-unsolved homicides with fresh eyes and with renewed energy. They reinterview witnesses, run DNA samples through crime labs, mail out letters to those witnesses who are difficult to locate. They may erect billboards highlighting an officer's murder to get people talking about the case again. They do this with the hope, and many times with prayers, that the one break they need in the case will occur, no matter how long ago the crime took place. Such was the situation in the murder of two police officers from the El Segundo, California, Police Department.

In 1957, two young police officers, Richard Phillips and Milton Curtis, were shot and killed after stopping a vehicle for running a red light. What the officers didn't know was that the driver had just raped a teenage girl after robbing the two young couples at gunpoint. Detectives had no leads in the case until 1960, when two watches and a gun were recovered in the backyard of a Manhattan Beach, California, home.

It was determined that the watches had been stolen from two of the teenagers. The gun was traced back to Louisiana. But there the trail went dead—again. Moving ahead 40 years, basically two police generations, investigators finally got a break when a tipster provided the name of the alleged killer. The tip proved false, but as a result, detectives took a closer look at the case. Aware that the FBI had just released a new computerized database for fingerprints collected across the nation, detectives decided to submit the fingerprints they had on file.

It worked! The prints led to Columbia, South Carolina, where in 2003, 45 years after the murders, police arrested Gerald F. Mason, a 68-year-old retired gas station owner living in a comfortable suburban home of the city. In 2003, the suspect was convicted of both murders and through a plea agreement, the remaining counts of rape, robbery and kidnapping were dismissed. Mason was sentenced to life in prison.

This is one of the reasons for this book. By breathing new life into these unsolved homicides of police officers, justice may be served and the perpetrators finally made to pay for their gutless acts. When I decided to research this subject, I was appalled to discover that there was no centralized database that listed the name of each officer killed in the line of duty and the disposition of the case. While the FBI does maintain records going back to the 1980s, no agency has a definitive listing of the names of these brave officers, their departments and the basic information about the cases since the beginning of policing in the United States. After two years of comprehensive research, I have been able to document the sacrifices of these officers and put them in one place—this book.

However, there still are serious problems. In my research, I have identified 708 unsolved cases where it is nearly certain that the suspects were not apprehended. But I also identified an additional 1,052 cases where the outcome is unclear. For example, some officers are listed as killed in the line of duty but with no additional information. Because many of these murders occurred long ago, documentation is very difficult, if not impossible, to locate. In too many cases, the scant records state that officer so-and-so was killed outside a bar or in a fight with a drunk. And that is it—one sentence to describe the death of an officer in the line of duty. There is no mention of the circumstances or if the suspects were taken into custody. Nothing.

Still other cases, including some much more recent, do list the circumstances but fail to mention the disposition of the suspects. These cases can be investigated, but the time required would be too burdensome for one individual. That is why I am hopeful that each agency I have listed on my web page (www.unsolvedpolicehomicides.com) will take the time to identify a fallen comrade's case and determine exactly what happened as well as the disposition of the suspects. Were they arrested, did they escape, were they tried and found not guilty or convicted? With that completed, the information could be shared with me so I might update the master list and post the information online.

It is the very least we can do for these heroic officers who made the absolute sacrifice. And who knows where this might lead? When an unsolved law enforcement murder is cleared by an arrest, our family can celebrate and be stronger before moving on to the next one. We can never give up if there is hope that the killers can be brought to justice.

To the living we owe respect, but to the dead we owe only the truth.

—*Voltaire*

CHAPTER 1

The First

THE OFFICER:

Watchman Joseph Stoddard*
Cincinnati (Ohio) Police Department
End of Watch: Friday, September 10, 1852
Age: Not available

There inevitable had to be a first—the first Unsolved homicide of an American lawman. When Cincinnati incorporated as a village in 1802, it established a night watch. The primary duty of the watchman is to guard against fire, but just as important, to ensure the peace and safety of the community. The Cincinnati Police Department formed in 1859.

During the early-morning hours of Friday, September 10, 1852, Third Ward Watchman Joseph Stoddard was on patrol when he heard a loud commotion coming from the Blue Anchor Saloon on Front Street near Washington Street. Stoddard knew the bar well, as it was frequented by some of the most hard-core criminals of Cincinnati.

As Stoddard entered, the man responsible for the disturbance saw him, and took off through a side door. The watchman chased the suspect but lost him in a clump of bushes. Quickly forming a plan of action, Stoddard reported to his watch lieutenant and explained what had happened. Stoddard believed that the suspect was a counterfeiter. He asked the lieutenant if he could skip the end of watch roll call so that he could search the bushes to see what the man might have hidden. After that he would go home and return the next day to report the results of his investigation. The lieutenant agreed.

That was the last time anyone reported seeing Stoddard alive. At 5 a.m., a passer-by reported seeing a man who appeared to have been stabbed to death on Pearson Street between Third and Front streets, which was close to Stoddard's home. The night lieutenant responded and found Watchman Stoddard stabbed in the abdomen, lying in a gutter. Stoddard had fired his sidearm once, but no blood trail could be found.

It was later determined that Stoddard had been investigating William F. Chaffee (or Schee) for counterfeiting. Stoddard was due to meet the suspect the next morning. Chaffee was picked up and brought before the law of the city —the mayor, who promptly acquitted the man. After Chaffee's release, officers learned that the man who had run from the bar was Louis Dollman, another notorious counterfeiter. Besides making fake money, the suspect was also wanted for train robbery. Officials tracked him down in St. Louis, Missouri. When lawmen attempted to arrest him, Dollman pulled a gun and was killed. Although police believed Dollman might have been Stoddard's murderer, it was never determined if he was the guilty party. Consequently, the case was never solved.

Watchman Stoddard was survived by his wife and a large family, which was left destitute without his paycheck. Stoddard's funeral was one of the largest in the history of the city, with more than 800 police officers and firemen attending. It was never stated, but my guess is that a collection would have been taken up and given to the family. There were seven officers killed in the line of duty in the United States in 1852; Stoddard's was the first unsolved police homicide in law enforcement history that I have been able to uncover.

***Author's note**: Over the years, the Cincinnati Police Department had two listings of officers being killed near this time, "John Strother" in 1846 and "Joseph Stowder" in 1852. Through its research, the Greater Cincinnati Police Historical Society determined that just one officer, Joseph Stoddard or Joseph Stowder, died during this period, in 1852. Newspaper accounts of the day additionally gave the watchman's name as "Joseph Strowder" and "Joseph Strawder." City directories list "Stowders" on Front Street, where the watchman was reported to have lived.

SOURCES:

- https://www.odmp.org/officer/21547-watchman-joseph-stoddard/
- http://police-museum.org/line-of-duty/19th-century/patrolman-joseph-stoddard-cincinnati-police-department/

CHAPTER 2

"I am going to kill you"

THE OFFICER:

Special Officer Hank Frost
Nogales Police Department, Arizona Territory
End of Watch: Sunday, December 30, 1888
Age: Unknown

Officer Hank Frost was the law in Nogales, Arizona Territory, located just a stone's throw from Sonora, Mexico. Early in 1880, the town was established around a trading camp. The post office, which gave identity to a city, came in three years later. The border was wide open, and travelers moved freely between the United States and Mexico—including criminals. Arizona would eventually become a state in 1912.

On Monday, November 11, 1888, Special Officer Frost was busy arresting a loudmouth drunken gambler who was disturbing the peace. In those days, most departments could not afford police wagons, so officers had to walk, and many times drag their arrestees to jail. Along the way, friends, angry citizens and the like could intervene and the journey could become a perilous one.

As Frost was escorting "Antonio" to jail, the gambler pulled a knife and tried to stab him. Officer Frost reacted quickly, pulled his gun and shot the man dead. Not an uncommon night in the life of a Western lawman.

A month and a half later, Hank Frost was keeping warm by the stove in Crystal Palace saloon. At about noon, a "Mexican curbstone gambler" by the name of Doroteo Mejia, walked deliberately up to the seated Frost and proclaimed, "You (curse words omitted), you killed my friend, and I am going to kill you." With that, Mejia pulled a revolver and fired three shots into Officer Frost, killing him almost instantly. The assassin then ran out of the saloon, "across the line," where he paraded back and forth, with pistol in hand, screaming for anyone to hear that Frost had killed his friend and so he killed Frost in return. After a short time, the bandit faded into the depths of Mexico and was never heard from again. There was no arrest, and the case remains unsolved.

Very little is known about Hank Frost. What we do know is that he lived in Nogales in 1876 per the census, which only listed him by name and did not give any further details, and that Frost served in the United States Army. Nothing else about him has surfaced. There are no newspaper accounts of his murder, his burial, his life or his background. Like so many others from the era, he is just a statistic and another unsolved homicide of a lawman whose job was to protect the citizens of Nogales.

Nogales, Santa Cruz County, showing boundary between Arizona Territory and Mexico. General view of town from hillside, looking west along International Street. Circa 1899. Library of Congress.

SOURCES:

➡ Newspapers.com
➡ Ancestory.com
➡ http://www.odmp.org/officer/5149-special-officer-hank-frost

CHAPTER 3

Hobos

THE OFFICER:

Patrolman Jacob Neibert
Muscatine (Iowa) Police Department
End of Watch: Saturday, June 13, 1896
Age: 55

Patrolman Jacob Neibert walked past the Hershey Lumber Company every day when going to and from work as a patrolman for the Muscatine Police Department. It was also a place he used to work. He would have no idea that this was also where his life would end.

It was in the early morning hours of Saturday, June 13, 1896, that Neibert was walking his footbeat on Muscatine's streets overlooking the Mississippi River. As he was passing the Hershey Lumber Company, he spotted two tramps loitering. It was not unusual to come across transients on his beat. He probably thought, here are two more that I will be taking to jail in the police wagon.

As he approached the men, things quickly went sideways as the two attacked Neibert, pulled a gun, and shot the officer in the abdomen. As they ran, Neibert remained calm, pulled his gun and shot back at the fleeing tramps. It appeared to the dying officer that he may have hit one. With the sound of gunfire cutting through the quiet of the night, help arrived quickly from the station a mile away.

Neibert would die 10 minutes after being shot, but before he did, he muttered that the suspects were "hobos." Responding officers discovered a blood trail leading from the crime scene. They followed it for a mile before they lost track of it. Muscatine County Sheriff H.E. Wiley wasted no time in forming a posse to search for the suspects. Bloodhounds were also brought in from a neighboring town, but the trail had grown cold, and the dogs could not get a scent. The posse also had no luck.

The consensus of the investigators was that the fleeing suspects, one no doubt with a bullet wound, jumped onto a train as indicated by the direction they had run. The theory was given credibility when a train conductor, "Kile," discovered a hobo bleeding from the head and his hands and kicked him off train at Fruitland, Iowa, 10 miles southwest of Muscatine.

A break in the case occurred four days later when officials from Monmouth, Illinois, arrested a man who had a bandaged hand and fit the description of one of the suspects. The mayor and marshal of Muscatine traveled to Monmouth, where they took the suspect into custody. One witness to the arrest of the hobo was a reporter from a newspaper who noted:

> *"The [hobo] denied ever having been in Muscatine in his life and assumed a total ignorance of the murder [but] he was very nervous and as he saw the crowd gather at the depot to take a look at him his eyes nearly popped out of his head he was so greatly excited."*

Other onlookers could see that the man had a cut on his forehead and another down the side of his face and a wound to his hand. The suspect was thoroughly questioned and shown to witnesses for identification purposes, but no one could identify him. Consequently, the man was released.

With no arrest made and hopes dimming each day that there ever would be, the editor of the Cedar Rapids Evening Gazette let the community know just how he and others felt:

> *Women will send him bouquets in jail and some attorney will be found who for $25, more or less, cash in hand will do his utmost to set the ravening beast again at liberty among defenseless people. Nine chances in ten the tramp would not be convicted of murder in the first degree, and if, under the tenth chance, he was so convicted the chance would again be nine to one that he would be pardoned or have his sentence commuted.*

Asinine legislatures do nothing to abate the menace. They are too busy with some political scheme and too much afraid of losing the vote of someone, who from ignorance or sympathy espouses the cause of the tramp.

Jacob Neibert was born in Germany in 1847 and immigrated to the United States in 1859. Neibert served his adopted county during the Civil War in the 35th Iowa Volunteer Infantry. After his first wife died, he married again in 1876; they had no children. His brother served on the Muscatine Fire Department and would later become chief.

The current location of the Hershey Lumber Company and the scene where Patrolman Neibert was slain.

SOURCES:

- Nancy Bowers, author, Iowa "Unsolved Murders: Historic Cases." http://www.iowaunsolvedmurders.com/the-murders/lumberyard-tramps-murder-of-officer-jacob-neibert-1896/
- The Carroll Sentinel, June 15, 19, 1896
- The Davenport Democrat and Leader, July 16, 18, 1896
- Cedar Rapids Evening Gazette, June 13, 16, 1896
- https://www.odmp.org/officer/17150-police-officer-jacob-neibert

CHAPTER 4

"I told you I'd get the son of a bitch"

THE OFFICER:

Assistant Marshal Pitt McClellan Doxsie
Independence (Iowa) Police Department
Date of Incident: Sunday, October 24, 1897
End of Watch: Tuesday, October 26, 1897
Age: 34

In the late 1890s, Independence, Iowa, became known as the "Lexington of the North" for its unusual kite-shaped horse track. So many race fans attended these horse races that a special trolley system was built to accommodate them. But with prosperity came criminals who demanded a cut of the action. During 1897, local police were pursing a network of gangs who were responsible for numerous burglaries and robberies around Independence.

Well aware of these crime trends, Assistant Marshal Pitt Doxsie was making his rounds through the business district early Sunday morning, October 24, 1897. As he was weaving his way in and out of the alleys, he ran into his boss, town Marshal W.M. Higbee, who happened to be walking to a social club. After a short conversation, both lawmen continued on their way.

It was pitch-black in the city, as the streetlights were turned off at this hour of the night. To compensate, Marshal Doxsie illuminated his path with a lantern. At 12:45 a.m., Doxsie turned down the alley behind what is now First Avenue West. Devoured by the total blackness of the alley, Doxsie stopped when he believed he saw two men prying open the back door to W.H. Littell's clothing store.

Doxsie drew his .38 caliber revolver while attempting to illuminate the area with his lantern. As he crept closer, he saw two men duck behind a stairway. He yelled out, asking what they were doing. His answer came in a flurry of bullets aimed right at him. Out in the open, the exposed marshal could only return fire toward the muzzle flashes, as he could not see anything else. Firing five rounds from his service revolver, Doxsie went down when he was struck in his right leg, just below the knee. The two men ran from the area.

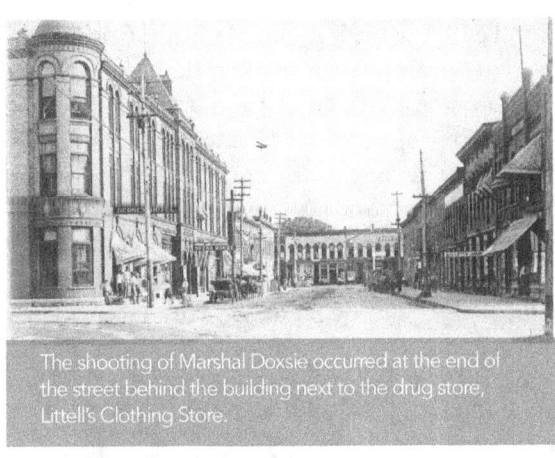

The shooting of Marshal Doxsie occurred at the end of the street behind the building next to the drug store, Littell's Clothing Store.

Unable to walk and bleeding profusely, the brave marshal dragged himself to the front of a cigar store and yelled for help. About the same time, Marshal Higbee, who had talked with Doxsie earlier, was leaving the social club and heard a cry for help. He ran to the location, only 100 feet away, and found his deputy lying on the sidewalk, bleeding heavily. Other citizens arrived at the same time. One of the men held up Doxsie's head and asked who had done this to him. His only reply was that it was too dark and that he could only make out shadows. A group of citizens carried the wounded marshal to his home.

Marshal Higbee began a preliminary investigation into the shooting, tracking the blood backwards from the cigar store to the alley and to the rear of the Littell Store. There he found a large pool of blood marking the spot where Doxsie had gone down. Higbee discovered the stairway where the burglary suspects hid and found bullet damage around the area. He located rounds in the wooden post, the stairway and the windows of the neighboring shop. He determined the burglars fired 12 shots and Doxsie five.

Buchanan County Sheriff Clyde Iliff was called in, and with the help of several deputies, he tracked a blood trail leading away from the alley to a bridge along a wagon road about a mile or so east of town. It became evident that Marshal Doxsie had managed to shoot at least one of the suspects.

At first his injuries were thought not to be life-threatening, but the bullet had struck an artery. With the large loss of blood, Doxsie passed away two days later. The marshal left behind three young children under the age of four, including one newborn, as he gave his life in the line of duty.

A week after his murder, the Independence City Council voted to hire a Pinkerton detective from Chicago. Only in town a few days, the detective shocked many when he claimed he knew who the two murderers were, based on his own investigation. The brash detective said they were two local men: John L. "Jack" McGready, a 27-year-old blacksmith, and his buddy Joseph "Joe" Hurley, age 19. It was reported that both were "desperate characters." McGready, the local paper stated, was "a morphine fiend, and shows plainly the effects of his being deprived of the use of the narcotic during his confinement."

Assistant Marshal Pitt McClellan Doxsie
Independence (Iowa) Police Department

During their separate interrogations, the men made conflicting statements about the Town Marshal W.M. Higbee, who assisted in the early investigation of the shooting. began five weeks after the shooting. Everyone retained an attorney. A man who ran a livery barn testified that he was at his business the morning after the shooting and saw McGready walk past and stop to talk with a local resident. The witness said he overheard McGready claim, "I told you I'd get the son of a bitch, and I got him." A second witness added that he heard McGready state, "Doxsie got his needlings [sic]."

No one came forward to put McGready in downtown Independence the night of the shooting, although one witness reported seeing his buddy, Hurley, at 10 p.m. Both had strong alibis and the charges were dismissed because of insufficient evidence to present to the grand jury. No suspects were ever convicted for the killing of Doxsie, and the case remains unsolved.

SOURCES:

- Nancy Bowers, "Iowa Unsolved Murders: Historic Cases." http://www.iowaunsolvedmurders.com/the-murders/down-in-the-dark-murder-of-officer-pitt-m-doxsie-1897/
- https://iowacoldcases.org/tag/iowas-fallen-police-officers/
- http://www.dps.state.ia.us/commis/pib/ipom/Line_of_duty_deaths.shtml
- http://www.odmp.org/search?cause=gunfire&state=iowa&o=75
- Ancestry.com
- Newspapers.com

CHAPTER 5

The Frontier Sheriff

THE OFFICER:

Sheriff George T. Young
Park County (Montana) Sheriff's Office
End of Watch: Friday, November 9, 1900
Age: 44

Grabbing the local headlines away from the 1900 presidential election held just three days earlier was the shooting death of a popular sheriff in Park County, Montana. The opening paragraph in the Red Lodge Picket exclaimed, "A terrible tragedy was enacted at Springdale, in Park County, last Friday evening, resulting in the instant death of Sheriff George T. Young of Livingston, and the serious wounding of Undersheriff Frank Bellary."

The tragic events began on November 8, 1900, when a gunman robbed a man in Garrison, Montana. The robber then hopped a "blind baggage car," (a car without a door) on an eastbound train. When the train pulled into Logan, a local rancher named E.V. Beaver boarded the same baggage car. It was speculated that the desperado mistook Beaver for a lawman and shot the unsuspecting citizen. Before he died, Beaver gave a detailed description of his killer. All lawmen along the train line were alerted. The next stop for the train was Springdale.

The train arrived in Springdale around noon on Friday, November 9th. The station agent, Mr. Carney, who had heard that a murder had been committed in Logan, was especially vigilant as he watched the passengers getting off the train. One man stuck out as looking rough, and he prominently carried a six-shooter on his hip. The stranger wandered around the waiting room and appeared uneasy. At times, he would drop off into a fitful sleep and suddenly awaken and throw his hand to his hip, where he carried the large revolver. Carney thought this was the wanted man and wired Logan for a better description. After getting a reply, he told officials the wanted man was in Springdale. Sheriff Young was notified.

A railroad depot in Livingston, Montana, which was typical of the stations at the time Sheriff George Young was gunned down by a wanted killer.

Around 1 p.m., Young and Undersheriff Bellary left Livingston for Springdale in a "private conveyance," arriving at 6:10 p.m., just after dusk. Scanning the depot for the wanted man, Young was not sure who or where the suspect was. He found the station agent, Mr. Carney, having dinner in an adjoining room. The agent left his table and accompanied the sheriff to the lobby. Carney spotted the stranger outside, standing next to the railroad tracks.

Both lawmen approached the suspect. Young had his handcuffs out, ready to slap them on, while Bellary had his gun drawn. The two officers had gone only a couple of feet when the gunman opened fire. Bellary was struck in the chest with the first shot. Young kept advancing and was within a couple of feet of the suspect when he was shot through the heart. The sheriff reeled and fell heavily to the depot platform. Bellary, although seriously wounded, fired at the fleeing murderer and then bent down to check on his friend. "Are you shot, George?" The sheriff pointed to his left-hand vest pocket and said, "That looks like it." With those words, the sheriff died.

Carney quickly telegraphed Livingston, where a posse of nearly 100 armed men was formed and immediately left for Springdale. Upon the posse's arrival, sentinels were posted at every escape point. Separate posses were also organized under the direction of the local deputy sheriff. Men were dispatched in every direction and messages sent up and down the railroad line. A posse of 20 men came across the possible killer two miles west of Big Timber, a town east of Springdale. When a deputy called out to the man, the suspect opened fired. The posse returned fire. In a telegram, the deputy in charge said "I believe we have him surrounded." They didn't. Once again, the desperado faded off into the night.

The Springdale newspaper reported that the 23-year-old suspect went by the name of Brown and had done prison time for killing "a half-breed." At the time of his conviction, he swore vengeance on all of "mankind" and boasted that when he was released he would start on a mission of murder. The convicted killer said he would start in western Montana and leave a trail of blood clear across the state. In the end, the killer of Sheriff Young did make his escape, and the case remains unsolved.

Undersheriff Frank Bellary survived his wound and was appointed sheriff to fill out the term of his friend. George Young was born in Canada in 1856 and immigrated to the United States in 1873. He was married in 1880 to Clara and at the time of his death had four children: Arthur, 19, George, 16, Clara, 14, and Vera, 6.

SOURCES:

➡ http://www.mtgenweb.com/deerlodge/young.htm
➡ https://www.newspapers.com/image/38534254/?terms=Sheriff%2BYoung
➡ http://www.odmp.org/officer/14620-sheriff-george-t-young
➡ Ancestory.com

CHAPTER 6

"Oh, Paul, help me, I'm hurt"

THE OFFICER:

Officer Charles "Karl" Mayer
St. Paul (Minnesota) Police Department
End of Watch: Saturday, February 1, 1902
Age: 41

With his graveyard shift almost over, Officer Karl Mayer was making one final trip down the alley near the intersection of University and Farrington avenues. It was cold, well below freezing, with snow on the ground. Mayer was "shaking doors" to insure that all the businesses on his beat were secure. At 2:20 a.m., he purposely went to the rear of Jessrang's saloon to try the door. As alleys go, it was mostly an open space with good visibility of the door. The only obstacle was a coal bin just to the left of the door. As Mayer walked past the bin, three men jumped from behind it and opened fire with a large .44-caliber handgun. Subsequent investigation revealed the men had been attempting to burglarize the saloon.

Mayer went down immediately from a bullet that entered his left side, just above the hip, and tore open his intestines. The three burglary suspects ran from the area, leaving behind a bottle of nitroglycerine with enough explosive component to have destroyed the entire building. Although fatally wounded, the officer managed to blow his whistle several times to summon help. When this did not work, he fired his weapon three times in rapid succession.

Paul Gerver, who lived nearby, heard the shots, quickly got dressed and ran to the scene. As soon as he appeared, Officer Mayer told him, "Oh, Paul, help me, I'm hurt. Run for a doctor." Mayer died three hours later at St. Joseph's Hospital, but not before giving detectives a description of the suspects and details of the shooting.

The men who killed Mayer were believed to be the same suspects who had fired on Minneapolis Officer Frank Ford in a similar incident a year earlier. The officer had discovered the men boring holes at the rear of a saloon. This was the MO of burglars who used explosives, such as nitroglycerine, to blow open doors and safes. When the officer surprised them, one of the men opened fired at Ford, with the round piercing his cap and slightly grazing his scalp. The men escaped, but all three suspects were eventually arrested in Kansas and returned to Saint Paul. After extensive questioning, all were released due to lack of evidence and a key witness's refusal to testify.

A busy commercial street in St. Paul, Minnesota, about the time Officer Karl Mayer was slain.

Seven years later, in 1909, one of these suspects, Jack Havlin, aka Jack Curtin, aka Albert Clark, had a confrontation with an officer from the Omaha Police Department. Ms. Annie Wilson was minding her own business as she casually strolled down the sidewalk. Suddenly, without warning, Clark walked up to her and ripped a diamond necklace from around her neck. Wilson's friend, Jennie Smith, went after the desperado. As she approached him, Clark cracked her across the head with his gun and kept moving.

Seeing the commotion, Officer Lafayette "L.A." Smith rushed toward Clark, who turned and shot him twice in abdomen. Although mortally wounded, Officer Smith fired multiple shots, hitting Clark in the leg. Shortly after the shooting, two detectives began a search for the assassin. As they headed downtown, they saw a man duck behind a pillar. The two detectives split up and moved around to each side of the suspect's hiding place. As they closed in, Clark opened fire on Detective Devereese, a round striking him the chest (which he survived). Then Detective Heitfeld, along with a bloody Devereese, fired on Clark, taking him down with wounds "in each groin." Still conscious, the crook lamented that he had not killed more officers: "If my gun hadn't gone back on me, neither of those policemen would've taken me nor gotten away alive."

A native of Ireland, Clark was a hard-core criminal who did time in Wyoming for a stagecoach robbery. He was also arrested for safe blowing and attempted murder in 1896. Clark was sent to prison, where he escaped from his confinement but was soon recaptured. The cop killer died from his wounds nine days after he was shot by the detectives. No one was ever convicted of killing Officer Mayer, and the case remains unsolved.

A mug shot of Albert Clark

Charles Mayer was born in 1861 and raised in Silesia, Prussia. He trained as a machinist and immigrated to America in 1880, arriving in St. Paul two years later. He joined the police department in 1888 and worked out of the Rondo Avenue Substation, assigned to the bicycle squad. He was survived by his wife, Bertha, and seven children ages 17 to just 3 weeks old. Regrettably, his oldest son had died just one month before his own death, and even worse, one of his other sons, who had been sick, died just four days after his death. No family should have to endure that much misery.

On a positive note, Mayer's only daughter, Matilda, would later marry St. Paul Policeman Gustave Barfuss, who would go on to be a key figure in the police department corruption cleanup in the 1930s. He was later appointed Commissioner of Public Safety. Officer Mayer would have been very proud.

SOURCES:

- http://www.spphs.com/honor_roll/mayer.php
- http://www.omaha.com/news/crime/in-the-line-of-duty-more-on-the-officers-on/article_b5133610-1e9f-11e6-b66e-bba20375aead.html
- http://www.odmp.org/officer/8736-police-officer-charles-mayer
- Newspapers.com
- Ancestry.com

CHAPTER 7

Victim of a Strike

THE OFFICER:

Patrolman Paul Mendelssohn
Waterbury (Connecticut) Police Department
End of Watch: Sunday, March 8, 1903
Age: 26

Paul Mendelssohn was born in Germany on September 10, 1876, and after immigrating to the United States, he joined the Waterbury Police Department in 1900. In February of 1903, workers from the Connecticut Railway & Lighting Company began a strike by walking off their jobs. The labor action immediately turned violent when 19 drivers were either pulled from their trolleys and beaten or were hit with flying glass and rocks thrown by the strikers. Consequently, the governor called out the Connecticut National Guard. The soldiers were instructed to ride the trolleys during the evening hours to protect the non-union drivers and the passengers. Supplementing the troops were patrolmen from the Waterbury Police Department.

Reporting to work on the night shift of March 8th, Patrolman Mendelssohn was assigned to ride car No. 66, the North Main Street trolley. It was day 56 of the strike. He was instructed to protect the riding public and the non-union driver from the brutal strikers. As the trolley reached the end of its route in the area of Bucks Hill at 9:50 p.m., four masked men boarded the trolley and without hesitation opened fire on Officer Mendelssohn, striking him in the head, neck, and chest. The driver of the trolley quickly jumped and fled, leaving Mendelssohn dying on the front passenger seat. A subsequent autopsy revealed Patrolman Mendelssohn was struck by bullets fired from .22, .32, and .38-caliber handguns.

As word of the shooting reached police headquarters, a manhunt and investigation was hurriedly launched. But simultaneously, officers from the police department were called out to another murder at a rooming house where an argument at a card game had left one person shot to death. Stepping up to assist with the depleted ranks of the Waterbury Police Department was the sheriff of New Haven County, who dispatched 70 deputy sheriffs to aid in the search for the killers.

A trolley like the one Patrolman Mendelssohn was riding when he was shot and killed.

It was too late, as the suspects in the shooting had made their escape. A few weeks later, 18 men were arrested for their alleged involvement in strikebreaking and union activities related to the railway strike, but no one was ever charged with Patrolman Mendelssohn's death. The crime remains unsolved.

The strike ended the following month.

Patrolman Paul Mendelssohn, badge No. 45, was just 26-years-old when he was killed, leaving behind a wife and two young children. On one positive note, his wife was awarded the first police pension by the City of Waterbury.

SOURCES:

- http://wtbypd.org/Media/Newsroom/tabid/59/ID/11/Paul-Mendelssohn--EOW-03081903.aspx
- http://wtbypd.org/Media/Newsroom/tabid/59/ID/3/Our-History.aspx
- http://www.odmp.org/officer/9210-patrol-officer-paul-mendelssohn
- Ancestry.com

CHAPTER 8

An Unsolved Homicide That Time Forgot

THE OFFICER:

Patrolman Charles Haggerty
Mobile (Alabama) Police Department
End of Watch: Wednesday, December 30, 1903
Age: 48

No officer left behind. Those of us in law enforcement live by that creed. If an officer is killed in the line of duty, we never forget. We pay homage to the fallen so they are not just another statistic, but individuals we shall long remember. We keep their memories alive through photographs displayed on our station walls, we name streets after them and we have anniversary dates to celebrate what the officer accomplished in a life cut short. "Lest we forget" is our battle cry.

But standing in the way of remembering is the haze of forgetfulness that gets thicker as decades pass. Time moves on, new generations of officers come and go, and sometimes, we do forget. In researching *Unsolved*, I have come across too many officers who have given the ultimate sacrifice, only to be lost in the depths of time. I have discovered numerous officers killed in the early 20th century who don't even have gravestones. Fortunately, as agencies discover these forgotten men and women, officers put on fundraisers and collect the necessary money to purchase a grave marker. Soon after, departments usually have a ceremony to revive the officer's life and story of his or her sacrifice. It should be the mission of each one of us to be vigilant to honor these forgotten heroes and take action if some remote clue pokes through the fog of history. Captain Roy Hodge of the Mobile Police Department did just that.

For Hodge, it began with a 115-year-old police souvenir book he has had for years. It was very common at the time for a police department to put together a book of photographs of each officer, pictures of police stations and usually a short history of the department. It's somewhat similar to today's high school yearbooks. As Hodge was preparing to teach an academy class, he was thumbing through the old book looking for historical details to share with the class. As he did so, he noticed a note scribbled next to an officer's picture. It said: "Your father was probably the last man that ever saw Haggerty alive at 2:30 a.m. He was murdered on Royal Street at Government Street."

This note sent Hodge on a mission to the city's library to dig through old newspapers from 1903. The captain wanted to see if Haggerty was indeed killed and, if so, why there was no mention of his sacrifice in the records of the Mobile Police Department. Squinting through the endless reels of microfilm, Hodge discovered an article describing what happened. It was December 30,1903, just before 3 a.m. Patrolman Charles Haggerty had just made an arrest on the west side of Royal Street. Moments later, four shots rang out, and just a few seconds after that, Haggerty was dead. The suspect escaped and was never found. The only witness to the shooting was a man operating a city sweeping machine who described the shooter as "a small, slimly built white man with a cap on."

Police took in several people for questioning, but each one was cleared of killing Haggerty. And just like that, the story was gone from the paper and, for whatever reason, the written history of the department. Hodge said that what bothered him the most about this whole affair was how Officer Haggerty was forgotten, how he was lost "in the mist of time."

In 2016, as officials in Mobile paused to remember fallen officers on their department as well as those from across the country, they added one more name to the list—an officer by the name of Charles Haggerty. Soon his name will be added to the National Law Enforcement Officers Memorial in

Washington, D.C. One small step to clear away the fog of time and resurrect the memory of a fallen brother. Lest we forget. Officer Haggerty was survived by his wife.

SOURCES:

- http://local15tv.com/news/local/unsolved-murder-of-mpd-officer-charles-haggerty
- https://www.odmp.org/officer/23157-police-officer-charles-haggerty

CHAPTER 9

The Truant Officer

THE OFFICER:

Truant Officer Claude R. Ball
Calhoun County, West Virginia
End of Watch: Unknown date in 1905
Age: 40s

Skipping or missing school in the early 20th century was not taken lightly. Truancy is loosely defined as any intentional unauthorized or illegal absence from compulsory education. Unlike today, when a computer auto-dials a family whose child missed school, in an earlier era there were truant officers who would visit the homes of those absent from school. Many feared the truant officer, as he could impose a fine on the family for truant violations. Many of these truant officers were constables or sheriffs, some concurrently. Today the position of truant officer has gone the way of the dial phone. But this was not the case in 1905, in a rural area of West Virginia.

Truant Officer Claude Ball was riding his horse along a primitive ridge road from Mount Zion to Hur, on his way to interview a family for not sending their children to school for an extended length of time. When Ball was just two-tenths of a mile from the home, he was shot off his horse and landed near a large tree—dead. His body was later discovered by the Calhoun County assessor.

Officer Ball was not without his detractors. He is mainly remembered for his change of personality after being appointed as county truant officer. Many said the "authority went to his head." An acquaintance of Ball stated, "Ball had a reputation of being a big-headed guy, who liked to command those around him." This same individual also was quoted as saying that Ball was murdered by a member of the family he was sent to interview. They lived in a hollow and were the closest family to the location where Ball was shot to death. No one was ever arrested for the crime.

The only surviving photograph of the murder of Officer Claude Ball. Photo courtesy of Bob Weaver.

Of all the murders this author has researched for *Unsolved*, this homicide narrowly escaped being enveloped by history—to remain interned with the people from that generation. It was the publisher of *The Hur Herald* internet newspaper, Bob Weaver, who preserved the memory of this 1905 murder and shared it with others. I could not find any other record of this unsolved homicide, even after calls to officials from the county. Because of Mr. Weaver, the killing of Officer Ball will live for future generations to review and discuss.

SOURCES:

- Interview with Bob Weaver, editor of *The Hur Herald*. http://www.hurherald.com/
- Interview with officials from Calhoun County, July, 2016

CHAPTER 10

"Blackie"

THE OFFICER:

Policeman Herman Myron Personius
Valley City (North Dakota) Police Department
End of Watch: Tuesday, August 28, 1906
Age: 43

When hobos trains and the police come together, too many times it results in an unsolved police homicide. In several situations (as documented in Unsolved), the vagrant kills an officer and disappears immediately, jumping a train to the next city and beyond. The vagrants easily blur into the background with their stealthy use of mostly freight trains. The death of Policeman Herman Personius is a case in point.

On August 27, 1906, two hobos armed with handguns robbed two railroad employees of their money and belongings while riding in the caboose of the Cooperstown train in Sanborn, North Dakota. To escape, the robbers successfully switched trains, taking one that was just heading out for Valley City. Somehow the crew got the word out to the authorities in Valley City that the robbers were headed their way. Chief of Police Burt (no first name given) gathered a small group to meet the train: Policeman Personius, Policeman Swanson and Policeman Dan Moore. The lawmen formed up at the west end of the rail depot.

At approximately 4 a.m., the train arrived. Chief Burt and Swanson took the north side of the tracks while Moore and Personius took the south side. The four men carefully walked the length of the train but were unable to locate the suspects. Finally a crew member came forward and pointed out the boxcar in which the desperadoes had taken refuge. With guns drawn, the officers opened the door of the freight car and quickly captured two suspects. Personius, thinking that there were additional crooks, left the group and proceeded down the train when four shots rang out in rapid succession.

A photograph taken in the 1950s of the railroad depot in Valley City, North Dakota, where Policeman Herman Personius was shot.

The other members of the party hurried to the scene of the shooting. As Moore arrived, Personius called out, "They have got me, Dan. He went that way," pointing to the southwest. A witness saw two men run past his house heading southwest. Personius had been shot through the mouth and upper chest, both shots proving fatal. Personius died at the scene.

One of the men arrested was Tom Connors, who admitted to the robbery, and he implicated his companion, known to him only as "Blackie," as the man who shot Personius. The other suspect in the boxcar was not involved in the robbery.

Additional information allowed Chief Burt to draw the following conclusions: As Policeman Personius ran down the side of the train looking for additional suspects, he found Blackie running from the boxcar. At this time Personius yelled for help "two or three times." It appeared from the evidence that there was a fight between Personius and Blackie while he was attempting his escape. It was reasoned that the suspect thought Personius was attempting to get his gun or that both men might have been attempting to get their guns, which were both concealed in their pockets. Blackie managed to get his gun out first and shoot Personius. When Personius was found, his gun was still in his pocket.

A few months later, Connors was convicted of two counts of "highway robbery" and sentenced to 30 years in prison. Connors cooperated with authorities for a slightly reduced sentence, but nothing he added helped move the case forward. Over the next year, no fewer than 13 "Blackies" were detained. Many of these suspects were transported to Valley City, but no witnesses could identify the men, and all were released. Blackie was never caught, and the case remains unsolved. Policeman Personius was survived by his wife, five sons and two daughters.

SOURCES:

➡ Newspapers.com. (Several newspaper accounts provided notable details regarding the death of Policeman Personius. Without these, there would have been no article about the death of Personius as I could not locate any other detailed articles of the shooting. Note the *Bismarck Daily Tribune* and the *Ward County Independent* stand out.)

CHAPTER 11

An Assassin on the Loose

THE OFFICER:

Detective George W. Wilson
Council Bluffs (Iowa) Police Department
End of Watch: Monday, July 29, 1907
Age: 50

On today's police departments, with the exception of unusual occurrences, when a police officer goes home, he is seldom called back to assist with police emergencies. In the early 20th century, this was not the case. At 10 p.m. Monday, July 29, 1907, Officer W.H. Richardson, an Army veteran, was patrolling on his footbeat. In communication with police headquarters, using a call box, Richardson received conflicting information about a person either causing a disturbance or committing a burglary.

Richardson answered the call to the North First Street bridge area. Upon arriving, he spotted the possible perpetrator. The patrolman approached the suspect to question him. As he did so, the man abruptly drew a revolver from his pants pocket and shot Officer Richardson in the chest. Although seriously wounded,

Council Bluffs City Hall and Police Department, circa 1910.

Richardson returned fire, missed, but with his dwindling strength, ran after his assailant. After traveling a quarter of a block, Patrolman Richardson collapsed at the corner of Washington and First Street. A horse-drawn ambulance was summoned and took the wounded officer to Edmondson Memorial Hospital.

Edmondson Memorial Hospital where both officers were taken. Circa 1910.

Word quickly went out by telephone, calling in all off-duty personnel to assist in the search for the suspect. At 10:25 p.m., Detective George Wilson, a 10-year veteran, was summoned to join the search. Wilson, determining that he was very close to the scene of the shooting, quickly began his search for the gunman from right out his front door.

At approximately 10:30 p.m., and only two blocks from his home, Wilson reached Elliott Street, where he observed a suspicious man hiding in a ditch. When he approached the individual, the suspect shot at Detective Wilson, who immediately returned fire. Wilson was struck by one round in the abdomen and went down. As nearby officers responded to his location, he told them he thought he had hit the assailant in the foot, as the man was limping badly as he fled the scene.

Detective Wilson was transported to his home, then to Edmondson Memorial Hospital, the same hospital that was treating Patrolman Richardson. When the two officers' descriptions of the suspect were compared, they matched, indicating the same man had shot both officers.

Wilson was rushed into surgery to remove the bullet, but he died a short time later. Patrolman Richardson evidently recovered from his wounds. The search for the suspect by over 200 mounted men brought in some possible suspects, but no one was arrested for the murder of George Wilson and the shooting of Officer Richardson. The case remains unsolved.

George Wilson was born in 1857 in Missouri and married Edith Moore in 1898. Sharing their home was his wife's 12-

year-old brother and George's niece, Edna Wilson, who was 7. They had no children of their own.

In researching what happened to Patrolman Richardson, I could find no reference to him on the Council Bluffs Police Department, but did find a W.H. Richardson as a city marshal in Clarinda, Iowa, in 1911-1912.

SOURCES:

- "Iowa Unsolved Murders: Historic Cases" by Nancy Bowers
- https://www.odmp.org/officer/17160-detective-george-w-wilson
- Newspapers.com
- Ancestry.com

CHAPTER 12

The Jungle

THE OFFICER:

Patrolman Joseph Nelson Allen
Fort Collins (Colorado) Police Department
End of Watch: Wednesday, July 3, 1907
Age: 45

In the first decades of the 20th century, sugar beets were the primary business of Northern Colorado and of Fort Collins, a growing city of 8,000 people. Surrounding the city's sugar beet factory was an area known as "the jungle," where liquor flowed freely and crime was widespread. It was where Patrolman Joseph Allen would be killed.

Allen was from Kansas, and it was claimed that he rode his bicycle all the way to Fort Collins to get a job and earn money so he could send for his wife. He found that job on the local police force. It wasn't long before the 45-year-old was assigned to the jungle. Gaining experience and confidence, Allen said he could deal with any problem that arose. That

Patrolman Joseph Allen with his wife, Dana Ellen, who were married in 1894.

was true until the night of July 3, 1907. While walking his regular beat, he was suddenly attacked from behind by an assassin who beat him with a brick until he fell unconscious. The suspect stole his revolver, nightstick and knife. A passerby heard someone moaning, found the fallen officer and called the police. Allen died a short time later in the hospital.

As detectives put the case together, they discovered that an hour before Allen's murder, a doctor making a house call in the area reported having seen the patrolman talking with two men that were later arrested for investigation of his murder. The doctor said the conversation appeared to be casual and friendly. Later the two men were arrested, but no charges were brought against them, and no one else came forward with any leads.

The monument at the Fort Collins Police Department honoring the two officers killed in the line of duty.

Over the years, the city rid itself of its "plague spot": The jungle disappeared, as did the sugar beet factory. As the city of Fort Collins grew by leaps and bounds, Allen's name and story faded away like a name on an old tombstone. But while the city may have forgotten, the Fort Collins Police Department didn't. The name of Patrolman Allen is engraved on a beautiful monument at police headquarters, along with that of Charles Brockman, the only other Fort Collins officer to die in the line of duty. While the murder went unsolved, Patrolman Allen, the bike-riding man from Kansas, will remain a part of Fort Collins history—forever.

SOURCES:

- http://www.coloradoan.com/story/news/2014/01/12/a-walk-through-history-who-killed-joseph-allen-the-policeman-who-biked-to-fort-collins-/4447977/
- Ancestry.com. It was here that two photographs were found of Patrolman Allen, filling a void of images of the brave officer.

CHAPTER 13

"Tell all the boys goodbye. I had bad luck"

THE OFFICER:

Patrolman Friedrich "Fred" P. Widmann
Waterloo (Iowa) Police Department
End of Watch: Sunday, October 11, 1908
Age: 30

Patrolman Fred P. Widmann was a gentle giant in an imposing body who patrolled the city streets of Waterloo, Iowa, on the midnight shift. The local newspaper said, "His kindness in life was as unfailing as the water that springs up from a perpetual fountain and his gentleness and loving disposition are more commonly found in women than in men."

The 30-year-old officer was single and had mentioned when he came on duty that Sunday, October 11, 1908, how he was looking forward to taking his "lady friend" to the Cedar River for a picnic. Unfortunately, there would be no picnic, and no lady friend would ever become his wife, for this day was his last.

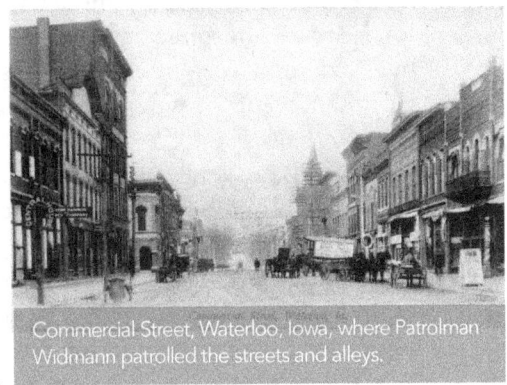

Commercial Street, Waterloo, Iowa, where Patrolman Widmann patrolled the streets and alleys.

Patrolman Widmann was working a footbeat in the alleys and sidewalks in the business district along East Fourth Street. With only his police-issued whistle to signal for help, at 3 a.m. Widmann stopped by the police station to report that all was well on his beat. He then headed to the alley behind the Security Savings Bank.

This particular alley was dark and cluttered. Little light penetrated the dark spaces between the different walls that jutted out, creating natural hiding places. One could not see what was going on at the rear of the business unless specifically walking around the wall and peering into the store. This was the situation when Widmann came around a wall and surprised burglars breaking into the Coburn and Son Bicycle and Gun Shop. What happened next occurred like a blur. The suspects brazenly opened fire on the officer with a .38-caliber revolver. Widmann was struck by two rounds. One bullet lodged in his ribs and the second to the left side of his abdomen. Although mortally wounded, Widmann emptied his six-shot .38-caliber Colt revolver in the general direction of his assailants who fled the scene.

People in nearby homes and hotels reported hearing as many as a dozen loud bangs. One report was that it sounded like someone pounding a board on the side of a building.

Fighting for his life, Officer Widmann bravely pulled himself 100 feet out of the alley to Main Street and shouted for help. At the police station, three officers heard the bangs but did not recognize them as gunfire. Patrolman Tom Hartman went outside to investigate and heard Widmann's cries for help.

Quickly, several people responded. Someone ran for a doctor, another hurried for a stretcher from the nearby fire station and a third organized a posse to find the suspects. Widmann, still conscious, spoke to Patrolman Hartman, "Well, Tom, I guess he got me. He shot me twice in the stomach, and I fired twice at him behind the boxes at Coburn's."

Widmann was taken to the hospital, where it was obvious to the doctors that his wounds would be fatal. His family was notified and rushed to his side. He said goodbye and told them how to dispose of his property and conduct his affairs. When Police Chief E.A. Leighton and other officers arrived at his bedside, Patrolman Widmann spoke his last words, "Tell all the boys goodbye. I had bad luck, but I hope none of them will meet with the misfortune I did while performing their duty." Hearing this, several of the street-hardened cops broke down and cried.

Patrolman Fred Widmann calmly looked death in the face just as he had the bullets fired at him just a few hours earlier. He was a remarkable example of a police officer who keeps fighting, no matter the circumstances. As a reporter from the *Waterloo Reporter* newspaper wrote, "The dying officer bade his parents, brothers, and sister an affectionate good-bye, then closed his eyes forever upon the earthly scenes. The closing hours of his life were as calm as summer's dying day."

Dozens of men were brought in for questioning, suspects were taken off trains, outlying departments were all on the lookout, but to no avail. The suspects were never identified, and the case remains unsolved.

In 2002, Widman's niece, Eunice Wilson, who was born after his death, and the Waterloo Police Protective Association restored his gravesite. They removed gnarled tree roots, straightened his headstone, and attached a plaque to document the information about him that was slowly being lost to time. It reads:

OFFICER FRED WIDMANN
WATERLOO POLICE DEPT.
KILLED IN THE LINE OF DUTY
OCT. 11, 1908
FOREVER VIGILANT

Through the efforts of Patrolman Widmann's niece, Eunice Wilson, and the Waterloo Police Protective Association, a commemorative plaque was placed on the restored headstone. Courtesy photo findagrave.com.

Unsolved, Cold-Case Homicides

SOURCES:

- Iowa Cold Case: Iowacoldcases.org
- "Iowa Unsolved Murders: Historical Cases" by Nancy Bowers
- http://www.findagrave.com/cgi-bin/fg.cgi?page=gr&GRid=77230941
- http://www.wikitree.com/wiki/Widmann-49
- https://www.odmp.org/officer/14149-patrolman-fred-p-widmann
- Newspapers.com

CHAPTER 14

"Don't get excited; we're officers of the law"

THE OFFICER:

Chief Deputy Seymore L. Clark
Weber County (Utah) Sheriff's Department
End of Watch: Friday, November 27, 1908
Age: 37

For as long as anyone can remember, Uintah, in Weber County, Utah, has been a railroad town. As if to prove the point, the train tracks bisect the small city right down the middle. In the early 1900s it was noted for bars and the accompanying brothels. Many unsavory characters traveled illegally in the boxcars as a means of getting around.

In the fall of 1908, traveling by horse and buggy, Sheriff's Deputy Seymour Clark and his partner, John Murphy, were transporting a very sick man to Ogden. As they trotted past the railroad station they observed a man seemingly hiding behind some boxes next to an open boxcar. Deputy Murphy called out to the suspicious man, "Don't get excited; we're officers of the law." As soon as those words were uttered, the suspect opened fire with a .32-caliber handgun at the two deputies sitting in the wagon.

All three men in the wagon were immediately struck. Murphy was hit in the hand, and Clark was pummeled with several rounds to his upper body, while the passenger was struck by yet another round. Murphy and the ailing man survived their wounds, but Deputy Seymore Clark died at the scene. Quickly, a posse was formed and 50 armed men began a search for the suspect. As the local paper reported, "It is believed that if the murderer is captured that he will be lynched, as the dead officer was a popular man and the people of Ogden are greatly incensed over the cowardly manner in which he was killed." Despite a large reward, the perpetrator was never found and the case remains unsolved. According to Utah records, Deputy Clark is the only fatality the Weber County Sheriff's Office has ever experienced.

At a ceremony held in 2014, over 100 years after the shooting, today's Weber County Sheriff's Department awarded the deputies families with Purple Hearts for the sacrifices of the two men. Melissa Ladene Castleton, Murphy's granddaughter, traveled from California to attend the event. On her finger was a ring with a cracked stone that she was told had saved her grandfather during that fateful night.

"You always wonder," Castleton said, "was it exaggerated? Did it really happen? Now we know it really happened and this is the only possession I have from my grandfather. Never knowing my grandfather, I feel the last couple of months I've come to know him and this has been a very sweet experience for our family."

Clark's great-nephew, Robert Elbert Smith said he heard the story of Clark's death from his mother when he was growing up. He said he is glad to see his great-uncle recognized. "I think it quite an honor not forgetting people, the service that they did, the ultimate sacrifice," Smith said. "I'm a Vietnam veteran myself, so those things mean a lot to me." "Even though it has been over 100 years," said Sheriff Terry Thompson, "it's a reminder the sacrifices of others in law enforcement are never forgotten."

Before joining the department, Clark had served as a Utah Fish and Game officer. He left behind a wife.

SOURCES:

➡ Findagrave.com. http://www.findagrave.com/cgi-bin/fg.cgi?page=gr&GRid=26614426
➡ Newspapers.com
➡ "Uintah, Images of American" by Sue Bybee, page 61
➡ https://www.odmp.org/officer/17320-chief-deputy-seymore-legrande-clark

CHAPTER 15

"If I had only been a little quicker"

THE OFFICER:

Patrolman David Brooks
Los Angeles Police Department
End of Watch: Friday, April 8, 1910
Age: 38

Friday nights in Los Angeles have changed little in the past 106 years—it gets very busy for LAPD officers. So it was on that Friday evening, April 8, 1910, at 10:30 p.m., when two young gunmen, dressed in black clothes, black hats, and wearing black handkerchiefs covering their faces, entered Conrad Winter's saloon at 3725 Central Avenue. John Edwards, the bartender, was the only man in the bar when he looked up and saw the masked men, with guns drawn, approaching him. "Throw up your mitts," hollered the man who appeared to be in charge. Edwards, seemingly unfazed by two guns pointed at him, replied, "Go to the dickens!" When the leader growled that he meant it, the bartender quickly raised his hands. As the leader kept his gun on Edwards, his accomplice went around the counter to the till and removed $50 in silver but missed $200 in gold, which was hidden in a drawer.

As a result of numerous robberies in the area, Patrolman David Brooks, 38, a seven-year veteran out of University Station, working plain clothes, was walking his footbeat north of Grand Avenue, approaching 30th Street. It was less than an hour after the robbery and a distance that the suspects could have easily covered. As the two gunmen walked past a witness who was somewhat out of sight, leaning against a telephone pole, he overheard one of them point out that a man was coming and say, "Let's rob him." The witness noticed they were both wearing all black.

Unknown to the bandits, the man they randomly selected was a Los Angeles police officer. As the suspects' guns came out, Brooks was ordered to put his hands up. The streetwise veteran complied, but only raised his left arm as his right went for his gun. With that motion, the officer's jacket pulled back, revealing his badge pinned to his chest. "He's an officer," one of them yelled. "That's nothing," said the other. "Hold him up anyway."

Central Station where Patrolman David Brooks was first transported.

Patrolman Brooks began to pull his gun out. At the same time, both suspects opened fire at near point blank-range. One round struck Brooks on his left side, just below the ribs, and exited on the right side, cutting through his intestines and liver and severing an abdominal artery. The mortally wounded officer refused to give up and fired two shots at the fleeing bandits, who returned fire. Loosing strength in his legs, Brooks fell to the ground but managed to empty his revolver at the suspects.

Quickly, there were 20 people surrounding the fallen officer. One was Dr. T.E. Taggert, who had run to the corner after hearing the shots from his nearby home. Dr. Taggert knew there was not time to wait for an ambulance, including LAPD's, which was horse-drawn. The doctor flagged down a passing auto and directed the driver to Central Hospital. This was the infancy of gasoline-powered cars, and they were quite bumpy and slow. Despite being only minutes from death, Patrolman Brooks managed to utter what he was thinking in those fleeting moments. "If I had only been a little quicker," he said between gasps, "I would have got those fellows."

When the driver of the car was unsure where the entrance to Central Hospital was, he stopped in front of Central Police Station. Captain Avery Bradish came running out and with help from others carried Brooks around the corner to the hospital entrance. As they carried the officer into the emergency room, a doctor asked what was going on. Captain Bradish said, "It is some private watchman, I guess. Shot somewhere by thugs." But then, as if coming back from the dead, Brooks lifted his head and said in a clear discernible voice, "Captain, I am a patrolman. I belong to University Station. Brooks is my name—David Brooks. I am one of your men." The captain quickly told the officer that indeed, he now recognized him, and taking his hand, calling him Davy, he tried to be positive and cheer up the stricken officer.

After just eight minutes on the operating table, Brooks uttered his last words, "I ought to have got 'em, but I was a little nervous—I was a little shaky, you know, I—." His head fell back onto the table, and Patrolman David Brooks was dead. LAPD detectives made several arrests, but after questioning, all of the men were released. The hunt for Brooks' killers continued in earnest for months, but eventually all leads failed to reveal the killers. Over the years, the suspects were never identified, and the case remains unsolved.

David Brooks was born March 6, 1872, in Ohio, the eldest of five children whose father was a farmer. After moving to Los Angeles in 1896, Brooks worked as a streetcar conductor. In 1898, he married and had three sons—David Jr., born in 1899; Walter, born in 1901; and Frederic, born in 1903 at about the same time that Brooks joined the LAPD.

A month after his death, LAPD hosted a concert and ball to raise money to benefit his widow and children. Nearly 3,000 people attended, including the mayor and Chief of Police Alexander Galloway. The event raised $4,000, which in today's money would be $100,000.

Officer Brooks was buried at Inglewood Park Cemetery. His widow, Ottilie, died in 1948 in Los Angeles at the age of 71. She is buried next to her husband.

SOURCES:

- Newspapers.com.
- http://www.cemeteryguide.com/LAPD-Brooks.html
- https://www.flickr.com/photos/66577054@N00/9549333863
- http://www.odmp.org/officer/2299-policeman-david-brooks

CHAPTER 16

"There was another report and a spurt of flame from the revolver"

THE OFFICER:

Patrolman William Henry Cunliffe
Seattle (Washington) Police Department
End of Watch: Saturday, June 17, 1911
Age: 45

Seattle, Washington, was one of the most dangerous cities for police officers in the early 1900s. Within five months, Seattle lost three police officers to gunfire, and two of the shootings have remained unsolved. The first of these was the murder of Patrolman Cunliffe.

William Henry Cunliffe was born in England in the 1860s. He loved the rugged outdoors and immigrated to the United States, where he lived on the Great Plains of the Midwest, making ends meet as a cowboy. Moving north to Canada, Cunliffe joined the Royal Canadian Mounted Police for five years. Working his way south again, this time to Seattle, Cunliffe found work as a "carman" and drove a streetcar just before he was commissioned as a Seattle police officer in 1907.

Working the graveyard shift on Saturday, June 17, 1911, the three-year veteran was doing what he always did, walking his footbeat and making sure his assigned area was safe. At roll call that night, he had received information of an increase in burglaries where cash, jewelry and clothing had been stolen. There had been two burglaries just the night before. At 1:40 a.m., on the northwest corner of Summit Avenue and Columbia Street, he encountered at least one male suspect, but most likely two. The premise soon after the shooting was that Patrolman Cunliffe had his revolver drawn on one suspect when a second man approached from his left and fired three shots from his .38-caliber handgun from just a few feet away. One round hit next to the patrolman's badge, missing his heart but puncturing his left lung and lodging in his other lung. Although mortally wounded, Patrolman Cunliffe, a crack shot, steadied himself and fired three shots from his Colt revolver at the fleeing bandits, likely striking one of them. He then collapsed and died a few hours later. The two men fled toward Madison Street. Soon every detective and available officer was dispatched to comb the city.

A few days later, detectives located a witness who had an ideal position to observe the events of that night. Mrs. J.H. Brown, a guest at a local hotel, saw the shooting from her room overlooking the area where Patrolman Cunliffe was shot. She stated that she was asleep with her window open when she was awakened by the loud sound of a gunshot. Brown headed for her second-story window to see what was going on. As she reached the window, a second shot rang out. Mrs. Brown saw a man standing almost directly under a streetlight. Brown stated, "On looking out I saw a man standing in the middle of the street, holding a revolver in his hand. Instinctively I looked in the direction in which the pistol was pointed and saw a policeman standing in the shade of the tree. There was another report and a spurt of flame from the revolver. I saw the patrolman turn round on his feet and fall backward."

Subsequent investigations supported her statements when detectives located a spent round in the pillar of one home and another having gone through a window of a local resident. The third was recovered from the officer's body.

"The man who did the killing," said Mrs. Brown, "was easily the coolest of any of the people who were present in the events immediately after the tragedy. After firing the shot that caused the policeman to fall he coolly walked past his victim on the sidewalk, down Columbia Street and into the alley."

Officers checked a boarding house and arrested two men and two women but later released them, as there was no connection to the case. Another witness who was just disembarking from a streetcar when the firefight began only saw Cunliffe back into the street, fire several shots, then collapse. The manhunt continued, and police questioned every guest who arrived at their rooms after 2 a.m. Each had to explain why they were out so late. Another witness saw two men pass his house and noted that one man was supporting the other as if he were injured. There were other leads in the case, but no arrest was ever made. The case remains unsolved.

Officer Cunliffe was survived by his wife, Rebecca, and his two-month-old daughter, Mary. The two continued to live in Seattle. His daughter married in 1932 and had three children. Rebecca never remarried. She lived in Seattle until years later when she moved to Los Angeles to live with her daughter and son-in-law. She died in 1966 at the age of 84. Mary died in 1988 at the age of 77 and is buried near the father she never knew.

SOURCES:

- Retired Seattle Police Officers' Association. "Officer Down-Officer William H. Cunliffe." By Officer Mike Severance-North Precinct. http://rspoa.org/index.php?officer-william-cunliffe&highlight=cunliffe
- RCMP Graves, "True and Fascinating Canadian History, Constable William H. Cunliffe." http://www.rcmpgraves.com/memorials/cunliffe.html
- Seattle Post-Intelligencer. P-1 archive: "The oldest unsolved Seattle police homicide."
- Newspapers.com.

CHAPTER 17

"Walk in the paths of righteousness"

THE OFFICER:

Town Marshal Joseph Kaschmitter
Alton (Iowa) Marshal's Office
Date of Incident: March 25, 1911
End of Watch: March 27, 1911
Age: 53

In the early 20th century, railroad depots and the trains that traveled these routes allowed for a quick escape for any criminal transient drifting across America. Numerous unsolved homicides of law enforcement officers were the direct result. Town Marshal Joseph Kaschmitter was one of these victims.

Because of criminal activity around train depots, law enforcement officers made them an essential aspect of their patrol activities. Marshal Kaschmitter was no different. On patrol during the early morning of Saturday, March 25, 1911, he was checking to insure that the late night train got off with no problems and that there were no problems left behind. As the train pulled away, the marshal walked down a dark alley to make sure that there were no transients hiding out or breaking into stores.

A contemporary photograph of the train depot where Marshal Kaschmitter was patrolling the night he was murdered.

Kaschmitter would later describe how he had walked behind some businesses, when two men jumped from the shadows with guns pointed at him. The men ordered him to raise his hands. As the plain clothes marshal complied, his badge and gun were revealed. Without warning or any spoken words, the men opened fire, striking the marshal on his side. Kaschmitter fell face down into the dirt. While the lawman lay there mortally wounded, one of the men stood over him and shot him again in the back.

Main street of Alton, Iowa, at the time Marshal Kaschmitter was killed in the alley behind these businesses.

While most mortals would have just given up, Marshal Kaschmitter rolled to his side, drew his sidearm and fired at the two vagrants as they sprinted from the area. With no blood trail, the severely wounded officer apparently missed his targets. Struggling to his feet, Kaschmitter, still clutching his weapon, stumbled to a nearby restaurant, which the mayor owned. He was seeking help and wanted to inform the head of the city what had just happened. But with no answer, the dying man staggered down the street to two more restaurants, but with no luck.

A few citizens reported seeing him but did not recognize the marshal in plainclothes, and they were concerned to see a bloody man carrying a gun. Finally one of the spectators recognized the town marshal and rushed to help him. Notifications were quickly made to the sheriff, the town doctor, and the Kaschmitter family.

Arriving first were two doctors and a registered nurse. With the help of townsfolk, they carried the wounded man to his home. Over the next two days, Kaschmitter, with his family at his side, told his children to be obedient in their lives and

The Kaschmitter family circa 1883 in this recently discovered photograph. There would be eight more children after this image was taken.

admonished the older boys and girls "to walk in the paths of righteousness." After forgiving his assailants, he died.

Soon after the shooting, a posse was formed, and the search began for the killers. Unfortunately, a second night train had arrived just after the ambush, and it was feared the two assailants had made their getaway on the departing train. No arrests were made for the murder of Marshal Kaschmitter, and the case remains unsolved

Joseph Kaschmitter was 12 years old when his parents emigrated from Austria-Hungary. He was married and had 10 children. He had worked for the Omaha Railroad as a section foreman until 1904, when he was appointed town marshal. Kaschmitter was a devoted Catholic and sang in the church choir. Over 800 people attended his funeral. In 2014, the State of Iowa and the governor honored Kaschmitter and three other officers who were killed in the line of duty.

SOURCES:

- Iowa Cold Cases. https://iowacoldcases.org/case-summaries/joseph-kaschmitter/
- The Dark Side of Iowa. "Unsolved: Joseph "Joe" Kaschmitter. http://www.thedarksideofamerica.com/unsolved-joseph-joe-kaschmitter.html
- https://www.odmp.org/officer/19733-town-marshal-joseph-kaschmitter
- Ancestory.com
- Newspapers.com

CHAPTER 18

"Beware! The last notice!"

THE OFFICER:

Patrolman Joseph Raimo
Kansas City (Missouri) Police Department
End of Watch: Tuesday, March 28, 1911
Age: 33

The newspaper headline summed up the shooting of Patrolman Joseph Raimo in four words: "ASSASSINS GOT THEIR MAN." On Tuesday evening, March 28, 1911, Raimo was returning home to his wife and four young children. He was on a rare day off. He had spent an enjoyable night playing cards with some friends at a saloon at Fourth and Holmes streets. As he strolled down Holmes Street, his hands were in his pockets, and he was happily whistling. As he walked past a dark area, four quick shots flashed in rapid succession from behind a low brick wall 20 feet away. The patrolman fell to the sidewalk, dead, his body riddled with buck-shot fired from two shotguns. The sawed-off weapons were tossed away by the assassins as they escaped down the alley.

Mr. G.W. Fay, who lived in the area, happened to be at the end of the alley and said he saw two male Italians run past him. As the first patrolman reached the scene of the shooting, he noticed there were "several Americans...but no Italians were in sight" and that all the houses in the predominantly Italian neighborhood "were dark."

The motive for the killing of Patrolman Raimo had its genesis three months earlier. Mrs. Paulina Pizano, an Italian woman who was known for her "sharp tongue," refused to pay members of the Black Hand gang who were attempting to extort money from her. On December 14, 1910, as she stepped in front of her store, she was shot and killed by a shotgun blast at close range.

The Black Hand was an extortion racket run by immigrant Sicilian and Italian gangsters in large cities such as New York, Chicago, New Orleans and Kansas City from 1890 to 1920. The mobsters, MO (modus operandi) consisted of sending threatening notes to local merchants and other wealthy citizens. The notes were printed by hand and featured drawings of black hands, daggers or other menacing symbols. If the recipient did not pay, he or she was threatened with death or destruction of property. For as long as anyone could remember, the mob was a simple fact of life, something almost as old and established as the city itself.

One month before his death, Raimo, an Italian, was working undercover at a saloon called Little Italy. It was a known hangout for members of the Black Hand. Raimo overheard three men talking about the Pizano murder, and he heard the name of the man who pulled the trigger. When one of the gangsters looked up to see Raimo, he happened to recognize him as the cop who usually walked a beat in the area. Raimo, feeling the stares from the men, quickly left the bar, but he knew he was made. Since that encounter, Raimo was never free from the expectation of an attack.

One night while playing cards with his friends, he appeared to be upset and would not laugh or joke as he usually did. One of the men asked him what was wrong. Raimo replied, "I know who killed Paulina Pizano, that's what's the matter. And they know I know. Some day they will get me." Warnings concerning his premonition came immediately. Evidently, the gangsters were not quite sure what Raimo looked like, and over the next several weeks two officers were fired on while walking their beats, both in dark areas, bordering alleys, with shotguns being used. One of these officers was A. Johnson, who was walking the same beat as Raimo on Fourth Street. Two shots from a shotgun narrowly missed killing Johnson, with lead shot lodged in his wooden club. A shotgun was recovered from the alley, but the suspect got away. It was a month later that they found the man they were looking for.

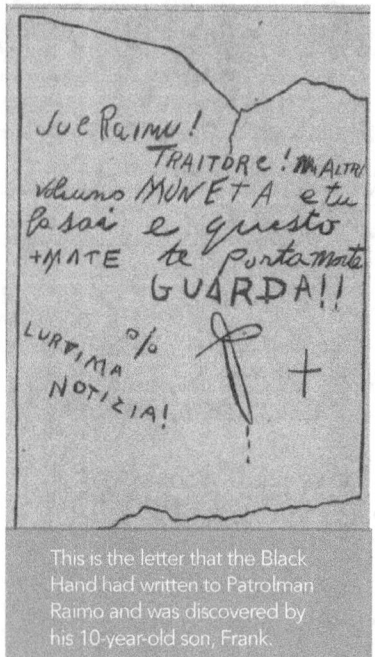

This is the letter that the Black Hand had written to Patrolman Raimo and was discovered by his 10-year-old son, Frank.

Two days after Raimo's murder, his body was taken to his home for the funeral. A reporter doing a follow-up article arrived at the home about the same time and was met by Raimo's 10-year-old son, Frank. He was looking through the window on his front porch as his father's casket was brought in. As the reporter came up the steps, Frank asked, "Say, Mister, do you think the — what you call it—the Black Hand, killed my papa?" The reporter told him yes, it was possible. The young boy said, "But what is the Black Hand? Does it sign things with a cross?...Because if it does, I've got a letter from the Black Hand, written to my papa."

The boy went to the corner of the porch, appeared to pull a brick from the foundation, and returned with a bit of crumpled paper. "I found it this morning, all crumpled up, back under my papa's bed," he explained. "I can read English—oh yes, I go to school; I'm in the third grade. But I can't read Italian, and so I don't know what it says very much. I didn't show it to anybody, 'cause I thought they might tell my mamma, and she is crying all the time now as it is. She mustn't have any more trouble now." Frank gave the note to the reporter and said to give it to the police.

The letter appeared to have been written with red ozocerite, a sort of red pencil used by contractors. It read, "Joe Raimo, Traitor: The others want money and you know it, and this notice brings you death. Beware! The last notice!"

The Kansas City Police Department did everything it could to apprehend the men responsible for the death of Raimo. The chief of police led the investigation and assigned 25 officers to the case, including 10 of his top detectives. During a raid in the

Italian section of the city, 60 people were arrested and taken in for questioning regarding the killing of Raimo. Even after the huge roundup, there were no arrests. The chief of police also ran a notice in the paper:

> *Special Notice. Officer Joseph Raimo was assassinated at 11:15 p.m. March 28, 1911, on Holmes Street, between Fourth and Fifth streets. The officer was noted for his bravery and diligence in the performance of his duties. He had been especially assigned to the various Italian cases, and his untiring efforts aroused considerable enmity among the criminal classes of that nationality. Officers will use every means to bring to justice the perpetrators of this foul crime. Wentworth E. Griffin, Chief of Police.*

Despite all the efforts of the department, no arrests were ever made, and the murder of Patrolman Joe Raimo remains unsolved. Kansas City would have to endure nine more years of the Black Hand until the passage of the 18th Amendment brought on Prohibition and bigger fish to fry for the Mafia.

SOURCES:

- http://www.kcpolicememorial.com/pages/1911_joseph_raimo/
- The Literary Digest, Volume 61. "The Murders and Mysteries of Kansas City's Little Italy." Edited by Jewitt Wheeler, Isaac K. Funk, William S. Woods.
- Newspapers.com
- Ancestry.com

CHAPTER 19

"He got what was coming to him"

THE OFFICER:

Patrolman Henry Lee Harris
Seattle (Washington) Police Department
End of Watch: Tuesday, July 4, 1911
Age: 29

Just a few weeks after the killing of Patrolman Cunliffe (chapter 16), Patrolman Henry Lee Harris was senselessly gunned down while working crowd control on Independence Day.

On July 4th, working the night shift, Harris was assigned crowd control at the intersection of South Washington Street and Occidental Avenue South, known today as Pioneer Square. By 9 p.m. many of the 2,000 partygoers were heavily intoxicated, and Harris was having a difficult time keeping the mainly male crowd on the sidewalks, and out of traffic. As Harris was using his baton to push one particularly rowdy man onto the sidewalk, an unknown suspect snuck up behind the officer, placed the muzzle of his revolver next to his head, and pulled the trigger. The bullet entered his brain. Grabbing at the wound with his hand, Patrolman Harris instinctively went for his sidearm and unconsciously fired five rounds into the ground as he fell to the pavement. Harris never regained consciousness and died an hour later at the local hospital.

As the police swarmed the area, most witnesses refused to cooperate, and officers found it difficult to even get a description of the suspect. One gray-haired old man stood over the dying officer and instead of giving aid, slurred, "It serves [him] right. He's been pushing people around here all day. He got what was coming to him."

In the ensuing confusion, the cowardly murderer ran from the location with no one in the assembled mass reaching out to stop him. Many present were not celebrating America's independence but were protesting the government and what it stood for. Several in the crowd were from the Industrial Workers of the World (IWW), an extremely radical group founded just a few years earlier. One sober witness stated he saw the suspect run into offices of the IWW, but a subsequent search was met with little cooperation. The suspect was described as "southern European, 35-40 years of age, 5-foot-7, dark hair, wearing laborer's clothing." The suspect was never seen again, and the case remains unsolved.

Born in Fergus Falls, Minnesota, on May 26, 1882, Harris found his way to Seattle and served as a railroad locomotive fireman before joining the police department in 1910.

SOURCES:

- http://www.behindthebadgefoundation.org/roll-call/harris-officer-henry-l
- https://www.odmp.org/officer/6127-police-officer-henry-lee-harris
- Newspapers.com

CHAPTER 20

"Killed on a footbridge over English Ditch"

THE OFFICER:

Marshal Frank Peak
Loveland (Colorado) Police Department
End of Watch: Tuesday, July 13, 1915
Age: 35

Loveland, Colorado, located just north of Denver, was a sleepy little town of approximately 4,000 in 1915. While many police departments had absorbed the city marshal's office, in Loveland it was still the marshals who patrolled the city. There were just two, one working the day shift and the other at night.

Marshal Frank Peak was a rookie officer, having just been hired by the city 10 months earlier. He had not received any formal training, which was normal during this era. He was on his own, learning as he went. On Tuesday, July 13, 1915, Peak was walking his footbeat, jubilant about the new "spotlight" (flashlight) he had just received. At 1:30 a.m. he took the time to demonstrate it to a mechanic who was working late that evening.

As he left the garage, Peak came across an anxious citizen who asked him to walk her home. Marshal Peak obliged and left the woman with her sister at 2 a.m. Twenty minutes later, heading back to town, Peak was walking across the footbridge over English Ditch. While on the 40-foot-bridge, Marshal Peak had a heated argument with one or two unidentified suspects, culminating with gunfire. Six shots were fired in quick succession. Then silence, followed by two to four more shots.

Two hours later, two citizens walking to work discovered the body of Marshal Frank Peak on the footbridge. The day shift marshal was called in, and he roped off the area. Peak's

Colt .38 revolver lay at his side containing six discharged casings. No suspects were arrested, and the case remains unsolved. He is the only Loveland officer ever to be killed in the line of duty.

But the story does not end there. One hundred years later, in July 2015, interest in the unsolved case was renewed. A crusty old retired private investigator, Alan Rosenburg, made a shocking declaration, announcing that he knew who killed the marshal. His interest in the murder began six years earlier when he was contacted by the granddaughter of Marshal Peak. She said before she dies, she wants to know who killed her grandfather on that footbridge so many years ago.

That is all the private eye needed. According to Rosenburg, the case began nearly a month before Peaks was shot down when two twenty-somethings from Loveland, William Frank Reynolds and William Fletcher Query, were involved in a good ole drunken brawl at the county fair, exchanging blows with Ed Strong and Mark Derby.

Although evidence indicated that Reynolds and Query were the victims, Marshal Peak arrested them and hauled them off to jail for the night. Rosenburg indicated that perhaps Peak didn't arrest Strong and Derby because the Derby family was politically connected and a force in the community. Feeling they were persecuted by the marshal, Reynolds and Query filed assault and battery charges against Strong and Derby. The case went before the local judge, who fined Strong and Derby each $5, the minimum allowed. Query and Reynolds were not placated by the slap on the wrist that Strong and Derby received.

Rosenburg theorizes that Query and Reynolds were out drinking beer around town on the night of the

Retired private investigator Alan Rosenburg, who took up the case of the killing of Marshal Peak, 100 years later. He is convinced he knows who did it. Photo courtesy of the Loveland Daily Herald.

murder when they happened to run into Marshal Peak on that small bridge on a pitch-black night. He believes the marshal tried to arrest the two men for public drunkenness. This was substantiated by a boisterous exchange between them that a witness later testified to. Additionally, Marshal Peak had two beer bottles in his pockets which he apparently confiscated from the suspects as evidence. It was a brand of beer that could only be purchased in another town and one which Query was known to consume frequently. It is unknown exactly what happened next, but Marshal Peak was shot to death on the footbridge.

Just seven hours after the marshal was gunned down, Query and Reynolds abruptly quit their well-paying jobs at the local sugar factory and hopped a train to Denver. When the sheriff heard this, he had authorities detain the two men as they got off the train. The two agreed to return to Loveland to testify at an inquest that would be held the following day to investigate the murder of Peak.

A two-hour inquest was held the day after the murder. The entire investigation hinged on the testimony of Query and Reynolds. If there were transcripts, Rosenburg could not find them. Most of the information came from the two newspapers in Loveland. When asked about the fresh abrasions on his arms that could have been a result of an altercation with Peak, Reynolds stated that he had gotten into it with a guy at work the day before. When asked why they left town so suddenly, as both were employed at the sugar mill, they answered that they were leaving the state to seek better-paying jobs. When the inquest was completed, there were no restrictions put on the

The headlines in the Loveland Daily Herald announcing the murder of Marshal Peak, just one of two marshals who patrolled Loveland.

suspects while the investigation continued. Consequently, both men immediately boarded a train and were gone—forever. Rosenburg followed their paper trail to Iowa, where they both showed up on the Iowa census that same year.

Rosenburg requested the autopsy report of Peak, and even though the coroner's office has records going back to 1877, Peak's file was somehow missing.

A Footbridge once crossed the English Ditch, now known as Chubbuck Ditch, where Marshal Frank Peak was murdered. A plaque honoring the hero ensures that no one forgets. It reads: "In Memory of Fallen Officer, Marshal Frank Peak, Killed in the Line of Duty, July 13, 1915, Night Marshal Frank Peak was shot by unknown assailant(s) on this site while serving and protecting the citizens of Loveland."

More than 100 years has passed since the murder of Marshal Peak, the leads have faded away and the case remains officially unsolved. But Rosenburg, who spent six years investigating the shooting, has his own conclusion. In an interview with this author he confidently stated, "I am 99.99 percent sure that Query and Reynolds killed Marshal Peak that night on the footbridge." This author would not disagree, except I would make it 100 percent.

SOURCES:

- ➡ http://mv.ancestry.com/viewer/9358e4d7-77b5-4789-af4e-c80b7471c0fc/15047730/209913344. Numerous articles about the death of Marshal Peak.
- ➡ https://www.odmp.org/officer/10471-marshal-frank-peak
- ➡ http://www.reporterherald.com/news/loveland-local-news/ci_27263089/tour-de-pants-commemoration-honor-100-year-anniversary
- ➡ http://www.reporterherald.com/news/loveland-local-news/ci_28478076/police-family-honor-fallen-officer

- https://www.youtube.com/watch?v=tIY8zVCIlG4
- https://www.coloradohistoricnewspapers.org/cgi-bin/colorado?a=d&d=LLR19150714-01.2.2
- Author's interview of Mr. Rosenburg in 2016

CHAPTER 21

"The other fellow shot me from behind"

THE OFFICER:

Patrolman Lawrence E. Kost
Seattle (Washington) Police Department
Date of Incident: Friday, December 10, 1915
End of Watch: Sunday, December 12, 1915
Age: 24

The lead paragraph of the *Seattle Daily Times* summed up the police shooting: "Patrolman Lawrence Eugene Kost, 24 years old, lies desperately wounded at the City Hospital with a bullet lodged in his spine and every available policeman of the Seattle department is searching for three alleged bandits, one of whom fired the shot."

On the night of the shooting, Friday, December 10, 1915, it seemed that every criminal in town was out breaking the law. For the night watch of the Seattle Police Department, it started with the arrest of a man with a loaded pistol, the collar of another with a pipe bomb and an attempted robbery at gunpoint by two armed suspects of a man stopped at a traffic signal. From there it only got more chaotic.

Rookie Patrolman Lawrence (Larry) Kost, with four months on the job, soon found himself in the midst of that crazy shift. Assigned a footbeat in the area of Boren Avenue and Terrace Street, Kost was not assigned a partner, but a friend, Lyle Smith, was tagging along. It was 11:35 p.m. Thirty minutes earlier, Mr. F.A. Twichell had called the Seattle Police Department and reported his automobile stolen. Twenty-five minutes later, three armed suspects driving the stolen Ford robbed the Moline Drugstore on Yesler Way. The owner of the store called police to report the robbery and gave a detailed description of the three suspects.

Although a rookie, Patrolman Kost was quickly proving his acumen for the job of a street cop. Walking his beat, Kost alertly spotted a suspicious-looking, unoccupied Ford, which was conveniently parked directly across from a police call box (there were no police radios at this time).

Phoning in, Kost gave the desk officer the plate number of the vehicle and was told it had just been stolen and was used in a robbery of the Moline Drugstore. Kost made a mental note of the descriptions of the suspects given to him and set off on a search for the three men.

Patrolman Kost and his friend headed toward Broadway. At approximately 11:45 p.m., Kost saw three men matching the descriptions of the robbers walking just in front of them. Using a side street, Kost hurried to get ahead of the suspects. His timing was perfect. As he turned the corner, the three men were just walking up to him. Meanwhile, Smith had peeled off and was watching from a distance.

The suspects, eyeing the uniformed Kost, promptly stopped in the shadow of some trees. Kost carefully walked up and asked the men where they were going. At the same time, he began to search one of the three men. The suspect being searched resisted Kost, and a struggle ensued. With Kost's attention focused on the combative man, one of the other suspects pulled a handgun and fired one shot, striking the officer on the right side of his waistline. The bullet lodged in his spinal column. As he was falling to the ground, paralyzed from the waist down, he managed to pull the suspect down with him.

The bandit swiftly freed himself, and the three men took off running. Although paralyzed and spread out on the ground, Kost refused to succumb to his wound and emptied his revolver at the fleeing suspects. Lyle Smith, who was a wide-eyed witness to the events, rushed to his friend's side.

Patrolman Kost, unconscious, was rushed to the hospital, where he drifted in and out of consciousness throughout the next two days. When able to fight through the pain, he gave a detailed description of the suspects and exactly what occurred. The captain of detectives, William B. Kent, showed Kost a photograph of one of the possible suspects and asked, "Does this look like one of the men who shot you?" "I should say it does," replied Kost after he carefully scrutinized the photograph.

Captain Kent reminded the young police officer, "Now don't say so if you are not absolutely sure." "It's the man, all right," insisted Kost. "That's the one I was shaking down when the other fellow shot me from behind." The man, George W. Gunther, was a young Californian who was wanted for a previous armed robbery. He was also identified as a gang member who had robbed a clerk at a local pharmacy in Seattle one week earlier. It all fit together.

After the detective left and Kost drifted off, the decision was made not to operate. It was thought that any attempt to remove the bullet would probably kill the officer. By not doing the surgery the doctors hoped that Kost might live for at least a few days if not weeks. Sadly, Kost died the next day.

A break in the Kost murder occurred a few weeks later when Los Angeles Police detectives arrested several suspects following an armed robbery. Detectives became suspicious when two of the suspects, Thomas Green and James Murray, seemed overly anxious to admit to a petty robbery and start serving their prison time. It was subsequently determined that the men were part of a gang known as the "automobile bandits." The thugs were responsible for the murders of two police officers and an old man who had confronted them. Additionally, the bandits were wanted for scores of other robberies and burglaries. One of the LAPD detectives stated that the gang was "unsurpassed" in police records for the level of their crimes and violence handed out.

A short time later, a third arrestee, Howard Dunnigan, decided to talk. He stated that the gang had been up and down the West Coast. Along the way they committed numerous robberies, including, he said, the Moline Drugstore robbery in Seattle. Dunnigan admitted to being present for three murders, including the shooting of Patrolman Kost, but swore he did not pull the trigger. Their modus operandi (MO) was always the same. The gang used a stolen car going to and from the robberies, and they took only Fords—just as they had done in Seattle.

Dunnigan went on to admit that the gang had committed a robbery in San Francisco, just weeks before the Seattle robbery. The police in San Francisco had chased the suspects in their stolen Ford until it crashed into a wall at the Presidio. Three of the four suspects escaped. The forth, the leader of the gang, Harry Wilson, decided to shoot it out with the police. In the firefight, Wilson shot and killed San Francisco Patrolman Corporal Frederick Cook, but not before Cook returned fire and fatally wounded his attacker.

The gang then headed north to Seattle, where they committed several robberies and murdered Officer Kost when he attempted to arrest them. From Seattle, they returned to San Francisco, where they murdered a senior citizen who caught them burglarizing the building they were staying in. Their next move was to Los Angeles, where they were captured.

Seattle Police Department detectives were certain that at least two of the suspects, Thomas Green and James Murray, were involved in the murder of Patrolman Kost. The third suspect might have been George W. Gunther, the suspect that Kost had identified as the man he was searching when he was shot.

Green and Murray were convicted of crimes in California, and both were sentenced to life in prison. Other members of the gang were sentenced to long prison terms in California, but no one was ever tried for the murder of Patrolman Kost. The case remains officially unsolved, but in this author's opinion, if the gang members had been extradited to Seattle, there was enough evidence to convict them of the murder of Patrolman Kost.

SOURCES:

- http://www.behindthebadgefoundation.org/roll-call/kost-officer-lawrence-e
- http://historylink.org/File/3786
- http://rspoa.org/index.php?end-of-watch&listpage=9
- Newspapers.com

CHAPTER 22

A Long Death

THE OFFICER:

Patrolman George William Mattern
Des Moines (Iowa) Police Department
Date of Incident: Tuesday, August 7, 1917
End of Watch: Sunday, May 12, 1918
Age: 27

Des Moines, Iowa, in 1917 was a city where horses competed with automobiles for space on the busy streets. In the heart of the city around Court Avenue and Third Street was the tough part of town. Many of the factory workers went there to escape after a hard day of work. It was an area where black smoke came bellowing from the huge industrial smokestacks like freshly lit cigars. The laborers enjoyed an ample choice of bars and restaurants at prices they could afford.

Located in the 300 block of Locust Street was one such bar, the Temp, and it happened to be the beat of two-year Patrolman George Mattern. It was getting late on the evening of Tuesday, August 7, 1917, when Mattern heard gunshots. He knew he was close, and he did as police officers have always done, he ran toward the sound of the shooting. As he was sprinting down one alley, he met up with a gunman running down the same alley coming right at him. Patrolman Mattern and the suspect spontaneously began shooting at one another. Mattern got off three shots but missed his target while the suspect's last round struck Mattern in the abdomen, coming to rest against his spine. Mattern went down. The bandit ran from the location and escaped. The officer was quickly transported to Mercy Hospital and underwent surgery.

Just moments before the shooting, the suspect had walked into the nearly empty Temp Bar as the bartender was cleaning up in preparation for closing. Standing at the bar, the man asked for a drink. As the bartender turned around to accommodate him, the suspect pulled out a gun and ordered him to raise his hands. The bartender was prepared for just such a robbery and quickly ducked behind the counter and grabbed his own gun and fired at the suspect. The bartender missed and the man took off running until he ran into Patrolman Mattern.

Mattern was operated on that night, and although the surgery was touch-and-go, by the following day the doctors thought the wounded officer would have a full recovery.

Meanwhile, detectives arrested 30-year-old Chester Scott, who lived on Walnut Street, very near the Temp Bar. Scott fit the description given by the bartender and was known to detectives for a previous robbery with the same MO. The bartender later identified Scott as the man who robbed him.

In an earlier case, Scott had robbed a lounge in the same area as the Temp, using the same distraction technique. He ordered a sandwich, and as the cook turned to make the order, Scott pulled a gun and robbed the store. After being captured, Scott pleaded guilty to that case and received a 10-year suspended sentence. He was paroled under the supervision of a local clergyman.

Just a month after being almost killed in the shooting, Mattern had recovered enough to travel with his wife and two children to visit a relative. Mattern celebrated his 28th birthday in January 1918, but the wound never fully healed, and he began to have serious complications. On May 12, 1918, nine months after being shot, Mattern died from a peritonitis, an infection caused by the robber's bullet. Neither Scott, (no explanation was ever given) nor anyone else was ever charged, and the case remains unsolved.

George Mattern was born January 26, 1890, in Lee Township of Polk County, Iowa, the first child of German immigrant Anna Gobeli and Ohio native William J. Mattern.

He had two siblings: Carol Joseph Mattern and Marie Mattern Christiansen.

Mattern, worked as a drug clerk before becoming a patrolman, married Grace Demoss. The couple had two daughters, Helen was 5 and Marcella was not quite 1 when their father died. Grace never remarried. She worked for 22 years as a telephone operator for the very same department her husband had served.

SOURCES:

- https://iowacoldcases.org/case-summaries/george-mattern/
- "Iowa Unsolved Murders: Historical Cases" by Nancy Bowers
- http://www.findagrave.com/cgi-bin/fg.cgi?page=gr&GRid=52423158
- http://www.desmoinesregister.com/story/news/crime-and-courts/2014/06/28/carlisle-teacher-anthony-garza-digs-unsolved-murder-des-moines-police-officer-cold-case-george-mattern/11583161/
- Newspapers.com

CHAPTER 23

The Second Deadliest Day in Law Enforcement History

THE OFFICER:

Detective Frank Caswin
Milwaukee (Wisconsin) Police Department
End of Watch: Saturday, November 24, 1917
Age: 30

THE OFFICER:

Detective Frederick Kaiser
Milwaukee (Wisconsin) Police Department
End of Watch: Saturday, November 24, 1917
Age: 39

THE OFFICER:

Detective David J. O'Brien
Milwaukee (Wisconsin) Police Department
End of Watch: Saturday, November 24, 1917
Age: 53

THE OFFICER:

Detective Charles Seehawer
Milwaukee (Wisconsin) Police Department
End of Watch: Saturday, November 24, 1917
Age: 45

THE OFFICER:

Operator Edward Spindler
Milwaukee (Wisconsin) Police Department
End of Watch: Saturday, November 24, 1917
Age: 35

THE OFFICER:

Detective Stephen Stecker
Milwaukee (Wisconsin) Police Department
End of Watch: Saturday, November 24, 1917
Age: 36

THE OFFICER:

Detective Albert Templin
Milwaukee (Wisconsin) Police Department
End of Watch: November 24, 1917
Age: 39

THE OFFICER:

Station Keeper Henry Deckert
Milwaukee (Wisconsin) Police Department
End of Watch: November 24, 1917
Age: 28

THE OFFICER:

Detective Paul Weiler
Milwaukee (Wisconsin) Police Department
End of Watch: Saturday, November 24, 1917
Age: 38

In what remains the second deadliest day in U.S. law enforcement history (after September 11, 2001), nine Milwaukee police officers were killed in a bomb blast at Central police station on November 24, 1917. On that Saturday morning, the daughter of the church cleaning woman discovered a questionable package outdoors, alongside the Italian Evangelical Church in downtown Milwaukee. The suspicious item laid around the church until that evening when two young church members took the package to the local police station. Station Keeper Henry Deckert took the 20 pound device from the young men and brought it to the lieutenant's office and then into the assembly room.

A number of detectives were just arriving for roll call. According to a police department report, "As detectives examined the package with a fury of haste, it exploded, immediately killing [nine police officers]." Of the 10 officers who were in the room, eight were killed and two were injured. A watch on one of the men stopped at 7:57 p.m.

Above the assembly room was the operator's room where Edward Spindler was killed by shrapnel blasting through the floor. A citizen filing a complaint and one of the men who brought the package to police headquarters were also killed.

The bombers were never apprehended, but police linked the bombing to a group of anarchists who were seeking revenge against the pastor of the church. The bomb was not intended to kill police officers.

Officials exam the aftermath of the bomb explosion at Milwaukee Central Police Station that killed nine officers.

SOURCES:

- https://en.wikipedia.org/wiki/Milwaukee_Police_Department
- http://rapidcityjournal.com/november-milwaukee-police-station-bombing/image_24f9d30c-8fa5-11e4-a9f1-8ba9ff42d734.html
- http://archive.jsonline.com/news/crime/victims-remembered-98-years-after-bomb-at-milwaukee-police-station-killed-11-b99622224z1-353168381.html
- http://milwaukeepolicenews.com/hero/paul-2/

CHAPTER 24

"Ma"

THE OFFICER:
Chief of Police John J. Sturgus
Anchorage (Alaska) Police Department
End of Watch: Sunday, February 20, 1921
Age: 60

Anchorage, Alaska, in the depth of winter can be a very unforgiving city. For police officers it is like working a never-ending night shift because the sun is up for such a short time. For Chief of Police John Sturgus, it was his first winter, and it would be his last. On January 1, 1921, Anchorage became a municipality, and the city council hired John Sturgus as the Anchorage Police Department's first chief of police. Sturgus had previous experience as a law enforcement officer in the states of Washington and Montana.

Early Sunday evening, February 20, 1921, Chief Sturgus, the only officer on the police force, was trudging through the snow in the alley at the rear of the Anchorage drugstore. At some point the chief encountered one or more persons at the foot of the stairs leading up to second-floor residences. It appears an altercation took place, as Sturgus was disarmed and was shot in the chest with his own weapon. The suspects escaped as the chief fell into the snow. No one reported hearing the single shot.

Around 9:15 p.m. the chief was found moaning by a civilian "special night watchman" who was hired by the local merchants to watch for fires and unusual activity. John McNutt saw the chief's body but did not examine him closely and thought he was just a town drunk. He later testified he did not recognize the chief but said, "the man was moaning."

Ironically, McNutt set off to find the chief to report what he had seen. During his search, he came across Mrs. Baxter, who was returning to her home above the drugstore. Hearing about the "drunk," Mrs. Baxter went to investigate for herself. She immediately recognized the chief and knelt down beside the dying man. Sturgus was still moaning but called out to her as "Ma," a nickname she was known by. Baxter hurriedly ran to a nearby store to get help. The chief, still semiconscious, was groaning, "Oh, my head," and "Oh Bobby, Bobby."

Local citizens got the chief to the hospital, where he was placed on an operating table. He was asked repeatedly by two U.S. marshals who had shot him, and though he talked about being cold and how the bright lights hurt his eyes, for some reason he did not answer them, and died, leaving behind a mystery that has not been solved to this day.

Around town, several theories circulated. The one having the most credibility was that he was killed "by members of an illicit liquor gang." The conjecture was that he was killed for revenge because he had assisted the local marshal's office during the previous week in making several arrests of moonshiners. The law enforcement group had pulled the plug on 12 moonshine outfits in one week. The identity of the killer as well as the motive were never determined despite a reward for $2,000.

Jack Sturgus was born December 24, 1861, in Mansfield, Ohio. He was a peace officer in Montana and Everett, Washington, before moving to Alaska in 1913. He relocated to Anchorage in 1916 and was employed as special U.S. deputy until his appointment as Anchorage's first chief of police. To date, his death is the only unsolved police murder in Anchorage history.

SOURCES:

- http://www.findagrave.com/cgi-bin/fg.cgi?page=gr&GRid=20923219
- *Forgotten Heroes: Police Officers Killed in Alaska*, 1850-1997 by William Wilbanks. Page 33-40.
- http://www.muni.org/Departments/police/Pages/History.aspx
- http://www.muni.org/Departments/police/Pages/SturgusBio.aspx
- http://www.odmp.org/officer/12947-chief-of-police-john-j-sturgus

CHAPTER 25

"Negro cop shot by white man"

THE OFFICER:

Patrolman William Whitfield
Indianapolis (Indiana) Police Department
Date of Incident: June 18, 1922
End of Watch: November 27, 1922
Age: 37

The newspaper headline reads "Negro Cop Shot by White Man." In the first half of the 20th century, African American law enforcement officers were being hired in greater numbers, with most assigned to predominantly black areas of their communities. Patrolman William Whitfield was an exception. The 12-year veteran had a brilliant performance record and was assigned to the largely white area of Indianapolis, the first black officer to have been so assigned. The new assignment was not well received by many in the white community and even among some within the police department.

Working plainclothes in an alley near College Avenue at 36th Street at 11 p.m., Patrolman Whitfield observed a white man who "was roughly dressed" and did not fit the area. Whitfield attempted to stop the man and question him. As he did so, Whitfield pulled back his jacket to show the unidentified man his police badge. Upon seeing this, the suspect quickly took off running. Patrolman Whitfield went into a foot pursuit.

Having just initiated the chase, the suspect abruptly stopped, turned and fired one shot at the pursuing officer, striking him in the abdomen. Patrolman Whitfield fired two rounds and went down. The suspect continued running. Struggling to his feet, Whitfield managing to reach 36th Street, where he stopped a passing streetcar and its operator notified police. A soldier who saw the commotion took Whitfield to a nearby hospital. Officer Whitfield struggled with his agonizing wound for five months, finally succumbing to his injuries on November 27, 1922.

His death remained virtually unpublished at the time, and he was buried in an unmarked grave as the family could not afford a gravestone. Seventy-six years later, an article detailing the circumstances of Officer Whitfield's death and burial appeared in an Indianapolis Police Department newsletter. Almost eight decades after Officer Whitfield was interred, it took only three hours for the generous officers of the Indianapolis Police Department to raise the necessary funds to purchase a headstone. On a cold, wet day in November 1998, hundreds turned out for a ceremony with full police honors. Four years later, through the efforts of a longtime resident who had dedicated himself to researching the murder of Patrolman Whitfield, additional money was raised to place a sundial and plaque in a nearby park.

The suspect was never apprehended, and the case remains unsolved. Officer Whitfield was divorced, and he and his four children lived with his father.

SOURCES:

- http://www.odmp.org/officer/14114-officer-william-whitfield
- http://www.indystar.com/story/news/2013/09/20/list-of-indianapolis-area-police-officers-killed-in-the-line-of-duty/2841565/
- https://www.newspapers.com/image/106402076/
- Ancestry.com

CHAPTER 26

The Colorado Rangers

THE OFFICER:

Colorado Ranger Edward P. Bell
Colorado Mounted Rangers
Date of Incident: October 14, 1922
End of Watch: Monday, October 16, 1922
Age: 33

Following the establishment of the Colorado Territory in 1861, the Colorado Rangers were formed. They were loosely based on the renowned Texas Rangers. In the early years, the Rangers assisted both law enforcement and the state militia and since 1941 have been an all-volunteer auxiliary force, assisting local law enforcement agencies across the state. In 1921, the Rangers traded in their horses for Harley-Davidson motorcycles and were very active during the violent years of Prohibition (1920-1933). The Rangers paid special attention to the bootleggers who were running illegal booze throughout the state.

With their vigorous enforcement of Prohibition, they were not popular with the gangsters who ran the operations. When the law got in the way of profits, the gangsters turned to intimidation and violence. Colorado Ranger Edward Bell was likely a victim of just such an attack.

On the evening of October 16, 1922, Rangers Bell and his partner, George Jennings, received an anonymous telephone tip that a gas station west of Limon was about to be robbed. The Rangers left immediately on their new Harley-Davidson motorcycle, which was equipped with a sidecar for the second officer. As the two rushed to Limon, they were abruptly run off the road by an automobile, causing them to crash.

Ranger Edward Bell on the motorcycle with sidecar (right). Not long after this photograph was taken, Bell and his partner, George Jennings, were run off the road, robbed and beaten. Ranger Bell died from his injuries.

They survived the wreck but were then attacked by unknown assailants, who beat them severely and stole their wallets and service revolvers. A passersby found them a short time later, and they were rushed to St. Luke's Hospital in Denver. Bell was beaten so badly that he died in the hospital two days later. Jennings survived his wounds but could not recall anything about the attack because of his beating.

The circumstances of what happened were never officially determined. It was theorized that bootleggers in the area were responsible, as both Rangers had made several large raids on nearby stills the previous month. In 1999, Ranger Bell's name joined those listed on the Colorado Law Enforcement Memorial. To date, he is the only Colorado Ranger to be killed in the line of duty. Bell was survived by his wife, parents, and three brothers.

SOURCES:

- http://www.odmp.org/officer/20444-colorado-ranger-edward-p-bell
- https://www.coloradoranger.org/history
- http://www.leg.state.co.us/CLICS/CLICS2016A/commsumm.nsf/b4a3962433b52fa787256e5f00670a71/e3c2ca198356686c87257fa2005a7d5f/$FILE/16HouseState0427AttachB.pdf
- http://www.teapartytribune.com/2011/07/12/colorado%E2%80%99s-oldest-law-enforcement-organization/

CHAPTER 27

"Killed by thugs"

THE OFFICER:

Night Watch Officer John "Jay" Gould
Oxford Village (Michigan) Police Department
End of Watch: Friday, February 13, 1925
Age: 52

It was a typical February morning in the village of Oxford, Michigan—bone chilling cold on that Friday the 13th in 1925. Making his rounds, Night Watch Officer John "Jay" Gould was shot point-blank in the chest by a 12-gauge shotgun. On his death certificate, it simply reads: "Killed by thugs."

Officer Gould was sworn in as a night watch officer in 1912. His duties were tending to the village by foot during nighttime hours. This included checking the village jail and fire hall, patrolling the downtown businesses, and assisting other law enforcement agencies in the village if needed. During the day, the village marshal handled these duties. Night watch officers were appointed by the village council and were paid $15 per week.

As the years passed, community members came to call Officer Gould "Jay." He was an officer who earned a reputation of being "fearless." Gould once boasted that he was afraid of nothing, and did not fear death. His attitude would be on a collision course with the "Purple Gang." This was a bunch of hoodlum bootleggers and hijackers from Detroit who used Oxford as a hideout when on the run. According to an unsubstantiated rumor, the gang told Gould to stay off the streets the night of February 12.

Retired Captain James Malcolm and Sgt. Michael Solwold of today's Oxford Police Department never forgot. They led a movement to raise money for a gravestone for Night Watch Officer Gould, who had been buried in an unmarked grave.

Despite the warning, Gould went out on patrol as he always did. That night at 3 a.m., the watchman observed a suspicious vehicle parked alongside the Oxford Savings Bank at Burdick and Washington streets. It was later reported to be a stolen car containing six gangsters. A witness, Mr. Macomb, who lived in an upstairs apartment across the street from the bank, saw Officer Gould standing next to a "large touring car." After hearing shouts, Macomb started for his front door when he heard a loud gunshot. Macomb reached the street just in time to see the touring car speeding away. He found Officer Gould lying face down in the road, bleeding from a shotgun wound. He died where he fell. The suspects were never identified, and the case remains unsolved.

Gould was born in Toronto, Canada, on May 18, 1872, and moved to the United States as a young boy. He was survived by his wife and two children and was buried in an unmarked grave. In 2015, 90 years after the murder, two dedicated officers from Oxford Police Department, retired Capt. James Malcolm and Sgt. Michael Solwold, helped to raise money for the purchase of a headstone. "There are still some things that need answering," said Solwold, "Just because we're going to have a gravestone doesn't mean we're done."

SOURCES:

- http://www.theoaklandpress.com/article/OP/20150511/NEWS/150519937
- http://www.cincinnati.com/story/news/local/oakland-county/2015/05/11/oxford-police-mystery-officer/27096269/
- Newspapers.com

CHAPTER 28

"Iowa City cop is killed in chase"

THE OFFICER:

Motorcycle Officer Edward M. Leeney
Iowa City (Iowa) Police Department
End of Watch: Thursday, April 29, 1926
Age: 32

Hanging in the Iowa City Police Department headquarters for as long as most can recall, is an old tattered frame surrounding a faded newspaper clipping from 1926. The headline reads, "Iowa City Cop Is Killed In Chase." It is one of the few records of the death of an Iowa City police officer killed on duty. The story could have ended in 1926 as a simple unfortunate accident but for the determined efforts of several Iowa City officers 85 years later.

Nationwide, one of the leading causes of death for officers killed in the line of duty is traffic accidents. And for the first 50 years of the 20th century, motor officers were killed disproportionately to their patrol car colleagues. On most police departments, hard helmets did not become mandatory until the 1950s. If they had been, perhaps Motorcycle Officer Edward Leeney would have lived a long life and retired.

Main street, Iowa City, Iowa. Circa 1900.

Unsolved, Cold-Case Homicides

At 10 p.m. Thursday, April 29, 1926, Officer Leeney was pushing his motorcycle hard. He was in pursuit of a speeding Ford coupe, roaring through the streets at nearly 50 miles per hour. With limited overhead lighting, his view was restricted. As he approached the intersection of Market and North Dubuque streets, he collided with a city streetcar.

The impact was horrific. Leeney struck hard against the side of the streetcar, bounced off, and slammed into the pavement, fracturing his skull. The married father of three young children died a short time later at a local hospital. Meanwhile, the Ford sped out of town and was never seen again.

For years the incident was treated as just an unfortunate accident until 2011, when Iowa City, Chief Sam Hargadine researched the incident further. He specifically looked at current law outlined in Code Chapter 707. In part, the code, which was not the law in the 1920s, states: "Murder defined: A person who kills another person with malice aforethought either express or implied commits murder….The person kills another person while escaping or attempting to escape from lawful custody."

The argument in Leeney's case was simple. When a law enforcement officer must resort to chasing a fleeing suspect through a city at high rates of speed, a collision involving someone is a strong possibility. Had the officer not been chasing the Ford that night, the question could be asked would he have collided with the streetcar and died? Extremely

IOWA CITY COP IS KILLED IN CHASE

Edward Leeney Suffers Fractured Skull

IOWA CITY, April 30.—(U.P.)—Motorcycle Officer Edward M. Leeney. 33. of the local police force, was struck by a street car while chasing a speeding Ford coupe here and fatally injured.

He was thrown against the street car and struck his head on the pavement several feet away, suffering a skull fracture from which he died 10 minutes later in a local hospital. The accident occurred about 10 o'clock last night.

The motorman of the street car declared that Leeney was traveling at a high rate of speed. Witnesses estimated that he was going 48 miles an hour. He leaves a widow and three small children. His mother and two brothers also survive.

A copy of the newspaper clipping hanging in Iowa City Police Department headquarters.

unlikely. The Iowa City Police Department has reclassified Leeney's death as an unsolved murder.

SOURCES:

- https://iowacoldcases.org/case-summaries/edward-leeney/
- https://www.facebook.com/iowacoldcases/posts/901823226507525
- Ancestry.com
- Newspapers.com

CHAPTER 29

A Casual Drive Turned Deadly

THE OFFICER:

Patrolman Arthur H. Bassett
Rockford (Illinois) Police Department
End of Watch: Thursday, September 22, 1927
Age: 29

The 29-year-old, three-year patrolman for the Rockford, Illinois, police department could not wait to get off work. Arthur Bassett had made plans to pick up his fiancee, Pearl Johnson, at 11 p.m. and go for a short ride. Patrolman Bassett was in such a hurry, he didn't even change out of his uniform.

After he picked up Miss Johnson, they took a short drive down Montague Road. The delighted husband-to-be turned onto Michigan Avenue near the intersection of South Central Avenue. In no hurry, the couple decided to pull over to the side of the road in this remote area surrounded by large fields.

After stopping for just a few minutes, Bassett noticed a car pull up directly behind them. Suddenly, four men jumped from

The remote area where the shooting took place. The "X" marks the spot where Bassett was gunned down. The cross is where one of the suspects was wounded. (All photos from the Rockford Register Republic.)

The car driven by Bassett with a bullet-shattered window.

their vehicle and surrounded the young couple. Without warning, the men started pounding on Bassett's car and yelling obscenities. Bassett hollered, "What do you want?" To this one of the thugs answered, "Get out of the car and you'll see." Bassett was always prepared for the unknown. He kept a .45 automatic right under his seat, and he was also carrying his service revolver, as he was still in uniform. As Bassett sprang from his vehicle armed with both weapons, one of the suspects simultaneously jumped into the car and told Johnson to "get down." Bassett confronted the other three, and everyone starting shooting. When the smoke cleared, the man in the car quickly got out, at which time Johnson heard one of the men cry, "For God's sakes, Ralph, get me in the car quick, I am bleeding to death!" Johnson saw the other men pick him up and carry him back to their car.

Pearl Johnson ran to her fiancé who was lying in the middle of the dirt road with a growing pool of blood spreading out from under him. In shock, she ran down the street screaming for help. When Bassett's colleagues arrived, it was too late to help their fallen comrade. Police searched the area with no luck. The officers noticed blood all over the area around the car. It appeared to them that the gunfight was at very close range and it appeared that another man had been shot.

Just a short time after the shooting, a local

Arthur Bassett's fiancee, Pearl Johnson.

doctor was awakened in his home by a loud pounding on his door. Outside a man was yelling that his friend had been shot and needed help. The doctor told the young man that he did not have the proper equipment or facilities to help him. He told the man to take their friend to the local hospital. The man left. It was theorized that at least one suspect knew the area because he was able to locate the doctor's home in a residential neighborhood. The police contacted hospitals and doctors, but no one had seen the wounded suspect.

Bassett had been struck two times, with one round going through his chest and cutting his aorta and exiting under the right shoulder blade. Although there was plenty of evidence to go on, there were no arrests made, and the case remains unsolved.

SOURCES:

- http://www.bassettbranches.org/tng/getperson.php?personID=I31715&tree=1A
- http://www.odmp.org/officer/1569-patrol-officer-arthur-h-bassett
- http://rockrivertimes.com/2015/01/14/voices-from-the-grave-the-unsolved-murder-of-rockford-police-officer-arthur-bassett/
- http://history.rockfordpubliclibrary.org/localhistory/?p=13837
- Newspapers.com

CHAPTER 30

"I'm afraid the bootleggers are going to get me."

THE OFFICER:

Patrolman Norman L. Schoen
Indianapolis (Indiana) Police Department
End of Watch: Tuesday, March 6, 1928
Age: 29

During Prohibition, Patrolman Norman Schoen made it his duty to go after criminals involved with bootlegging in his community of Indianapolis. A man who, according to his wife, never brought the job home with him and talked very little about anything that happened at work, told her the day before his death, "I'm afraid the bootleggers are going to get me."

The following day, at 11 p.m., Tuesday, March 6, 1928, Patrolman Schoen was shot and fatally wounded by an unknown assailant just a few feet from his house. Schoen was just getting home after his shift when he was shot in the back by an assailant who was lying in wait behind a large tree. Schoen fell with his flashlight in his right hand and his gun still in its holster. The bullet had pierced his heart. A witness reported hearing a single shot and then an automobile door slamming shut and the car speeding off. A Chrysler automobile was seen by another witness leaving the crime scene.

A young man who heard the loud shot, came outside and found the officer lying between the street and the sidewalk. Schoen was carried into his home, where he died a short time later, never regaining consciousness. All cities east of Indianapolis were notified to be on the lookout for the killer, and a police emergency squad (specially trained detectives armed with Thompson submachine guns) went as far east as Greenfield in search of the Chrysler. The dragnet failed to turn up any leads or suspects. The detective in charge stated that he was without "any tangible" evidence that might lead to an arrest. Detectives believed that revenge was the motive for the slaying. Schoen took his job seriously. As one friend stated, "From the day he became a patrolman, he felt as if the entire responsibility for the welfare of Indianapolis was on his shoulders."

IMPRESSIVE MILITARY SERVICE IS HELD FOR SLAIN POLICEMAN

AMERICAN LEGION GUARD HEADING THE NORMAN L. SCHOEN FUNERAL CORTEGE AS IT LEFT THE IRVINGTON M. E. CHURCH.

The American Legion led the funeral cortege for Patrolman Norman Schoen.

Schoen also had made enemies. During the preceding summer, Schoen accidently shot a 5-year-old girl when firing at a fleeing felony suspect in a vehicle. Although he visited the young girl daily while she was recovering, some in the community refused to forgive the officer for his misdeed. Patrolman Schoen also drew the derision of the underworld for his aggressive policing of the local bootleggers and producers of liquor on his beat. To the detectives, the motive for his killing had to be revenge. They shook down numerous mobsters, but once again, came up with no arrest. His murder remains unsolved.

Norman Schoen was a lifelong resident of Indianapolis. He enlisted in the Army in October, 1917, a few months after the United States entered World War I. He joined the 147th Aero Squadron as an ambulance driver and spent 14 months in France. At the conclusion of the war, Schoen worked in a manufacturing plant. He soon grew bored and told his friends that he wanted more "action," so he decided to join the police force. Schoen had 13 months on the force at the time of his murder. His military funeral was attended by hundreds of friends and members of the Indianapolis Police Department. He was survived by his wife and two young daughters.

SOURCES:

➡ http://www.indy.gov/eGov/City/DPS/IMPD/About/Memoriam/Pages/nschoen.aspx

➡ Newspapers.com

CHAPTER 31

"My God, I'm shot"

THE OFFICER:

Patrolman Paul Miller
Indianapolis (Indiana) Police Department
Date of Incident: Tuesday, July 17, 1928
End of Watch: Wednesday, July 18, 1928
Age: 36

Just three months after the slaying of Patrolman Norman L. Schoen (chapter 30) of the Indianapolis Police Department, Patrolman Paul Miller, also of IPD, was gunned down. In both cases, the killers were never apprehended.

Miller, a seven-year veteran and his partner, John Banks, were on duty at Substation No. 6 at Vermont Street and Sherman Drive. The officers received a report of two

The newspaper headline highlighting the shooting of Patrolman Miller.

suspicious men who appeared ready to rob a drugstore. The two patrolmen responded in their police car and pulled up in front of the Schaller & Cole drugstore at 2502 Station Street. Banks quickly jumped from the vehicle and ran into the store. The suspects were gone, but as he started to exit, Banks heard gunfire. Outside, Banks found his partner lying in front of the police car a short distance away. As Banks reached his partner, Patrolman Miller moaned, "My God, I'm shot." Banks looked

FELLOW-POLICE, HEADS BARE, FORM FUNERAL LANE FOR HONOR TO MILLER, SLAIN ON DUTY BY BANDITS

Officers from the Indianapolis Police Department pay their final respects to their fallen comrade.

up and saw two suspects running from the area. Banks went into a foot pursuit. As he was chasing the suspects, Banks fired three shots. One of the suspects must have been shot, as evidenced by a short blood trail leading from the area. Later, a witness reported he saw one of the men stumble and fall in the alley, then get back on his feet and continue to run from the area. As the two men ran, one of them turned and fired at Banks but missed. Banks lost track of the two suspects.

Miller was shot four times, once in his chest, abdomen, left arm and back. He was transported to a local hospital. When he arrived, the brave officer fighting unconsciousness, was able to give a detailed description of the two suspects and the circumstances of the encounter. Patrolman Miller said he was shot by two white men, one of whom approached him from the front while the other came up from behind. The man in the front fired a large-caliber revolver. This struck Miller in the chest, with the impact knocking him to the ground. After he fell, the second man stood over Miller and fired several bullets into him from a revolver at point-blank range. As the two suspects ran from the location, Miller emptied his own revolver at the fleeing men. Seventeen hours later, Miller uttered his last words, "I hope they get them, Doc. I hope they get them before they shoot someone else." Although over 100 possible suspects were taken in and questioned, the killers were never found, and the case remains unsolved.

Paul Miller was born in Kentucky on June 18, 1892, and moved to Indiana when he was 9. He joined the police department in 1921. Chief of Police Worley praised Miller's record, exclaiming, "His record was unusually good and he has made many good arrests. He has been commended on several occasions because of his devotion to his duty." Miller was the second policeman in the Miller family to die while serving on the IPD. Fourteen years earlier, his brother John died of pneumonia.

SOURCES:

- https://www.odmp.org/officer/9354-officer-paul-p-miller
- Newspapers.com

CHAPTER 32

The Secret Boarder

THE OFFICER:

Deputy Sheriff Louis H. Dayton
Clay County (Iowa) Sheriff's Office
End of Watch: Wednesday, March 20, 1929
Age: 54

Spencer, Iowa, resident Mrs. Emma Jensen was a light sleeper. She had no choice. When you have two boarders who are men, and one has to walk through your dining room to get to his room, you can't be too careful. On the night of Wednesday, March 20, 1929, it was no different. Emma Jensen knew she had one boarder in bed, but not the second—which was very common.

Mrs. Jensen knew why but was sworn to secrecy and was not to tell anyone—not even her husband. A mysterious man who said his name was Bert Cook (an alias, hereafter referred to as Louis H. Dayton) had approached her three weeks earlier to rent a room. He told her that he was posing as a door-to-door salesman selling a spot remover but was actually a special deputy working undercover to unearth the illegal manufacturing, and sales of liquor in the county. It was a time in the nation when almost anything to do with liquor was illegal. It was the era of Prohibition.

At 11 p.m., she heard the undercover agent climb the stairs to his room. She listened to him use his water bowl and then promptly leave again. As he did so, he slammed the door so hard that it flew open. Mrs. Jensen looked out the window and saw Dayton almost running down the street toward downtown.

About 20 minutes later, Mrs. Jensen got back into bed. Then she heard someone on the porch of her home. She again got up and peeked out the window. She saw Dayton just standing on the porch. Suddenly, he walked off in the same direction as before.

A short time later, she heard Dayton return. She listened as he stopped in the dining room and heard him say, "Is this Chris's place?" Jumping from bed, she met Dayton standing in the darkened room. "What is the matter with you?" she asked. Dayton said, "I feel funny; it seems like I can't hardly see. It seems like I am half-blind. I must have fell or something like that. I'm bleeding."

She instructed Dayton to use the kitchen sink and clean up. As he finished, she noticed that the sink was full of blood. As she talked with him, she noticed that he seemed confused and was swaying where he stood. The deputy told Mrs. Jensen that the last thing he could recall was encountering two men and waking up on the sidewalk near the post office. He had a deep wound under his chin and commented that he got "hooked." The deputy then threw a punch in the air to demonstrate how he was struck down.

When Dayton complained that he felt "queer all over," Mrs. Jensen suggested that he go see the town doctor. Dayton stubbornly refused. He turned and walked up the stairs to his room, followed by Chris, Emma's husband. Outside his room, he opened the door, turned on the lights and collapsed in the doorway—dead.

After the authorities arrived, they found a watch and some cash on Dayton's body and made the assumption that robbery was not the motive for the attack. The coroner noted that the victim's skull was not fractured but that Dayton most likely died from a blood clot in the brain from being struck on the head. That type of injury would be consistent with his confused and dazed behavior. The subsequent autopsy would prove this to be correct. The sheriff went to the area where Dayton said he was attacked and found two large pools of blood 30 feet from the post office. It appeared to officials that the suspects had used brass knuckles to work Dayton over.

Speculation ran rampant on who had beaten Dayton senseless. Shortly before his death, Dayton had confided to

Mrs. Jensen that he had gathered incriminating information on local bootleggers, and the authorities were getting ready to "make a cleanup." After he turned in the names of the guilty parties, he would be leaving Spencer.

Even the local paper revealed the facts of the case for all to read:

> *That [Dayton] had secured evidence against Spencer bootleggers and expected to report some liquor sales on them within a few days was his statement made shortly before Wednesday, the evening he was beaten. He had been hanging around pool halls and other places watching bootleggers and told some acquaintances that "he had the goods" on some of the liquor vendors and was about ready to "turn in the list." Reports of [Dayton's] statements may have reached some of the bootleggers, police think, which prompted the beating.*

Law enforcement officials made an exhaustive search for the perpetrators, but to no avail. Dayton's homicide remains unsolved. As a local paper summed it up:

> *Into the category of "unsolved murders," local officials have placed the slaying of [Dayton], Special Investigator. State Agent Hi Yackey has spent much of the time since the slaying here assisting local officers, yet the solution of the mystery seems as remote as it did the night [Dayton] staggered into his rooming house and mumbled a story of being beaten in front of the Post Office.*

Louis Dayton was born January 15, 1875, near Washington, Iowa. He married in 1896 and had nine children. His ex-wife said he had very little education but liked detective stories; he would read them aloud. His daughter was quoted as saying:

> *He always had an inkling to be a detective and believed he had the ability to make a good one. He liked nothing better than to get a problem to work out that required detective work, and I've always known that he would like to be engaged in work that would give him a chance to do secret investigations.*

SOURCES:

- Nancy Bowers, "Iowa Unsolved Murders: Historic Cases."
- http://www.iowaunsolvedmurders.com/the-murders/undercover-murder-of-louis-h-dayton-1929/
- http://www.claycountysheriffsoffice.com/fallenofficers.htm
- https://www.odmp.org/officer/17598-deputy-sheriff-louis-h-dayton
- Newspapers.com

CHAPTER 33

Prohibition Party Takes Life of Town Marshal

THE OFFICER:

Marshal Edward Luton
Hamilton (Washington) Marshal's Office
End of Watch: Sunday, December 15, 1929
Age: 51

When the United States alters the Constitution that this country was founded on, the enforcement of the amendment can have an impact on every law enforcement officer in the nation. There is no hiding. When Prohibition was taking effect in 1920, the new law put a nationwide ban on the production, importation, transportation and sale of alcoholic beverages. The law made criminals of most Americans, who chose to keep drinking. In New York City alone, there were an estimated 100,000 speakeasy clubs where one could party and drink an endless supply of illegal liquor. On the opposite coast in Hamilton, Washington, a drinking party cost the life of a town marshal, one of scores of law enforcement officers to die as a direct result of enforcing the 18th Amendment.

On Sunday, December 15, 1929, during the height of Prohibition, Marshal Edward Luton, a 13-year veteran of the one-man police force of Hamilton, population 252, received a complaint of a rowdy drinking party in his jurisdiction. Everyone in Skagit County knew the marshal. With a smile that was endless and a personality to match, he was a popular lawman.

Arriving at the party, Luton noticed that many people were drunk from the illegal alcohol that was being served. In his usual reserved mode, Marshal Luton didn't call for backup from the local sheriff, but chose to handle the situation calmly and quietly. He announced that he was not going to make any arrests, but was simply going to dispose of the illegal booze by pouring it down the kitchen sink.

After Luton completed his job, a disgruntled reveler picked up a unknown object and beat the marshal to death in the kitchen. Luton's body was then dragged to the main thoroughfare near the house and dumped on the roadway. To make his death look like an accident, several attendees got in their cars and purposely drove over the marshal.

The subterfuge didn't work. In a subsequent autopsy, the results proved Luton was killed by blunt-force trauma to the head in the kitchen and died instantly. To destroy the evidence of the murder and illegal drinking, the house was burned to the ground by unknown suspects. Although some of the attendees were identified, including the daughter of a prominent politician, the only arrest was one partygoer for drunken driving. No arrest was made for the murder of Marshal Luton. The case remains unsolved.

Bessie Luton, the wife of slain Marshal Edward Luton, who chose to finish her husband's term, thus becoming one of the first female law enforcement officers in Washington state.

Marshal Luton's expectant wife grieved for her husband but through the tears picked up a shotgun and demanded to fulfill her husband's term, which was set to expire in a few months. No one argued. She became the town marshal for three months, one of the first women in law enforcement in the state.

Bessie Luton had her child, their fourth. Bessie never left Hamilton and raised her children and even some grandchildren. She passed away in 1970 at the age of 84.

SOURCES:

- http://www.odmp.org/officer/8344-marshal-edward-luton
- http://behindthebadgefoundation.org/rollcall/luton-marshal-edward/
- http://www.skagitriverjournal.com/upriver/uto-conc/hamilton/town/ham05-photos2.html
- http://blog.seattlepi.com/seattle911/2008/09/04/who-are-the-other-fallen-skagit-county-deputies/

CHAPTER 34

"The Skipper"

THE OFFICER:

Town Sergeant Harry Valentine Smeeman
Ashland (Virginia) Police Department
End of Watch: Saturday, June 29, 1929
Age: 39

Harry Smeeman was the Ashland, Virginia Police Department —the towns only officer. Although he went with the title of town sergeant, he was ostensibly the chief of police. Smeeman was a familiar and popular figure in the small town of Ashland. During the era of Prohibition, it was a railroad resort that was a hotbed of gambling, prostitution, narcotics and bootleg liquor. The likable chief, known as "The Skipper," enjoyed giving rides to local kids on his motorcycle's sidecar. Although small in stature at 5-foot-5, the chief could handle himself. He was skilled in the arts of judo and jujitsu, which he often put on display at civic functions.

On the evening of June 29, 1929, Smeeman planned to attend night court, collect some fines that were due, and end his shift by patrolling the town square. He told his wife he would be home early.

It was hot that Saturday night, and there was much going on around town. Leading the list was a craps game at the back door of Cross Brothers Grocery store in an alley behind the square. At around midnight, a single shot echoed across the town. With a shrug of the shoulders, people showed no concern and went back to having a good time.

Not everyone was in a party mood. When her husband failed to return home, a worried Mrs. Smeeman went out to find him. It was after midnight when she discovered his parked squad car by the train tracks that ran through the town square. The door to his car was open, but there was no sign of her husband.

A few hours later, a garbage collector discovered the body of the chief behind Cross Brothers Grocery store with a single gunshot wound to the head. His lead-filled blackjack was strapped to his hand, and his unfired gun was on the ground at his side. His handcuffs and keys were missing. As word quickly circulated, the crime scene was overrun by curious onlookers who trampled over any possible evidence. With Ashland's only cop murdered, the neighboring city of Richmond took on the investigation. Meanwhile, voting not to stand on the sidelines, the Ashland Town Council hired a private detective. Col. Frank Morgan was an investigator who had a penchant for long trench coats and tenacious investigative tactics. He was one of the best.

Initially, there was a substantial debate over whether Smeeman might have committed suicide. This theory was soon discredited, as there were no powder burns on the chief's face or hands to indicate he had shot himself. A subsequent autopsy further disproved the theory of suicide.

The mayor of Ashland, B. Morgan Shepherd, an extremely popular politician, argued that his chief was murdered in the line of duty. This was given credibility, as Shepherd was the town's coroner, and he directed an inquest into Smeeman's death. A reward was quickly posted for information leading to the arrest of the killers.

In Ashland, everyone had an opinion on how the chief was murdered. In an article headlined "Called By Death," the local newspaper speculated that Smeeman had been killed in the alley while trying to apprehend a criminal. But the hired private detective believed the body had been moved from the actual crime scene, hidden for hours and then dumped in the alley early in the morning. The private dick noted in his report that blood from the bullet wound had drained down inside Smeeman's clothes, which indicated he had been held upright for some time.

Although not supported at that time, Col. Morgan's theory was proven correct years later during a reexamining of the case. A paperboy who had been through the alley just before Smeeman's body was discovered said he saw nothing. "My brother and I were delivering papers. We didn't see anything. If he had been there, we would have saw it. We had a big collie dog and that dog, would have smelled it and went right to him."

As Morgan's investigation slowly moved along in the months after the murder, he came across an alleged eyewitness to the crime residing in a juvenile reformatory. The 16-year-old boy claimed that he had seen two men kill Smeeman during a fight off U.S. Route 1 about a mile north of Ashland. The teen stated that the chief attempted to arrest one of the men and had put his handcuffs on him when the second man, named "Joe," shot the chief in the head. The suspects loaded Smeeman into his police car and dumped him in the city where he was found, the boy said.

Corroborating the story was the fact that an investigating police officer found a button from Smeeman's police cap at the site off Route 1, exactly where the boy said the slaying took place. Two indictments were later handed down, and one of the suspects, Joe Clayman, was acquitted when the young man could not identify him as the murderer and charges were dropped. The other suspect was never found.

A generation later, the Ashland Police Department founded an award in honor of Smeeman. The award recognizes leaders in the agency who display tenacity, commitment to community and dedication to professionalism as displayed by Smeeman. Harry Smeeman was survived by his wife and two daughters.

SOURCES:

➡ https://www.findagrave.com/cgi-bin/fg.cgi?page=gr&GRid=6235599
➡ http://ashlandmuseum.org/explore-online/people/harry-v-smeeman-1890-1929
➡ Newspapers.com

CHAPTER 35

The Bootlegger's Car

THE OFFICER:

Policeman Peter Muller Jr.
Los Angeles Police Department
End of Watch: Sunday, April 13, 1930
Age: 28

It was like something out of a dream for shoppers in downtown Los Angeles one day in 1930. Seemingly out of nowhere, beautiful flowers rained down from the sky. All around, flowers floated to the sidewalks like a gentle spring shower. And for just a moment, the blossoms turned the drab concrete into a picturesque flowering garden. Those who bothered to look skyward would have seen a Los Angeles Police Department airplane circling the area and dropping its floral payload. Standing at attention amid all the excitement were scores of uniformed police officers along with a spit-and-polish color guard. Citizens walking past instinctively asked what was going on. Their reply came as a whisper that the police department was paying a final tribute to Policeman Peter Muller, who was shot to death five days ago. Sadly, it was the second time in two weeks that such an event had taken place. On April 3rd, Policeman James Costello was shot and killed by a crook. His assassin was captured; Muller's was not.

Policeman Muller was a man of action. When he was just 16, he enlisted in the Army and served in Europe during World War I, where he was wounded in combat. The Army veteran joined LAPD in June 1929. By Sunday, April 13, 1930, Muller had just 10 months on the job—but they were busy ones.

Muller was to begin work by calling in on a Gamewell call box at 3:30 a.m. But at 3:15 he had called the police reporting operator, Miss Mildred Tucker, at Georgia Street Police Station and told her he was at Ninth and Hope streets "staking out a bootlegger's car." At 4:03 a.m., he called back and said "he was still on the car." At 4:20 a.m. the driver of a street sprinkler truck drove past 1116 South Flower Street. At 4:35 the truck drove by the address again and discovered the body of a uniformed policeman lying face down in the street. It was Muller.

The theory was that Muller had stopped the bootlegger's automobile and was standing on the running board with his flashlight and revolver in his hands to escort the occupants to the Georgia Street Station. During the drive, one of the suspects succeeded in wrestling Muller's revolver from him and fired one round into the officer's chest, where it lodged in his right lung. Muller either fell from the car or was pushed.

Corroboration of this theory came from three women: Mrs. B.M. La Fleur, the landlady of the apartments at 1116 South Flower Street, and two of her guests, Mrs. William Cook and her daughter-in-law, Mrs. Susan Cook. All three women said they thought they heard a shot. The two Cooks declared that they also heard a car stop and start up again immediately. They heard a "gruff" voice cry out: "Let's get the hell away from here." They saw a black roadster driving swiftly south on Flower Street.

As detectives went through Muller's officer's field notebook, they found that he had stopped 13 suspects from the time he went on duty until he was shot. Scores of men were brought in for questioning, but none of them was arrested. The captain of detectives, Edwards, (no first name given), announced that he was without a single clue "leading to the identity of the officer's murderers," according to a newspaper account at the time. Nearly nine decades later, there are still no clues, and the case remains unsolved. Muller was survived by his wife.

Note: The difficulty of finding unsolved police homicides, even within one's own department, is exemplified by Muller's death. LAPD had no record that Muller's murder was unsolved, or that of Patrolman David Brooks in 1910. I have seen many quotes over the past two years of other agencies with the same problem—specifically, not being aware of unsolved homicides within their own departments. I have a list of 1,052 law enforcement officers published on my website, unsolvedpolicehomicides.com whose cases need to be researched to determine if these murders are unsolved. (Please see the addendum for details.)

SOURCES:

➡ https://www.odmp.org/officer/9723-policeman-peter-muller-jr
➡ Newspapers.com

CHAPTER 36

Rumrunners

THE OFFICER:

Patrolman Michael Thomas Connolly
Portland (Maine) Police Department
End of Watch: Friday, August 15, 1930
Age: 49

During Prohibition, the criminals' favorite mode of transporting illegal booze across the nation was by truck. However, for some, the high seas proved profitable, as bootleggers developed a navy of boats to get their liquor to the desired locations. These pristine beaches, jammed with beachgoers during the day, were transformed at night into landing zones for the sophisticated high speed boats transporting illegal alcohol. The criminals were making millions during the Great Depression while most people struggled to put food on the table. Huge sums of money were used as bribes to anyone who might get in the way. From mayors to city council members to many chiefs of police, most everyone was happy—everyone except officers like Michael Connolly. He fought the bootleggers and would not take any payoffs offered to him. His dedication to his sworn responsibilities as an officer would cost him his life. There was just too much money involved to have some beat cop get in the way.

Heavy rain battered Portland, Maine, early in the morning of August 15, 1930. For Michael Connolly, no matter; he simply pulled his rain hat on tighter and leaned into the wind. He was still adjusting to his recent transfer from Portland's East End over to the waterfront, a rumrunner's paradise by night. It was the height of Prohibition, a year when more law enforcement officers, 307, would be killed in the line of duty than during any other year in history. Nine of these killings were unsolved.

The last known person to see Connolly alive was a dairy employee along Middle Street. It was 2:20 a.m., and it appeared to the witness that the officer was scrutinizing something or someone as he slowly moved to a corner and carefully peered around it. He repeated this several times before walking away. At 3:10 a.m., he made his required notification to headquarters using one of the numerous call boxes located throughout the city. His next call in was scheduled for 6:07. He never made the call. Per regulations, officers were allowed a 15-minute grace period before a search party was sent out. But it would not be the police who found Patrolman Connolly.

Later that morning, a man was lazily walking down the beach searching for driftwood when he discovered a body at the tide line, partially submerged in the sand and water. The police were called and fellow officers confronted a gruesome scene. Lying in the wet sand, was the corpse of Connolly. The officers wanted to pull their dead comrade from the water, but they were instructed not to touch the remains until the medical examiner arrived. For three and half hours, Connolly's body lay buried in the sand. For his colleagues, the time had to be heart-wrenching as they stood around and stared, unable to do anything for their friend.

Finally at 11:20 a.m., the medical examiner arrived, and the body was pulled from its watery grave. One can imagine what the officers felt when they saw that his hands were bound with his own cuffs. The patrolman's gun was found shoved in his left-hand pocket, not in his holster. Connolly was right-handed. The gun had not been fired.

During the investigation, officials came to believe that Connolly had had a confrontation with rumrunners, who overpowered him, took his gun from its holster, handcuffed him and forced him down to the beach. As his face was purple, they believed he was thrown in the water alive, struggled and drowned. The time would have been 4:07 a.m., as indicated by his stopped watch.

Although several suspects were brought in for questioning, including not only bootleggers but some hobos, no arrests were made, and the case remains unsolved. Patrolman Connolly joined the police department in 1918. He was married and had five children ages 3-11.

SOURCES:

- http://www.likes2write.com/stories-of-long-ago/the-unsolved-murder-of-patrolman-michael-connolly-portland-me/
- http://strangemaine.blogspot.com/2011/10/old-unsolved-portland-murder-resurfaces.html
- https://news.google.com/newspapers?nid=2457&dat=19880826&id=k6IJAAAAIBAJ&sjid=Ug4NAAAAIBAJ&pg=1001,4281839&hl=en
- https://www.odmp.org/officer/3362-patrolman-michael-thomas-connolly

CHAPTER 37

A Small City Marshal

THE OFFICER:

Marshal Virgil G. Untied
Minburn (Iowa) Police Department
Date of Incident: Thursday, July 23, 1931
End of Watch: Monday, July 27, 1931
Age: 33

Minburn, Iowa, is just a dot on a map in central Iowa. It's not a place that travelers seek out. A farm town, Minburn has changed very little over the years. During the Great Depression, it was not unusual for gangs to leave the big cities behind for the ripe pickings in the rural breadbasket of the nation. Just a couple of hours before sunrise on Thursday, July 23, 1931, off-duty telephone operator Lena Hagenstein was awakened by loud noises coming from Gottschalk Grocery store next to her home. This was unusual. Miss Hagenstein telephoned the town's only cop, Marshal Virgil Untied, who told her he would be there quickly.

Untied knew from what Hagenstein had told him that he would need armed backup. As in most small towns, there was no other law enforcement agency to call in on such short notice, so the marshal asked Lena Hagenstein's brother, William Hagenstein to assist him. Next he phoned his own brother, Jasper. All agreed to quickly meet at the Gottschalk Grocery store. As the marshal and two civilians approached the store, they found it empty: the suspects were gone.

The three men widened their search and went to the E.J. Shaw Grocery store near the railroad depot. As his two friends took up concealment near the store, Marshal Untied crossed the railroad tracks and approached the store. As he got close, a volley of shots rang out from the building. Untied collapsed from a shotgun blast, struck by five buckshot pellets. One of the shots went through his eye and lodged in his brain. His civilian backup returned fire, and at least a dozen shots were exchanged.

During a lull in the shooting, the three suspects ran from the Shaw Grocery to a parked automobile a block away. As the car sped away toward Des Moines, Hagenstein and Jasper

Baker Street Minburn Iowa, as it looks today. Google maps.

Untied noted that it had Polk County license plates. Surrounding agencies were quickly notified. When officers spotted a speeding automobile matching the getaway car between Grimes and Johnston, they went into pursuit. As they closed on the small car, a running gun battle took place. As the smoke cleared, the suspects had once again eluded police.

The Iowa Bureau of Criminal Investigation appointed a special agent to investigate the shooting. The agent discovered that a total of four Minburn stores had been burglarized before the shootout. Tires and inner tubes were stolen from the Minburn Oil Company, and $5 in cash from the Butler Garage. The Gottschalk Grocery safe had been blown open and $20 taken. At the Shaw Grocery, the suspects had opened the safe and gotten away with $200 in cash and assorted merchandise.

With his wife and three children at his bedside, Marshal Untied fought bravely. He died four days after being shot. The suspects were never apprehended, and the case is unsolved.

SOURCES:

- Iowa Cold Cases, https://iowacoldcases.org/case-summaries/virgil-untied/
- "Iowa Unsolved Murders: Historic Cases" by Nancy Bowers, http://www.iowaunsolvedmurders.com/the-murders/gun-battle-in-the-night-murder-of-virgil-untied-1931/
- https://www.odmp.org/officer/17192-night-marshal-virgil-g-untied
- Newspapers.com
- Ancestory.com

CHAPTER 38

Killed By One of His Own?

THE OFFICER:

Marshal George Coniff
Newport (Washington) Police Department
Date of Incident: Saturday, September 14, 1935
End of Watch: Sunday, September 15, 1935
Age: 53

There were so many contributing circumstances to the shooting death of Marshal George Coniff on the night of September 14, 1935, it was as if it were preordained. It was the height of the Great Depression (1929-1939) in America, and many turned to crime to enrich themselves at the expense of honest citizens. Thrown in the mix was an officer with questionable motives, or as some bluntly pointed out, a crook. All of these factors had an impact on the violent death of Marshal Coniff.

It was a typical Saturday night for Coniff, who was on patrol in the small eastern Washington city of Newport. Coniff was experienced, having served as chief of police in nearby Sandpoint, Idaho. He knew crime trends and where to concentrate his activities. Patrolling down a dark alley as officers have always done, Coniff spooked three men behind the closed Newport Creamery.

Spokane Police Department, Detective Clyde Ralstin, implicated in the murder of Marshal George Coniff.

During the Depression, cheese

and butter were rare commodities, often the targets of theft for the black market. As Coniff approached the bandits, they opened fire, striking him four times. One of the bullets ripped through the upper portion of his heart. The marshal died 10 hours later. The killers faded into the night and somehow avoided a massive manhunt and numerous roadblocks. Or did they?

As Newport was the county seat for Pend Oreille, Sheriff Elmer Black, on hearing of the shooting, quickly ordered roadblocks set up. Soon the city was sealed off. One driver caught in the web of barricades was Spokane Police Department Detective Clyde Ralstin. In what would later prove significant to the case, this particular roadblock was manned by two rookies. When Detective Ralstin became belligerent and waved his police identification at the young officers, he was allowed through without any questions being asked or the car being examined. The officers did make a note that the car was "boiling and hot and appeared as though it had been driven very hard."

The Spokane police took over the initial investigation of the murder of Marshal Coniff but just as quickly transferred the case back to the county of Pend Oreille. One positive outcome resulted from the abbreviated investigation: Detectives determined that Coniff was killed by a .32-caliber revolver, based on the bullets taken from his body.

Although this was a start, the first major breakthrough in the case occurred with the arrest of several suspects connected with creamery burglaries in Montana. The ringleader of the gang was Ace Logan, who just happened to be a close friend of Detective Ralstin, the same person who bluffed his way through the roadblock. It was concluded that the criminals operated out of Spokane. Many of the items fenced, such as butter, hams and bacon from these creameries, found their way to a mom and pop operation called Mother's Kitchen, a favorite hangout for cops from the Spokane P.D.

Mother's Kitchen had a dubious reputation, as many of the waitresses provided more than a refill of coffee. When Pend Oreille County Detective Charles Sonnabend conducted a follow-up investigation at the eatery, his boss, Sgt. Daniel Mangan, ordered a halt to his questioning. As a result of this, and with no other solid leads, the case went dormant for 20 years.

In 1955, the sheriff of Pend Oreille County was William M. Giles. He was familiar with the Coniff case and pledged to never give up in his efforts to solve the murder. He arranged a mini-task force. It was composed of former detective Sonnabend, who was the lead detective in the early investigation, former sheriff Elmer Black, and United States Marshal Darrell O. Holmes. The first order of business was to share their knowledge and opinions regarding the case. Detailed notes were taken.

Sonnabend, the one with the most previous knowledge, outlined the background of the case for the group. He revealed the large number of creamery robberies in 1935. Sonnabend had questioned the ringleader, Logan, over a three-

The corroded .32-caliber handgun believed to have been used in the murder of Marshal Coniff recovered 50 years after the crime by Sheriff Bamonte.

week period. Logan ended up serving time in a federal penitentiary for interstate motor vehicle theft. Logan broke down during questioning and admitted his participation in the creamery robberies. Most important, he identified Detective Clyde Ralstin as the one who funneled stolen goods through his ranch to Mother's Kitchen. Besides creamery goods, Logan

Sheriff Tony Bamonte on the bridge from where the murder weapon was thrown.

stole shoes from a boxcar and, in another burglary, cigarettes, cigars and tobacco, all of which were alleged to have been run through Ralstin.

The night of Coniff's murder, Logan admitted that he was with Ralstin at the blockade. Logan further stated that Ralstin was "in on all of the creamery robberies." Detective Sonnabend believed it was Ralstin who fired the shots that killed Marshal Coniff. At the time of his arrest, Logan's hotel room was searched, and a .32 revolver and a .38 Special were recovered. The guns were retained by the Spokane Police Department. Later, the .32 was signed out by Ralstin, who subsequently reported it stolen. It was rumored that it was tossed into the Spokane River. After Logan had made his confession to Sonnabend and the reports made their way to the chief of police, Ralstin was fired from the police department.

With the help of those involved in the Sonnabend interview and with additional facts collected concerning the murder of Coniff, it was hoped that arrests could be made in the 20-year-old case—but there were none. It would be 30 more years before the case was once again opened for investigation. And again this time, it was the sheriff of Pend Oreille County, Tony Bamonte, who was looking for answers.

Sheriff Bamonte was working on a thesis for his master's degree on the former sheriffs of the county. This information provided him with the background on the Coniff shooting. In 1989, Bamonte contacted the Spokane Police Department and outlined his suspicions about Ralstin and others who had covered for him. In its reply, the department stated, "We can find no employment records for any of the people and officers, and most of the principals involved in this are dead anyhow."

But the word was out. There was a new sheriff looking into the Coniff murder. One of the individuals who decided to come forward was a frail 86-year-old retired Sgt. Dan Mangan. He revealed that "I knew Ralstin…he was into something…I heard that he was involved in all the creamery burglaries and he was peddling." Mangan also confirmed that Ralstin hung with some "shady characters" and was mixed up with some dairy business at Mother's Kitchen.

Mangan closed the interview by stating that the Spokane chief of police "gave us a package. And said this was the Ralstin package….I knew about the murder…thought this might have been the murder weapon." Mangan threw the package into the Seattle River. "It's been on my mind ever since," he said.

Extremely fortunate for Sheriff Bamonte, about the time of his interview with Mangan, the Washington Water Power Co. ordered an inspection of the Spokane River in the area and stopped the flow of water. This rare event allowed the sheriff to walk out onto the now dry river bed to an area where Mangan said he threw the package.

Incredibly, within just 10 minutes, Bamonte found the corroded gun. It was a .32-caliber revolver, which was the same type of weapon used to murder Marshal Coniff a half century earlier. Sheriff Bamonte had the Washington Crime Laboratory in Seattle examine the weapon. The laboratory confirmed Bamonte's suspicions that deterioration of the metal was consistent with the gun having been in the water for 50 years.

Besides Sgt. Mangan, another person came forward and added to the mounting evidence against Ralstin and others. Pearl Keogh, now 85 years old, had known Ralstin quite well, as she worked for him at Mother's Kitchen. She was also acquainted with Mangan and Virgil Burch, who ran the day-to-day operations at the restaurant. Keogh recalled a dinner she hosted in 1940. She related how her boss, Burch, had bragged about being with Ralstin when he shot Coniff five years earlier. He bragged he was under a tarp in the back seat of the getaway car that was allowed to pass through the roadblock by the rookie officers. But her most startling revelation was how Ralstin boasted of shooting Coniff.

On January 23, 1990, the prime suspect in the murder of Coniff, Clyde Ralstin, died in Montana. He was a well-liked and respected man in his community. Sheriff Bamonte's reward for his diligence was to be hounded for going after Ralstin and, some say, causing his demise.

Despite over 50 years of solid police work in the attempt to bring justice to the murderer of Coniff, no arrest was ever made, and the case remains unsolved. I would suggest that if this information had been available back in 1935, the results would have been different, namely that the case would have been solved.

SOURCES:

- Tony and Suzanne Schaeffer Bamonte, History of Newport, Washington (Spokane: Tornado Creek Publications, 1998), 68-69.
- Tony Bamonte, Sheriffs, 1911-1989: A History of Murders in the Wilderness of Washington's Last County (Spokane: Arthur H. Clark Company, 1991), 123-147.
- Timothy Egan, Breaking Blue (New York: Knopf, 1992).
- Tony Bamonte, email to Laura Arksey, April 9, 2009, in possession of Laura Arksey, Spokane, Washington.
- http://unsolvedmysteries.wikia.com/wiki/George_Coniff.

CHAPTER 39

The Man With the Keys

THE OFFICER:

Special Patrolman August Mayford
Alton (Illinois) Police Department
End of Watch: Friday, October 16, 1936
Age: 66

For nearly two decades, Special Patrolman August Mayford could be seen making his rounds in the central business district of Alton, Illinois. In addition to his normal police equipment, Mayford carried a large collection of keys that jingled when he walked down the street. These keys were significant, as they

A view of Alton, Illinois, Third Street looking West, about the time Patrolman August Mayford was murdered.

allowed the special patrolman to gain entry to the businesses on his beat. If a display light had been left on after hours, he would enter the business and turn it off. The 66-year-old patrolman had an uneventful career until one fall night in 1936 when he went missing. Fifteen days later his body was discovered with eight bullet holes in his back. What happened that night remains a mystery to this day.

Mayford was well-liked by the citizens of Alton, and it did not bother him that some people simply referred to him as a "door rattler." Mayford was very proud that the business owners entrusted him with the keys to their stores so he could ensure that there were no problems.

On that ill-fated Friday night of October 16, 1936, Mayford did what he always did: He enjoyed his favorite "dinner" of bacon and eggs at the Illinois Restaurant. Around 11 p.m. near Third and Piasa streets, Mayford ran into Patrolman Claude Barkely, and they exchanged pleasantries. Barkely would be the last known person to see Mayford alive. When Mayford missed his 12 a.m. call to police headquarters, concern began to build. The veteran officer usually made the call from the Faulstitch Cigar store, but on this day, the phone did not ring. Chief of Police J. Uhle was immediately notified.

After being alerted, the chief realized he had not seen Mayford in the business district as he usually did. It was his habit to give the 66-year-old patrolman a ride home after work. The chief also noted that several stores had their display lights left on, an oversight Mayford would have taken care of. The chief traveled to Maul Shoe Store on West Third Street where Mayford usually kept clothing that he might need if the weather changed. Inside Uhle found an overcoat, a raincoat, some extra clothing and a wallet that contained $33, which was a large sum during the Great Depression. All patrol units were ordered to search for the missing patrolman.

On Tuesday, two sets of Mayford's keys were discovered in a closet at the Maul Shoe Store that had been missed on two previous searches. The prevailing thought of officials was that Mayford had surprised a burglary in progress at a business in the area and that he could have been kidnaped.

On Halloween, over two weeks after his presumed kidnapping, ranch hands at a local farm discovered Mayford's body lying face down on the edge of a corn field. He was by Cahokia Creek, near Edwardsville, Illinois, 15 miles from Alton.

The coroner and sheriff reasoned that Mayford was kidnapped after interrupting a burglary or preventing a robbery. The officer was severely beaten: His jaw was broken and his false teeth knocked out. He was dumped from a car near the creek by someone who had to be familiar with the area. The assailant then stood over the prone officer and fired eight rounds into him. The only property taken was the patrolman's side-arm. No suspects were ever charged in the murder, and the case remains unsolved. Mayford left behind a wife and daughter.

SOURCES:

- "10 Bizarre Unsolved Mysteries Involving Police Officers." http://viralbuzzme.com/2016/07/11/10-bizarre-unsolved-mysteries-involving-police-officers
- https://www.odmp.org/officer/8742-police-officer-august-mayford
- Newspapers.com

CHAPTER 40

"Two men in black Ford. Shot sheriff, myself"

THE OFFICERS:

Sheriff Lawrence I. Smoyer
Boone County (Nebraska) Sheriff's Department
End of Watch: Thursday, June 17, 1937
Age: 41

Constable William Wathen
Boone County (Nebraska) Sheriff's Department
Date of Incident: Thursday, June 17, 1937
End of Watch: Sunday, October 3, 1937
Age: 54

In a remote area of Nebraska, a small-town sheriff and his constable partner were gunned down as they investigated reports of two suspicious men who had been seen in the area the past two days. The officers, one dead and one clinging to life, were left in a field in the hot Nebraska sun to rot away.

Tuesday, June 15
Two days before the shooting, members of the Young family, ranchers in Boone County, were passing the evening on their front porch. At 10:30 p.m. they saw headlights on the road near their home. A moment later they heard an engine revving. By the sound, they could tell the car was stuck in one of the many sand pits that dotted their property. Knowing the car would have a difficult time getting out, two family members went to see if they could help.

As Louis "Scout" Smoyer, the brother of Sheriff Lawrence Smoyer, later reported from information he received from the Young family, "There were two strangers in a black Ford. One of them got out to help us push. He was about six feet tall, slim, and had on a light shirt and straw hat. I noticed he was wearing black and white shoes. He was a pretty tough customer. He kept cussing the other fellow. When the car was finally pushed out of the sand hole, the tall man barely mumbled thanks as they drove off."

Wednesday, June 16

Leonard Noble, a farmer near the Youngs, was out inspecting his fence line when he spotted two men in a Ford who had no business in the area. The car was parked amongst a clump of trees, well off the road. He noticed the men moving about the area and thought they might be cattle rustlers. He went home and called Sheriff Lawrence Smoyer. The 10-year veteran sheriff drove to the location, looked around, but was unable to locate the men or the Ford.

Thursday, June 17

Farmer Noble, aware that Sheriff Smoyer had not located the men in the black Ford, was on the lookout for them. Early in the morning, Noble observed the car a second time. He immediately called for the sheriff. This time Sheriff Smoyer took along Constable William Wathen to investigate the suspicious vehicle and suspects.

Arriving in the area where the men were last reported, Constable Wathen was just closing a cattle gate when the strangers came roaring over a hill directly toward the sheriff's car. Sheriff Smoyer sounded the car siren and the black Ford stopped. "I got out and started to the front of the car, and one of them, the slim fellow, stepped out of the car," Wathen later told investigators. "Smoyer got out and took a couple of steps when this slim fellow pulled a gun and shot him. He fell back, and as I was pulling my gun, the same fellow shot me. I fell down, and he shot me again but missed. I managed to empty my gun at them. The fellow who did the shooting came over and took my gun away from me, then went around and took

Smoyer's out of the holster. They backed out, went around us and out of the gate."

Wathen was shot in the groin, and the bullet lodged in his spinal cord, paralyzing him from the waist down. The constable was unable to help himself or his partner. Both lawmen were left for dead under the scorching sun. Fearing he was about to die, Wathen managed to write a note: "June 17, 1937. One tall slim man. One medium heavy. Car No. 7-489 Colo. Two men in black Ford. Shot sheriff, myself. Smoyer dead. Not able to move. Two men. Am not able to move. They shot me first. I fired three shots after down. Goodbye. Wm."

As part of the investigation of the murders of Lawrence Smoyer and William Wathen, officers re-enact the shootings at the location of the crime.

Wathen lay in the field all night and into the next day. He became so thirsty that he drank the ink from his pen. The second morning, a rancher, George Blankenship, noticed cattle roaming in his yard. He knew the cattle belonged to another rancher several miles away. Blankenship mounted his horse and drove the cattle back to where they came from. As he got close, he noticed the gate was open and a car was parked nearby. Thinking it belonged to the strangers he had heard about, he summoned authorities, who discovered the law officers more than 24 hours after they were ambushed. Sheriff Smoyer was shot through the heart and died instantly. Constable Wathen would suffer for four months before losing the battle with his injury.

Because so much time had passed, the two men in the Ford were long gone. A few days later, the black Ford, with five bullet holes, was found in Cheyenne, Wyoming. Investigators traveled to Colorado, Wyoming and California in compiling a case. The detectives learned that the Ford had been stolen one day before it was spotted in Nebraska, from a garage in Denver, Colorado. When investigators had gathered enough information to obtain a warrant, they started looking for two bank robbers, Marvin Cooley and Charles Doody, two ex-cons who had spent time in prison together. Cooley was located and arrested, Doody was never found.

Scout Smoyer, the brother of the murdered sheriff, looked just like his brother. Accompanying detectives to the jail where Cooley was being held, the look-alike brother walked in and stared Cooley in the eyes. The suspect in the murder "turned as white as a sheet. He was so petrified. He thought he was looking death in the eyes," reported the brother.

About to be sent to Nebraska to face murder charges in the shooting of the two officers, Cooley conveniently confessed to a 1932 bank robbery in Louisville, Colorado. As a result, authorities were prevented from bringing him back to face murder charges. He served 10 years and was paroled in 1948. Although the county attorney at the time of the murders stated, "There is strong set of circumstances pointing to Colley's guilt," the county attorney in 1948, when asked by the prison warden just before Cooley was paroled if there would be an indictment, replied that he "cannot find anything that indicates reason for taking the suspect into our custody." The probable murderer of the two lawmen walked free, and the case remains unsolved.

The funeral service for Smoyer was held on the courthouse lawn in Albion, where an estimated crowd of over 7,000 people paid their respects to the popular sheriff. Smoyer was a veteran of the Great War and was married with six children ranging from age 7 to 16. William Wathen was married with two daughters.

SOURCES:

- "Boone County Murder Mystery" by Sheryl Schmeckpeper
- https://www.odmp.org/officer/13882-constable-william-wathen
- https://www.odmp.org/officer/12512-sheriff-lawrence-i-smoyer
- http://www.nebraskalife.com/Boone-County-Murder-Mystery/
- Newspapers.com

CHAPTER 41

The Traveling Tent Show

THE OFFICER:

Deputy Sheriff James Duncan Reddicks
Hardin County (Texas) Sheriff's Department
End of Watch: Friday, June 30, 1939
Age: 64

The circumstances surrounding the shooting death of Deputy Sheriff James Reddicks read like a movie script. In fact, a fictionalized account of the deputy's murder has been turned into a screenplay, and the author is shopping it around to movie producers. The murder occurred during the Great Depression in Saratoga, Texas, a place so rural that it was scarcely a dot on a map.

Reddicks would not have been murdered if not for a traveling tent show. The large tent shows were especially popular in rural areas that could not afford to build a theater or opera center. When the shows came to town, most of the community would turn out to see a variety of amusements, from medicine acts to motion picture shows.

One of these tent shows set up in Saratoga, in Hardin County. On Friday night, June 30, 1939, 22-year-old E.B. Means and two friends arrived late for the movie and wanted in. Standing in their way was Deputy Reddicks, who was working the event. He bluntly told the boys to move on, that he could not let them in after the movie started. The young men became confrontational and refused to leave. Soon an argument turned into a shouting match, and it was reported that Deputy Reddicks hit Means over the head with his billy club. Means, enraged, shouted in front of several witnesses, "I'll get my dad's gun and come back and kill you." Means and his friends stormed away. A short time later Reddicks, who also owned a local café, was behind the counter tending to business.

Suddenly, a person with a shotgun fired two blasts through a window striking Deputy Reddicks and killing him instantly. The shooter escaped. Means' grandfather evidently thought his grandson was guilty of Reddicks' murder and turned him over to authorities. It was reported by some that law enforcement officers beat Means in an attempt to elicit a confession. That would not have been unusual. It was a time in America when the "third degree" was an accepted means of police interrogation, not unlike waterboarding in wartime settings years later. Despite his reported whipping, Means refused to confess and would not even give authorities his name.

A traveling tent show similar to the one that led to the killing of Deputy Sheriff James Reddicks.

It didn't matter. A grand jury was formed and indicted E.B Means for the murder of Deputy Reddicks. But after two years of preliminary hearings and a trial, murder charges against Means were dropped for lack of evidence. There were no other suspects, and Means was the only person ever arrested. Many in the community always believed that the authorities had the right man but that Means got off on a technicality. The case remains unsolved.

Note: In some sources Reddicks is spelled Reddick.

SOURCES:

- https://www.odmp.org/officer/22314-deputy-sheriff-james-duncan-reddicks
- Book based on murder of sheriff's deputy in 1939 that remains unsolved, by Cassie Smith, http://www.beaumontenterprise.com/news/article/Book-based-on-murder-of-sheriff-s-deputy-in-1939-5016538.php#photo-5521382
- Unsolved murder of deputy sheriff begins journey to the big screen, Texarkana Gazette, http://www.pressreader.com/

CHAPTER 42

The Bomb Squad

THE OFFICERS:

Detective Ferdinand Socha
New York Police Department
End of Watch: Thursday, July 4, 1940
Age: 35

Detective Joseph J. Lynch
New York Police Department
End of Watch: Thursday, July 4, 1940
Age: 33

The 1939-40 New York World's Fair opened with a slogan: "Dawn of a New Day." It allowed the nearly 45 million visitors a peek into the future. Keeping these millions of people safe was, among others, the New York Police Department. Whether looking into the future or remembering the past, one factor never changed: There were evil people meaning to do harm to others. Two members of NYPD bomb squad gave their lives to save thousand of others from a bomb.

At some point on July 4, 1940, unidentified individuals planted a time bomb in the British Pavilion. Because Britain was at war with Germany, Nazi sympathizers were suspected. Detectives from the NYPD were on alert inside the British Pavilion, as two days earlier a telephone caller threatened to blow up the pavilion.

One of these detectives, Frederick Morelock, received a tip about a suspicious package in a second-floor fan room and responded. Inside he found a canvas bag, and to protect others in the building, he risked his life by removing the possible bomb to the rear of the Polish building that had an area with very little activity. Emergency Service Squad personnel quickly cordoned off the location and called for the bomb squad.

Because it was a holiday, detectives from the bomb squad were on call from their homes. An hour before going end of watch, Detective Joseph Lynch received a telephone call telling him of the suspicious satchel.

A watery crater marks the spot where a bomb exploded, killing detectives Joseph Lynch and Ferdinand Socha from the NYPD bomb squad.

His partner, Detective Ferdinand Socha, was off duty but had told his partner to call if he was needed. Lynch did and picked up Socha while traveling on his way to the fairgrounds. Upon arrival, the two detectives were briefed by the incident commander. The bomb experts told the commander they were going to make an inspection of the device.

In this era of bomb squad service, protective suits were not widely used. Walking to the satchel, the detectives in their business suits carefully lifted the bag off the ground and began their examination to see what they had. Upon closer examination, the detectives heard a ticking sound coming from the satchel. The two professionals knew they had to see if it actually contained a live bomb. They made the decision to carve a 'small two-inch peephole to ascertain just what the satchel contained.

As Lynch was carefully pulling the material aside to look inside, he told his partner, "It's the business." With those words, there was a terrific explosion as the bomb exploded, leaving a large crater in the ground. Five other nearby officers were wounded, two critically. The police immediately implemented a major manhunt, believing the attack was perpetrated by Nazi or Irish Republican Army sympathizers. As time went by, no arrests were made, and the case remains unsolved.

Detective Lynch left behind a wife and five children, including one in the hospital at the time of his death with a chronic and painful bone infection. Detective Socha was married with no children. The Lynches made a funeral home out of their living room, and the caskets were covered with a blanket of roses given by the British government. More than 5,000 mourners paid tribute to the two officers, including Babe Ruth.

Every Fourth of July the officers are remembered by NYPD with a bouquet of roses that is left at a small memorial plaque in Flushing Meadows Park at the Queens Museum of Art, the last remaining building from the 1939 fair.

SOURCES:

➡ Published under the banner A Walk in the Park. "Detectives Socha & Lynch Honored In World's Fair Bombing Tragedy Anniversary," by Geoffrey Croft. http://awalkintheparknyc.blogspot.com/2015/05/detectives-socha-lynch-honored-in.html

➡ Queens Chronicle. "70th anniversary of World's Fair bombing" by Liz Rhoades.

➡ The New York Times. "Death at the World's Fair" by Michael Pollak.

➡ The Detectives' Endowment Association Inc. "Articles: Joseph J. Lynch."

CHAPTER 43

"Look out Charlie! He looks bad"

THE OFFICER:

Patrolman Charles H. Shaw
Nassau County (New York) Police Department
End of Watch: Friday, September 6, 1940
Age: 33

While on patrol officers are constantly vigilant for anything unusual. Accordingly, observation arrests rates as a highlight of any shift. These arrest don't usually result from answering a radio call, but from the instincts and training of an officer who observes something that just doesn't fit the surroundings. The ability to separate a law-abiding citizen from a criminal who has committed or is about to commit a crime is a special trait that many of a department's finest officers possess.

Charles "Charlie" Shaw was just such a patrolman, as was his partner, Sgt. Robert Kirk. On patrol in the early morning hours of Friday, September 6, 1940, they observed a parked automobile with a lone man sitting in the front passengers seat. The auto was located in a remote area that borders a golf course in Woodmere, Nassau County, New York. The vehicle was stopped in complete darkness, illuminated only by the headlights of the officers' patrol car.

Patrolman Shaw pulled his police car parallel with the parked car, which was pointed in the opposite direction. Shaw's door was now just three feet from the driver's door of the suspicious vehicle. As Shaw stopped his vehicle, Sgt. Kirk quickly focused his flashlight on the interior of the parked car, revealing a "colored man" whom they described as being shabbily dressed. He was wearing a "flat-topped soft hat, of a shape which is known as a pork pie, hamburger, or streamliner."

According to subsequent reports, as the light from Kirk's flashlight illuminated the suspect's face, he observed "an unusually vicious expression of the eyes." Kirk shouted out a warning, "Look out Charlie! He looks bad." Shaw promptly got out of his car and was standing between the two cars, only feet from the suspect. Kirk immediately stepped from the right side of the police car and was walking to the rear when a huge, blinding blast from a shotgun struck Patrolman Shaw point-blank in the chest and neck. Shaw died three hours later.

After firing one round from his 12-gauge shotgun, the suspect bolted from the vehicle and disappeared into the darkness. As he ran in pursuit, Sgt. Kirk emptied his revolver at the fleeing man. The suspect was not struck, and he escaped. The ensuing investigation revealed that the murderer had stolen a 1939 Oldsmobile from an apartment complex just a half-mile from where the officers encountered him. It appeared he had pushed the car to the location. At the time of the encounter, the suspect was trying to start the car by "jumping" the ignition wires. Despite a dragnet of more than 250 officers, the suspect was never apprehended, and the case remains unsolved. Shaw left behind a wife and 6-year-old daughter.

SOURCES:

- https://www.nassaupba.org/fallen/charles-h-shaw
- Newspapers.com

CHAPTER 44

More Than Deposits and Withdrawals

THE OFFICER:
Officer Arnold Kemp
Thomasville (North Carolina) Police Department
End of Watch: Monday, December 7, 1942
Age: 38

The First National Bank was the home and meeting place for the professional elite of the growing city of Thomasville, North Carolina. Built in 1922, the two-story building housed physicians, dentists and the city attorney. It was well known that many of the city's most prominent business and civic leaders took part in high-stakes poker games in the corner of the second floor. Booze was always the drink of choice, even though the city was in a dry county.

The bank was also popular with the local police department. With two substantial doors protecting the lobby of the bank, two smaller outer doors were usually left unlocked before midnight. Thomasville police officers would take the opportunity to go inside and warm up on cold nights and use the second-floor bathroom, saving a two-block walk

The First National Bank were the body of Officer Arnold Kemp was found.

Unsolved, Cold-Case Homicides

to the police station. The First National Bank would also become the crime scene of the murder of a Thomasville officer.

Officer Arnold Kemp was a rookie, in his 10th month working the night shift with his partner, W.C. Loftin. The two were patrolling the business district of Thomasville on the bone-chilling night of December 6, 1942. It was an uneventful evening for the two officers. Following their routine, they checked the doors of The First National Bank sometime around 2 a.m. and found them locked.

A couple of hours later, the two men stood next to their patrol car at the corner of Main and Salem streets. Loftin told Kemp he was going out to patrol the outlying sections of the city and would meet Kemp back at that spot 45 minutes later, at 4:45 a.m. This would allow time for Kemp to get to the police station to relieve the desk officer at 5 a.m.

When Loftin returned at the appointed time, Kemp was nowhere to be found. Loftin made a cursory search of the area including the bank, and despite its being 5:30 in the morning, the outer bank doors were unlocked. Checking the bank carefully, Loftin found it empty. With no sign of the missing officer, all eight remaining officers of the department began an extensive search. One of the officers checked the bank and found the doors locked again, even though Loftin never locked them.

With a light snow falling during the morning, Thomasville officers were joined in their search by the Davidson County Sheriff's Office and North Carolina State Highway Patrol. The large contingent of lawmen checked throughout the city and outlying fields. At noon, an all-points bulletin was broadcast across the state that Officer Kemp might have been abducted. Concern for the fate of the missing officer grew by the minute. A local newspaper proclaimed in the December 7 issue: "Policeman Missing at Thomasville."

Around 3:10 p.m., Mayor R.L. Pope, an executive of the bank, suggested to officials that perhaps they should look in the elevator shaft. Detectives had the elevator operator run the elevator car upward, allowing enough room to peer below into the shaft. As the elevator crept up, officials discovered the lifeless body of Officer Kemp, four feet below in the bottom of the shaft.

Detectives noted that Kemp's glasses were still on, all his police equipment, including his gun, was in place and his uniform was unspoiled. It appeared to the detectives that there had been no struggle before his death. The only wound on the body was a skull fracture over his right ear, 2 1/2 to 3 inches long. Murder was the apparent cause of Officer Kemp's death, but some speculated that he might have fallen into the elevator shaft while inspecting the bank.

Debunking this theory was the type of elevator in the bank. This particular unit could not operate if the door was open. For Kemp to fall into the shaft, the car would have had to be on the second floor, with the first-floor door open. When the elevator was tested, there were no mechanical problems. In fact, it had worked continually all day until his body was found that afternoon.

Leaving speculation behind, the county coroner formed a jury inquest that determined that Kemp's death was a homicide, even though city and police officials characterized it as an accident. Years later, the current city manager and police chief would not comment on the case for a newspaper article written in 2013. According to the police department, the case is closed—a statement that officials have repeated for decades.

Over the subsequent years, theories and opinions have generated a lot of discussion and speculation. The prevailing thought was a massive cover-up. Many feel Kemp was murdered when he came upon prominent residents, late at night at the bank, gambling, drinking and entertaining women. There was even a deathbed confession told secondhand in 1999 that Kemp's death was a murder. It would stand to reason that the elite of Thomasville accidently caught by Officer Kemp feared for their reputations and did not want the word to get out on what Kemp found.

Kemp's children would support this theory. His wife told the children years later that their father had told her with the strictest confidence and looking very troubled, "I am going to tell you something, but you are to never, ever tell anyone what I am about to tell you. Don't tell the boys; don't tell your brothers or sisters. But last night I walked in on a prominent crowd of Thomasville men...." He was interrupted when his sons came into the room, and never finished the sentence. He was found dead two days later. Kemp was survived by his wife and two sons, ages 10 and 12.

SOURCES:

- Winston-Salem Journal, "Chair City Mystery Part 1: Weeks before officer's disappearance in 1942 filled with omens." By Christopher Yarbrough. http://www.journalnow.com/news/local/chair-city-mystery-part-weeks-before-officer-s-disappearance-in/article_b18c10da-7e2e-11e2-9785-001a4bcf6878.html
- Winston-Salem Journal, "Mystery death of Thomasville patrolman remains closed." By Scott Hamilton. http://www.journalnow.com/news/local/mystery-death-of-thomasville-patrolman-remains-closed/article_b29f8f2e-9981-11e2-8b6b-001a4bcf6878.html
- http://www.odmp.org/officer/7445-officer-george-arnold-kemp
- Newspapers.com

CHAPTER 45

A Day Off

THE OFFICER:

Patrolman George J. Sperakos
Chicago (Illinois) Police Department
End of Watch: Thursday, April 24, 1952
Age: 41

I recently attended the National Police Collectors Show, where a man approached me with a question. He saw that I was writing a book on *Unsolved* police homicides and wanted to know if I had ever heard of his "Uncle George." The nephew, Dennis Daniels, was not sure of the spelling of his uncle's last name, but after several tries, we figured it out. I found that I didn't have George Sperakos listed as an *Unsolved* murder. In my records of 1,053 officer's killed in the line of duty where there is no mention of whether the perpetrators were apprehended, I did have a listing for Sperakos as being shot and killed, but like the rest, there was no disposition on the suspects. Well, make that 1,052, because with the help of George Sperakos' nephew, I'm able to officially list the incident as being *Unsolved* and shed some light on the tragic events of April 24, 1952.

It was a kick-back day for Patrolman George Sperakos—a well-deserved day off from his hectic schedule of working the graveyard shift with the Chicago Police Department. After attending a special training day on Wednesday, Sperakos, in street clothes, was still wearing his distinctive police hat as he paid a visit to his good friend Stanley Kozieniak, the owner of a small tavern in the 1800 block of Division Street. The two friends sat in a back room talking, while Kozieniak's wife was up front tending bar.

There were four patrons in the tavern when three men walked in and ordered drinks. For a few moments, the trio stood at the bar not saying much. Suddenly, two of the men drew revolvers, and one shouted, "This is a stickup!" Without hesitating, the third man walked behind the bar to the cash register, where he removed $200. As this was occurring, the other two suspects lined up the four patrons, along with Mrs. Kozieniak, and ordered them to "shut up."

Hearing the commotion, Mr. Kozieniak stepped quietly to the doorway, looked into the main room of the tavern and saw the three suspects robbing his bar. He turned back and told Sperakos. The off-duty officer pulled his gun and peeked around the doorway. One of the robbers saw Sperakos wearing his police hat and yelled to the others, "Copper!" Instantly, the two suspects fired at Sperakos, who returned three quick shots before ducking for cover. Coming up from his concealment, Sperakos fired three more shots at the robbery suspects before he was fatally shot in the head. It appeared he shot one of the suspects in the shoulder. Sperakos died several hours later in the hospital. The three suspects made their escape. Very little has been written about the murder of Policeman Sperakos, but what there is mentions that the case is unsolved. Policeman Sperakos was married, having just celebrated his one-year anniversary. He had one daughter and also was survived by a brother and, later, a nephew who refused to let his memory fade away.

SOURCES:

- http://www.cpdmemorial.org/fallen-heroes/p-o-george-sperakos-669/
- https://www.odmp.org/officer/12615-patrolman-george-j-sperakos
- Newspapers.com
- Interview of Dennis Daniels, the nephew of Patrolman Sperakos, August 2017

CHAPTER 46

A Thanksgiving Day Robbery

THE OFFICER:

Patrolman Richard S. Burchfield
Colorado Springs (Colorado) Police Department
End of Watch: Thursday, November 26, 1953
Age: 34

While most citizens were home that Thanksgiving night, enjoying quiet time with friends and family, others were out making sure their safety was insured by patrolling the streets of communities across the country. Patrolman Richard Burchfield was on the lookout for a man who had just robbed $6 from a citizen on a street in downtown Colorado Springs. It was Thanksgiving, November 26, 1953. It was approaching 8 p.m.

Burchfield was part of a team looking for the suspect who had committed this and several other street robberies over the past few weeks. At 7:55 p.m., the patrolman radioed to dispatch that he was returning to headquarters. He never arrived.

A citizen of Colorado Springs, Mr. Robert McVay, was returning home when he noticed a squad car parked at the curb near Bijou and El Paso streets, which was just a few blocks from the police station. He saw a man standing next to the police car, stooping down and looking in. His suspicions were piqued when he saw the man run up the street and enter another car. The police car remained parked. McVay drove two blocks and decided to go back and have another look. He saw the man still sitting in the other car. McVay continued to his home.

But things did not seem quite right to the inquisitive citizen, so he quickly drove back to the police car and again saw the same man looking in. McVay stopped alongside the police car and asked the man, "Do you need any help?" to which the man replied, "Hell no!" McVay again drove home, but this time he called the police. When he kept getting a busy signal, he decided to drive to the police station and report what he had seen.

Officers rushed the five blocks to the scene and were shocked to see Burchfield slumped over the steering wheel—dead. He had been shot eight times at close range behind the right ear, over the right eye, once in the right cheek, twice in the right shoulder, and three times in the right arm. The pattern of the shots suggested that he was shot by someone in the passenger seat or possibly the back seat.

Nine shells, which the FBI later determined came from a Colt Woodsman automatic .22-caliber pistol, were found in the car. Located near the officer's feet was an ID card stolen earlier from the robbery victim. The evidence indicated to investigators that Patrolman Burchfield apprehended the robbery suspect and was questioning him in his police vehicle when he was murdered.

Other officers assisting in the investigation were told by witnesses that a 1937-1941 Ford coupe had stopped near his vehicle around the time of the murder. The driver was described as a white male, tall, thin, and dressed in dark clothes, and his age was approximately late teens to early twenties. This corroborated what McVay had reported. Several suspects were taken in for questioning, but none was arrested. The case remains unsolved. Patrolman Burchfield left behind a wife and three children.

SOURCES:

- https://www.colorado.gov/apps/coldcase/casedetail.html?id=3861
- http://www.defrostingcoldcases.com/the-1953-cold-case-of-officer-burchfield/
- https://cspd.coloradosprings.gov/content/1953-burchfield
- Newspapers.com

CHAPTER 47

The Unassuming Sheriff

THE OFFICER:

Sheriff Hubbard "Hub" Ferguson
Gallatin County (Kentucky) Sheriff's Department
End of Watch: Friday, June 18, 1954
Age: 64

It was generally acknowledged throughout Gallatin County that Sheriff Hubbard "Hub" Ferguson was a quiet, kind, unassuming man who never did a mean thing, never harmed a soul and never knew he had an enemy in the world. He was a sheriff who did not even bother to carry a gun, deciding it was safer in the glovebox of his old Chevrolet. Why then was this carefree lawman found at the bottom of a creek, with a bullet hole through his head, a large gash on the top of his head and a 22-pound iron rail tied around his neck? That is the mystery that has endured and puzzled officials for over six decades.

Gallatin County is located on the fertile banks of the Ohio River in northern Kentucky, surrounded by Cincinnati, Louisville and Lexington. This was Ferguson's turf. While it is true that Ferguson was sheriff, his roots were in the dirt of Kentucky as a farmer. The sheriff had a tenant, Robert Dickerson, who operated the farm for him.

It was very difficult to go undetected in a small county with only a few thousand citizens in 1954. On the Friday night of June 18, 1954, at 6 p.m., the sheriff was noticed filling his gas tank in Sparta. At 7:30 he ate supper at Hall's Truck Stop. At 8 p.m. Ferguson paid a visit to the Dickersons. They talked for about 30 minutes, then Ferguson went into his barn to fetch some tobacco. At approximately 11 p.m., Jimmy

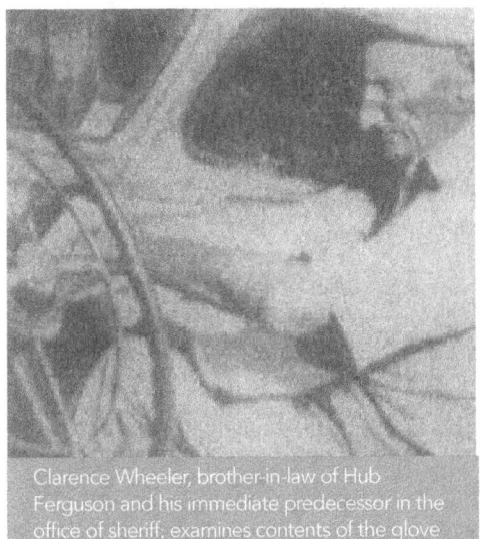

Clarence Wheeler, brother-in-law of Hub Ferguson and his immediate predecessor in the office of sheriff, examines contents of the glove compartment.

O'Connor, an 18-year-old who lived on a farm next to the Fergusons, came upon the sheriff's car parked on Lick Creek Road. The car was parked crossways, with the lights shining into a field, but the sheriff was nowhere to be seen. The car was parked where O'Connor had seen a broken fence earlier in the day. Thinking the sheriff was putting up wire so his cattle would not get out, O'Connor drove around the car and continued home.

The next day, Mrs. Dickerson, the wife of Ferguson's tenant, drove out a side road on the way to town. She also noticed the sheriff's car parked sideways. Mrs. Dickerson did not give it a second thought and drove on. When she returned at 10:30 that night, she noticed the car in the same location and called the police.

Before investigators arrived, the crime scene had been trampled by friends and onlookers. Sheriff Ferguson was missing. What investigators did find were the car keys lying on the seat. The glove compartment, where he always carried his gun, was open and the weapon gone. His hat lay on the ground 20 feet from the car. There was a blue coat in the back seat of the car that did not belong to him. There were no bloodstains and no signs of a struggle. Two things Hub never did was leave the car keys behind, not even for a second, and he never did anything without wearing his hat. Everyone recognized that this was a momentous event in a county where nothing much ever occurred.

Checking his home, investigators noted that Sheriff Ferguson's bed was not slept in Friday night. Not waiting to be told, friends of the sheriff organized a search party, and hundreds joined in. People on horseback, in cars and trucks and on foot, searched a large area around the abandoned car. On Monday afternoon, two searchers on horseback noticed how both animals shied away from a weed-infested area on Eagle Creek. The two men dismounted and discovered the body of Sheriff Ferguson. The sheriff had been shot above the right ear, with the bullet emerging near the top of the skull. There was a 1 1/2-inch gash at the top of his head that some speculated came from a hatchet. A 22-pound railroad tie plate was crudely fastened around his neck with baling wire. Ferguson was fully clothed, and his pockets contained half a box of 38-caliber bullets, $4 dollars, a flashlight, a blackjack and other personal items. He was still wearing his glasses.

Investigators in the water of Eagle Creek recover the body of Sheriff Ferguson, seen floating at the bottom of the frame.

The Gallatin County deputy coroner, U.P. Carlton, ruled the death of Ferguson a homicide, but could not conduct an autopsy because the body was too badly decomposed. A short time later, a Cincinnati pathologist, Dr. Frank Cleveland, made headlines when he criticized the lack of an autopsy. "They buried their case against any murderer" by not doing an autopsy, he said, adding that doing so was "a careless or foolish misuse of the coroner's authority."

Motive was the big unknown. The chief investigator, Harlan Heilman, working alongside state police detective Robert K. Gordon, was confident that the murderer was a local citizen because the suspect would have had to be familiar with the area to have put the body where it was found. Some in town thought it was the bootleggers who got him. The sheriff had several run-ins with one (unnamed) local bootlegger who, according to Ferguson's brother-in-law, "got him."

County Judge Earl Spencer said that "Hub just wasn't the type of man to get into trouble." The sheriff was somewhat of a loner, divorced and living in an apartment by himself. He never said much. The *Gallatin County News* described him as "Not the most popular man in the county, but the least disliked."

More than 25 suspects were given lie detector tests, but none provided any solid leads. Another 200 people were questioned. Neither Ferguson's gun nor the bullet that felled him were ever found. Meanwhile, the local citizenry, most of whom somehow counted Sheriff Ferguson as a friend, never gave up hope. As Charlie Chapman, a local citizen, prophesied not long after the murder, "He [the assailant] can't get away, especially if he lives around here. Lots of folks know everybody's business. I don't rightly know who will tell about it, but you mark my words, they'll find him." Regrettably, the criminals were never found, and the case remains unsolved.

SOURCES:

- http://www.angelfire.com/ky/roydwheeler/ferguson4.html
- http://www.angelfire.com/ky/roydwheeler/ferguson3.html
- https://www.supportingheroes.org/memorial/hero.php?hero_id=901
- http://www.enquirer.com/editions/2002/09/23/loc_recent_deaths_recall.html
- http://www.nkyviews.com/gallatin/text/ferguson.html
- http://www.nkyviews.com/gallatin/text/wheelers_ferguson.html
- Newspapers.com

CHAPTER 48

An Alibi for Murder

THE OFFICER:

Patrolman Frank W. Hardy
Seattle (Washington) Police Department
End of Watch: Friday, March 12, 1954
Age: 31

In police work, few radio calls raise the hair on the back of your neck and get the adrenaline pounding through your veins more than an "All units, a robbery in progress" or a silent robbery alarm at a bank. Law enforcement officers train endlessly for just such an event. There is diagonal deployment to consider, concealment and cover, what additional weapons to take and above all, communication with responding units . Patrolman Frank Hardy responded to just such a call. Regrettably, it would be his last.

What would go down in history as one of the most spectacular bank robberies in Seattle, began on Friday, March 12, 1954, at 10:40 a.m., when three middle-aged men entered the lobby of the Seattle First National Bank at 404 N. 85th St. wearing disguises. When they saw the large fake noses attached to black-rimmed glasses,

The Seattle First National Bank was the scene of a robbery and shooting that left one officer dead and two others seriously wounded.

Sgt. Howard Slessman was the first to reach the bank and was shot in the shoulder by one of the robbers. He is shown here recovering from his wounds in 1954.

many of the 20 customers inside thought it was some sort of prank. The snickering stopped when they saw the men were armed with guns. (Much of the following information was reported by the Behind the Badge Foundation which provides comprehensive support to Washington state's law enforcement agencies, families and communities after an officer has died or suffered serious injury in the line of duty.)

Once in the bank, Suspect No. 1 pointed a gun at the bank manager and ordered him to open the vault. Suspect No. 2 stood in the lobby as the lookout and kept an eye on the two entrances. Suspect No. 3 entered the tellers' cage area and starting loading money into brown paper bags he had brought with him. A bank employee lying on the ground, bravely used his foot to activate a hidden silent alarm. The call of the silent robbery alarm at the bank went out at 10:45. The closest unit to the bank was Sgt. Howard Slessman in Car 252. Officer Vernon Chase in Car 223 and Officer Frank Hardy in Car 213 arrived right behind Sgt. Slessman. Unfortunately for the officers, the glass in the bank's windows were all one-way, which made it nearly impossible for them to see inside while providing the criminals with a clear view of what was occurring outside.

Armed with a shotgun, Sgt. Slessman parked at the south side of North 85th and moved toward the main entrance. Officer Chase approached from the east side, also armed with a shotgun. Sgt. Slessman told Chase to take the east entrance. Slessman continued to the main entrance. Inside, the three suspects saw both officers approaching. The sergeant glanced inside the bank and saw several people in the lobby, none of whom appeared alarmed. He would later state it appeared like business as usual, and he thought this was probably just another false alarm. Slessman entered through the first set of doors. As he did, he saw a man moving toward him who he thought was the bank manager coming to explain the error in setting off the silent alarm. Suspect No. 2 stopped eight feet from the inner door, quickly raised his .45-caliber semiautomatic pistol and fired through the glass door. The bullet hit Slessman in the shoulder and entered his upper torso. The shot paralyzed his right arm. The sergeant went down. Suspect No. 2 walked over to the wounded man, leveled his gun directly at Slessman's head and, instead of executing him, calmly told him to stay where he was. He then strolled back into the bank.

Officer Vernon Chase, shot during the bank robbery, looking at the case file in 1963, the same year he was forced to take a disability pension as a result of the wounds he suffered.

Suspects No. 1 and No. 2 started to walk through the lobby toward the east door. As Slessman lay on the floor, he saw Officer Hardy moving from the sidewalk east of the bank toward the east entrance. Suspect No. 2, peering through the one-way glass, fired a shot through the quarter-inch plate-glass window, striking Officer Hardy in the head. Quickly, Officer Chase went to aid Hardy. Suspects No. 1 and No. 2 walked out the east door into the parking lot. Suspect No. 2 took aim and shot Chase in the abdomen. Chase went down. Not one shot had been fired by the three officers, and all were on the ground, bleeding. Suspect No. 3, the only remaining robber in the bank, used his pistol to smash out a window on the west side of the bank. He jumped out with a bag containing $6,900

A bank employee points to the bullet hole through which Sgt. Slessman was shot.

($63,000 in today's money) and left behind another bag, this one containing $90,800 ($831,000).

Suspects No. 1 and No. 2 sprinted to their stolen getaway car parked at the northeast corner of the bank parking lot. The late-model green Oldsmobile had Washington plates that had been lifted from a Studebaker in an auto wrecking yard. The two suspects drove north on Phinney Street as responding units pulled up. As Office G.D. Boyer arrived, a woman was yelling that a man had run behind a house on Phinney. Officer Boyer looked in that direction and saw Suspect No. 3 just getting into the getaway car. He chased the suspects on foot north on Phinney until he lost sight of the car.

At the bank, officers and citizens, along with several doctors and nurses from a nearby clinic, arrived to give aid to the three wounded men. The officers were loaded into three different ambulances and transported to nearby hospitals. Officer Hardy died while en route. Ninety minutes later, the getaway car was found abandoned in a parking lot. As the car was being recovered, one of the most intense manhunts in the history of the Pacific Northwest was underway.

Following the robbery and murder of Officer Hardy, a joint task force of the Seattle Police Department and the FBI, logged 10,000 hours in just two weeks of investigative work while following up on more than 700 leads. On the day of the shooting, a police bulletin detailing the robbery was sent to outlying agencies. After hearing of the Seattle robbery, Vancouver detectives who had been investigating a series of bank robberies were quick to note the similarities between the two. The MO (modus operandi) fit perfectly. A Canadian police superintendent promptly phoned the Seattle investigators.

Consequently, four months after the shooting, detectives had two of the three suspects identified: Clifford Dawley and John Wasylenchuk, both convicted criminals with lengthy rap sheets. Of the three suspects, Dawley, the apparent triggerman (Suspect No. 2), stood out as the leader. Despite the quick identification of the suspects, it would take nearly a decade for a grand jury to indict the two men for the murder of Officer Hardy and the bank robbery.

Authorities attempted to extradite Dawley, who was serving his first year of a nine-year prison sentence in Canada —but were turned down. Canadian law prohibited extradition until the full term of a sentence is served. Investigators were stunned. Nevertheless, Wasylenchuk, who was not in prison, was put on trial in a Seattle federal court in 1964. Prosecutors had a strong case and were going after the death penalty. But to everyone's disbelief, Wasylenchuk was provided an alibi by a retired sergeant of the Royal Canadian Mounted Police, who stated that Wasylenchuk was at his home the day of the shooting. This same Mountie had also been a defense witness in a previous bank robbery case in which Wasylenchuk was convicted. Through different informers, U.S. investigators learned that several Canadian officers had assisted criminals in setting up bank robberies in western Canada and, for a price, provided them with false alibis. With the alibi, Wasylenchuk went free. And with that acquittal, the second suspect, Dawley, was never brought to trial.

Postscript. Wasylenchuk had a heart attack and died in 1968. Dawley, who police always believed shot all three officers (Suspect No. 2), died in a boat fire in 1974. The RCMP sergeant died of natural causes four months after the trial. The third suspect was never officially identified.

Sgt. Slessman and Officer Chase both returned to work in July 1954. Chase never fully recovered from his wounds. After 19 surgeries and hospitalization for over three months, Chase retired on a disability pension in 1963. He died in 2002. Slessman was later promoted to captain and became head of internal investigation in 1977. His son, Mike, became a Seattle police captain. Howard Slessman died in 1981.

Frank Wallace Hardy was born in 1923 in Minnesota but lived most of his life in Seattle. He served in the United States Marine Corps from 1943 to 1946. He joined the SPD in 1951. Before his death, Hardy was remodeling the family home into their "dream house." Following his murder, fellow officers including the chief of police, along with tradesmen from throughout the area did a complete remodel of the Hardy home. It became known as "Project Hardy." His pregnant wife Rolene, and his daughter, Antoinette, moved into the completed dream house Frank had always wanted for them.

SOURCES:

- http://www.behindthebadgefoundation.org/roll-call/hardy-officer-frank-w
- Seattle Post-Intelligencer. http://blog.seattlepi.com/seattle911/2013/03/06/the-1954-seattle-bank-heist-that-exposed-a-political-scandal/#photo-211913 and
- http://blog.seattlepi.com/thebigblog/2010/09/20/p-i-archive-story-of-1954-greenwood-bank-robbery/
- The Seattle Times: http://community.seattletimes.nwsource.com/archive/?date=19931128&slug=1734219
- Newspapers.com
- A book was written on the shooting and robbery in 1994 titled: Cops, Crooks and Politicians by Neil W. Moloney, the former chief of the Washington State Patrol and a former Seattle police officer.

CHAPTER 49

The Politically Motivated Killings of Two Deputies

THE OFFICERS:

Deputy R. A. "Bob" Rogers
Polk County (Tennessee) Sheriff's Department
End of Watch: Saturday, March 8, 1958
Age: 65

Chief Deputy James Louis Wright
Polk County (Tennessee) Sheriff's Department
End of Watch: Saturday, March 8, 1958
Age: 49

Law enforcement officers face a variety of threats each day they walk out of the station to patrol the streets of America. Hidden dangers could be just around the next corner. This author has written in detail about officers who have lost their lives at the hands of robbers, burglars, tramps, drunks, gangs, thugs—and the list goes on and on. But to be killed for belonging to the wrong political party is almost beyond comprehension. However, this was apparently what happened in Polk County, Tennessee, when two deputies were slain and a third wounded.

It was a Saturday night in Copperhill, Tennessee, a once-thriving area for copper mines. The population had been declining since the 1920s, when it was 1,100. In 1958 it was down to 600. That Saturday night at 10 p.m., Deputies Bob Rogers, James Wright and Carmel Gibson pulled up to the

2 Polk Officers Die in Ambush; Another Injured

Unidentified Shotgunner Fires On Them Outside Tavern; Posse, Bloodhounds, Roadblocks Used

The page one newspaper headline from The Tennessean the day after the murders of Deputies Rogers and Wright.

Turtletown Grill—a cute name for a local beer joint off State Highway 68. The lawmen were there to check the bar, which usually had 15 to 20 patrons and an occasional drunk. As they stepped from their car, which was parked near the road, several shotgun blasts erupted from a gully just across the street. Deputies Rogers and Wright were hit in the head and were instantly killed. Deputy Gibson dived for cover and was only slightly injured. He returned fire but did not appear to hit anyone.

A posse was quickly assembled. Taking part were 50 men from Polk and adjoining counties, state highway patrol officers and bloodhounds from Cherokee County. The dogs picked up a scent from where the shooter had lain in wait and followed it 1,000 yards up the gully north of the tavern to where it abruptly ended. It appeared the assassin had a car waiting and escaped.

The following day, the talk in the press and on the street was that the killing of the deputies was politically motivated. "I think it was politics," Mayor Emil Greene of Copperhill declared. "And most of those with whom I have talked agree."

Polk County in the 1950s had a reputation for violence and death connected with local politics. It dated from a 1948 "revolution" by the Good Government League, which overthrew the iron rule of an unpopular sheriff. In 1951, 43-year-old W.A. Lewis returned home late one night from a day trip. As he got out of his car, he was killed by three blasts into his chest from a shotgun at close range. He managed to stagger to his doorstep, where he died.

Lewis was chairman of the mainly Democratic county's quarterly court. When the court had a meeting scheduled, armed "mountaineers" surrounded the courthouse, telling

Lewis, and anyone else attempting to enter, that there would be no meeting—or else. The Good Government League wanted the court shut down. The Democrats said they would get even. And so went the politics in the mountains of this small county, resulting in the deaths of two deputies and an innocent civilian. No one was ever prosecuted in any of the cases, and they remain unsolved.

Wright's granddaughter, who never knew him, hasn't forgotten the death of her grandfather. She learned about him from stories her mother told her, and she writes almost yearly on his *Officer Down Memorial Page*.

> *I sure miss you Big daddy. There's still no 1 been held accountable for you or Bob Roger's murder. The TBI [Tennessee Bureau of Investigation] failed you & him. There's still people who know the truth & I hope someday he will tell the truth. I love you. Take care of mother & Bigmama. Xixoxo*
>
> *Michele Gregory*
> *Granddaughter*
> *August 3, 2016*

SOURCES:

- http://www.odmp.org/officer/reflections/14541-chief-deputy-james-louis-wright
- http://www.odmp.org/officer/14541-chief-deputy-james-louis-wright
- http://www.odmp.org/officer/11455-deputy-r-a-bob-rogers
- Newspapers.com

CHAPTER 50

"Just give me a minute"

THE OFFICER:

Private Frank Henderson "Hank" Wall Jr.
Augusta (Georgia) Police Department
End of Watch: Tuesday, November 18, 1958
Age: 33

The front-page article in the *Augusta Chronicle* quoted a sergeant from the city police department about the recent murder of a fellow officer: "We'll get him." he said of the killer, adding, "A stocky gunman with a nervous trigger-finger violated the No. 1 rule of his profession Tuesday night. He shot a policeman without warning." A second officer added, "Yeah, but don't worry. We'll get him if it takes 10 years." Sadly, that comment proved too optimistic, as it has been 60 years, and there is still no one behind bars for the death of Private Frank "Hank" Wall.

Wall was driving his motorcycle down Walton Way on that Tuesday night in 1958 when an all-points bulletin was broadcast for units to be on the lookout for a black-and-white Chevrolet. The car had been stolen by a gunman just minutes earlier after he robbed Sheehan's package (liquor) store on Wrightsboro Road.

At just after 8 p.m., Private Wall observed a car matching that description and stopped it. As he dismounted from his motorcycle, Wall drew his sidearm. As he took a step toward the car, the driver jumped from the vehicle and fired five shots in rapid succession from a .32-caliber pistol. Wall was struck and went down on the roadway next to his motor. The gunman casually walked over to Wall and shot him again in the back. The assailant took Wall's weapon and fled the area in the stolen car, which was recovered a short time later. Wall was struck by two bullets to his abdomen—one from the front, one through his back—another round to his hand and one to his right ear.

Taken to the hospital, the dying officer told Lt. Thad Calhoun, "I know that face, Lieutenant. I'll bet I've seen it a thousand times, but I just don't know his name. It'll come to me in a minute; just give me a minute." Shortly after uttering these words, Private Hank Wall died.

As with almost all unsolved homicides of law enforcement officers, investigators were extremely busy in the early stages of the investigation. They followed up on hundreds of leads and interviewed 68 potential suspects—all without finding the killer. After a few weeks, the leads evaporated. But to their credit, detectives refused to give up. Investigators continued to work the case, and five years after the murder of Wall, the authorities charged Richard Hogan, a 30-year-old, in Wall's death.

Hogan maintained his innocence from the time of his arrest and supplied a weak alibi for the night of the murder. The alleged killer said there was a conspiracy to convict him and that detectives fabricated evidence. Despite Hogan's accusations, he was convicted by a jury for the murder of Officer Wall. As he was being hauled off to prison, the convicted murderer said, "They have put me in the vicinity of the crime but haven't been able to prove I had anything to do with it."

No sooner had the jailhouse door slammed shut on Hogan than his lawyers appealed the conviction to the Georgia Supreme Court. After reviewing the case, the court ordered a new trial, and this time, Hogan was found not guilty and walked out of the courtroom a free man.

From here the case went into a deep freeze. But somewhat surprisingly, in 2013, 55 years after Wall's murder, the case was thawed out when Richmond County Sheriff Richard Roundtree asked investigators to reopen it. This came after Roundtree learned of Wall's unsolved murder while preparing for Peace Officer Memorial Day, which is held every May. The sheriff acknowledged that finding new leads was not very likely, because most of the records were lost some decades ago in a flood. "It's a shot in the dark. We know that," Roundtree said. "Because it's a fallen officer, it's worth that shot." He went on to say that law enforcement officials owe it to Wall's family and the community to solve the case. And the hunt continues. Officer Wall was married with three children.

SOURCES:

- http://chronicle.augusta.com/sites/default/files/11191958SlainOfficerFront.pdf
- https://www.odmp.org/officer/13770-police-officer-frank-henderson-wall-jr
- http://chronicle.augusta.com/news-metro-latest-news/2013-05-26/slaying-augusta-police-department-officer-still-unsolved

CHAPTER 51

"Beat No. 2"

THE OFFICER:

Patrolman Douglas Eugene Cantrill
Davis (California) Police Department
End of Watch: Monday, September 7, 1959
Age: 23

It was a night they would never forget. Marguita Bourns and her boyfriend, Richard Sauers, were a young couple out on a date that Monday, September 7, 1959. It was still early, only 10:20 p.m., when driving through a residential area bordered by the Southern Pacific railroad tracks, they noticed a police vehicle that appeared empty with its red lights on. After driving another few blocks, Richard thought there was "something strange about the appearance" of the car, so he turned around and went back. Stopping next to the police vehicle, he saw a policeman's legs sticking out through the open driver's door. As Richard approached, he saw a .38-caliber revolver lying on the pavement next to the police car. Looking inside, he could see the officer was bloody and appeared to be dead.

The couple quickly drove to the police station, but no one answered their frantic knocking at the front door. So they went around the corner to the fire department to summon help. Soon, scores of officials were at the intersection of 10th and H streets.

The last contact Patrolman Eugene Cantrill had with the department was over the radio with Officer Victor Mentink, who would later serve as the Davis chief of police (1980-1988). Officer Mentink was assigned to Beat No. 1 in the center of the city, and Cantrill was patrolling Beat No. 2 on the edge of town. The subsequent investigation determined that

Nearly six decades later, not much has changed at the location where Patrolman Eugene Cantrill was murdered. Google Maps.

Cantrill had been murdered with his own duty weapon—shot once through the heart. There were no witnesses, and no one reported hearing a gunshot. It was thought that Cantrill might have been killed by a man and a woman who were acting suspiciously in the area.

Beginning the night of the murder, three different men were questioned, and in two cases, polygraph exams were given, but no one was ever charged in the murder of Cantrill. A forensic examination by the state division of criminal identification and investigation ruled out an accident or a suicide. Yolo County Coroner William C. McNary agreed Cantrill was shot and killed by someone else.

The 23-year-old officer left behind a nine-month-old baby and his wife. Today, the Davis Police Department is located at the intersection of Fifth Street and Cantrill Drive. The murder remains unsolved.

SOURCES:

- http://www.davisenterprise.com/forum/opinion-columns/1959-murder-in-davis-remains-unsolved/
- https://www.odmp.org/officer/2757-patrolman-douglas-eugene-cantrill
- Newspapers.com

CHAPTER 52

The Killing of a Small-Town Marshal

THE OFFICER:

Night Marshal William L. Meadows
Plainfield (Iowa) Police Department
End of Watch: Monday, January 23, 1961
Age: 36

In police work, it really doesn't matter what size of a town you patrol. The badge you wear on your chest comes with a large target on your back. While there is little crime in small- town America, when it does occur, these officers are hampered with similar problems. Heading the list is no backup for miles. Second, you work alone. Both of these circumstances applied to Night Marshal William Meadows that Monday morning, January 23, 1961. Meadows was the only peace officer in Plainfield, Iowa, population 445. As the only lawman, your phone can ring at any time—day or night. For Meadows, his fateful call came at 2:15 in the morning.

Mrs. Ernest Buckman owned a drugstore and lived above it with her husband. Both were awakened by a thunderous explosion at 2:10 a.m. At first she thought someone was breaking into their store. That was until both Buckmans looked out the window and saw two men inside the closed Hartmann Packing Plant that was directly across the street. In a town of just a few hundred, everyone knows one another and has their phone numbers. Mrs. Buckman called Ken Hartmann who owned the plant, with his father, Ted. Next she phoned Marshal Meadows, who lived 11 miles out of town with his aunt, Edna Voss.

After getting the call, Meadows quickly got dressed and told his auntie he would be right back. On the drive into

Plainfield, Meadows called for backup from the nearby Waverly Police Department who immediately dispatched two cars.

As Meadows arrived at the packing plant he could see that the front door had been smashed open. Getting out of his car, Meadows grabbed his trusted sawed-off shotgun. His duty revolver was already in his hip holster. With his backup still a distance away, Meadows entered the building. No sooner had he taken a step inside than the blast from a high-powered rifle echoed through the building. It was the last sound the marshal would hear, as the slug from a .30-30 caliber rifle ripped through his chest. The town marshal died instantly.

The Hartmann Packing Plant front door through which Marshal William Meadows walked and was immediately shot.

Just after Meadows was shot, Ted Hartmann arrived and parked at the front of the plant. As he was walking towards the door, a bullet whizzed through the front glass window, just missing his head. Then someone yelled, "Stay where you are, or you'll be shot too." Hartmann hid behind his car.

Meanwhile, Kenneth Hartmann parked at the rear of the plant. As he got out, he saw two men running from the building. The suspects ran north from the store, shooting as they fled. Mrs. Buckman counted four to five rapidly fired shots followed by a pause and then two more.

Roadblocks were set up on Highway 188, but the suspects had disappeared. As daylight broke, investigators, including detectives from Iowa State Bureau of Criminal Investigation, searched for evidence. The bullets from the building and one dug out of Hartmanns' car door came from two weapons: A high-powered rifle and a .38 revolver. In their haste to leave the building, the two killers left behind an impressive set of burglary tools, which they carried in a large knapsack. Also recovered were two gas masks the suspects used to protect themselves from the nitroglycerin the burglars had used to blow open the plant's safe.

The loud explosion that the Buckmans heard was the bandits blowing off the heavy 40-inch-tall safe door which flew across the room. When the marshal arrived, the suspects were preparing to blow the inner cash compartment. If they succeeded, they would have found only paper records, as Ted Hartmann had earlier taken all the cash for the day to the bank. A lengthy investigation turned up no additional clues, and the murder remains unsolved.

William Meadows was born in 1924 in Clear Lake, Washington. His father was a physician. During World War II, Meadows served with the Army Air Force. When the Korean War broke out, he again served his country. Meadows worked as the night marshal for five years and was not married.

SOURCES:

- https://iowacoldcases.org/wp-content/uploads/2011/02/1961-1-23-waterloo-dc-meadows-2pgs.pdf
- https://www.odmp.org/officer/9158-night-marshal-william-l-meadows
- http://www.iowaunsolvedmurders.com/the-murders/explosion-in-the-night-murder-of-william-l-meadows-1961/ by Nancy Bowers, "Iowa Unsolved Murders: Historic Cases."
- Newspapers.com

CHAPTER 53

The Fight for Integration

THE OFFICER:

Deputy Sheriff O'Neal Moore
Washington Parish (Louisiana) Sheriff's Office
End of Watch: Wednesday, June 2, 1965
Age: 34

Since 1791, thousands of American law enforcement officers have lost their lives in the performance of their sworn duty. Many were killed by gunfire, some while investigating robberies, burglaries, drunkenness and an assortment of other crimes. But few were ever killed because of the color of their skin. Deputy Sheriff Oneal Moore was an exception.

During the 1960s, the Civil Rights Movement was out to end racial segregation and discrimination against African Americans. The American South was in the crosshairs of fierce, and often violent, confrontations between the differing factions. In tiny Washington Parish, Louisiana, the black community joined in and demanded the integration of the all-white Sheriff's Department.

In 1964, Oneal Moore and David "Creed" Rogers were hired as deputies, making history as the first black law enforcement officers in the parish. They were hired to patrol the black areas of the parish's communities. Making clear its displeasure with the desegregation of the Sheriff's Department was the Ku Klux Klan, which had deep-seated influence in the parish. The result was numerous clashes between the races.

In the city of Bogalusa, Washington Parish, about an hour north of New Orleans, racial strife was making daily headlines in 1965. African Americans, flush with the success of integrating the Sheriff's Department, were demanding equal job opportunities and desegregation of other public institutions. They had several marches down main street. Many in the small community fought with the demonstrators. In just one week, 50 people were arrested for attacks against blacks.

On the evening of Wednesday, June 2, 1965, Deputy Moore and his partner, Deputy Rogers, were headed to Moore's house. Moore was at the wheel as they drove along the desolate Louisiana 21, near the small community of Varnado (on the Mississippi border).

Deputy Sheriff David "Creed" Rogers.

Both deputies were accustomed to harassment, so they did not give much thought to the dark pickup truck tailgating them on the empty road. As they crossed some railroad tracks, the truck pulled alongside. Rogers recalled the incident that changed his life: "It appeared to be a dark truck, a black truck. I noticed it had a white grille and a Confederate flag emblem on the front bumper." Suddenly, shots rang out from a shotgun and at least one rifle, striking both officers. Rogers continued, "Well, the car hit the tree, and they passed, still shooting, and evidently the last shot got him [Moore]; it knocked him over on me."

With every window shot out, blood splattered everywhere, and his best friend dead from a bullet to the back of his head, Rogers refused to give up. Fighting through his own serious injuries, including his right eye partially shot out and a hole in his shoulder, Rogers managed to put out an all-points bulletin on the truck. Within minutes, officers blanketed the area, looking for the black pickup. An hour later, a vehicle matching the description was stopped just 20 miles from the scene of the shooting.

The driver was Ernest Ray McElveen, a Bogalusa paper mill worker. Rogers description of the truck fit perfectly, right down to the Confederate flag. McElveen was well regarded in the community. He was a member in the racist and anti-Semitic Citizens Councils of America and of the even more savagely bigoted National States Rights Party. Police found two pistols in his truck. However, they were unable to find a rifle or shotgun. McElveen was arrested for questioning and investigation into the murder of Deputy Moore but was just as quickly bailed out by his friends, who put together the $25,000 bond. Two nights after the shooting, the chief deputy, a white man who was investigating Moore's murder, had his house sprayed with bullets. No suspects were ever identified.

For his part, McElveen was never prosecuted and no other arrests were made. Although many still believe the Klan was involved with the shooting, local leaders denied the accusations, and no evidence was ever presented against its members. The FBI has reopened the case several times over the years. In 2007 the FBI placed postcards and posters around the parish offering $40,000 for information leading to the indictment and arrest of anybody responsible for the shootings. There still has been no arrest, and the case remains unsolved. Moore was survived by his wife, Maevella and four young daughters.

"Somebody in the know is keeping it a secret," said Maevella Moore, 73, in 2009. A retired nurse, she was living in the same modest house that she shared with her husband when he was murdered in 1965. "I need some closure. I'm very frustrated."

Deputy Rogers recovered from his wounds and continued his career. He died at the age of 85 in 2007. The leading suspect, McElveen, died at the age of 79 in 2003. The other suspects in the truck were never identified. Deputy Moore gave his life that night in 1965, killed because of the color of his skin, but in death, he became a catalyst in the integration of law enforcement agencies in the South.

SOURCES:

- http://www.policemag.com/channel/patrol/articles/2010/10/chasing-ghosts.aspx
- https://www.youtube.com/watch?v=cUw4utwDQ7g
- Newspapers.com
- https://www.splcenter.org/fighting-hate/intelligence-report/2009/deputy-sheriffs-murder-still-unsolved
- https://en.wikipedia.org/wiki/Murder_of_Oneal_Moore
- http://unsolved.com/archives/o%E2%80%99neal-moore
- http://articles.latimes.com/2007/mar/04/local/me-rogers4
- http://nuweb9.neu.edu/civilrights/oneal-moore/

CHAPTER 54

The Prowler

THE OFFICER:

Police Officer Walter Franklin Stathers
Coral Gables (Florida) Police Department
End of Watch: Tuesday, December 18, 1967
Age: 45

Metro-Dade Police Detective Greg Smith investigated some of the most revolting, violent and brutal crimes while working three intense decades on cold case files. He handled hundreds of cases. As time has passed, names, charges and dates have become a little fuzzy for the retired detective. But one case file still haunts him—the 1967 unsolved murder of Coral Cables Police Officer Franklin Stathers. Despite the fact that decades have passed and witnesses have long since dried up, Smith and other detectives have never given up their search for the guilty party.

The ruthless killing of Officer Stathers on December 18, 1967, happened 15 years before Detective Smith joined the elite Cold Case Squad. Nothing eventful had occurred that Monday night for Officer Stathers, including a disturbance call at 2:59 a.m., at a prosperous Coral Gables neighborhood. Seemingly bored by the uneventful night, Stathers wrote in his log, "Talked to the Hughes boy and another couple and asked them to keep it a little lower." With few calls coming in, Stathers patrolled his beat, looking for anything or anyone that did not belong. If it walked, Stathers was on it.

About two hours after the disturbance call, a hurried transmission came from Stathers, requesting a K9 unit: "Get me a dog car." In his abruptness, the officer did not give his location. But others could guess where he was. When it was quiet, Stathers took special care to look after a house on South Alhambra Circle where Anthony Abraham, owner of a local car dealership, had an extensive Christmas light display that Stathers gave extra patrol.

Also working that night was Jim Harley, who would later serve as the chief of police of Coral Gables. Harley and others rushed to the area. As Harley came upon the scene, he noticed Stathers' car was across the street from the Abrahams' house. The engine was running and the driver's door open. The police car had veered out of control across the lawn and crashed.

Harley found the 45-year-old policeman, not next to his patrol car, but face down on the Abrahams' wet lawn. "It was pretty obvious he had been shot in the back of the head. It came out through his forehead. He was dead. No life in his body." The homeowner where the car crashed remembered, "I heard a big crash, and I looked out the window, and when I looked, I happened to see a blue flash and later on, I realized what that was—it was actually when Walter got shot." The live-in maid, Bertha Droquett, rushed to her window. She told investigators that a tall, thin black man wearing black pants and a white shirt had pedaled away on a 28-inch English-model bicycle with a chrome fender. Police speculated that Stathers had surprised a prowler and might have even jumped out of his patrol car, leaving it in gear in his haste to arrest the individual.

Detectives also believed there had been a violent fight, as Stathers' arm was twisted back and bruised. His .357 Colt Trooper revolver was missing and has never been recovered. As the winter sun rose that morning, officers had spread throughout the city and adjoining areas in a search for the suspect on a bike. More than 100 tips quickly came in. All were followed up, but no suspect was ever identified, and the case remains unsolved.

Stathers was born in 1921 in Allison, Pennsylvania, and served in the U.S. Navy during World War II. He was married in 1946 and had one son. He joined the Coral Gables Police Department in 1953.

SOURCES:

- http://jacksonville.com/apnews/stories/123007/D8TRNM1G0.shtml
- https://www.odmp.org/officer/12723-police-officer-walter-franklin-stathers
- http://boltoninvestigations.com/theunsolvedmurderofcoralgablespoliceofficerwalterstathers.html
- https://www.floridamemory.com/items/show/13754
- http://www.miaminewtimes.com/news/four-miami-detectives-recall-the-unsolved-murders-that-haunt-them-8399001

CHAPTER 55

A Department That Refuses to Forget

THE OFFICER:

Patrolman Robert Lawrence Tatman
Champaign (Illinois) Police Department
End of Watch: Saturday, November 25, 1967
Age: 27

The police radio transmission shattered the quiet of the early morning. "You got trouble out on West Church. You better get out here." Lt. J.O. Jones, was patrolling on the midnight shift for the Champaign Police Department that night, November 25, 1967, did not recognize the voice on the radio as one of his officers. He ordered all units to respond. Instantly, the sound of police sirens erupted as units rushed to West Church Street.

A few minutes earlier at 1 a.m., Patrolman Robert Tatman was on patrol when he radioed in that he was making a traffic stop at Church Street just west of Mattis Avenue. That was the last he was heard of. A passing motorist who saw Tatman on the ground near his police car used the officer's car radio to call for help. Lt. Jones was the first on scene. "Something I didn't want to see" said the man who would later serve as chief of police.

Patrolman Tatman was lying on his back in front of his car. The motor was running, the emergency lights flashing, the driver's door open. His flashlight was next to him; his hat was near the curb. Tatman had been shot in his right side. He died almost instantly.

Subsequent investigation suggested that his .38 revolver was taken from him and pushed into his ribs by the unknown assailant. Tatman would have tried to grab the gun, but investigator believe the suspect pulled the trigger, dropped the gun and fled in his car. The revolver was found next to Tatman. Roadblocks were set up, but with no results.

As hard as investigators worked the case, no breaks developed. Over the years, the case found its way to the back of a file cabinet, getting dusted off periodically, just in case somehow, someway, something was missed. It wasn't. But as anyone who has ever pinned on a badge knows, police work is unpredictable. Twenty years after the murder of Patrolman Tatman, the phone rang in the detective bureau. On the other end was an investigator from the Nebraska State Patrol. The ensuing conversation would keep the Champaign Police Department busy for years.

An unnamed woman who was seeing a therapist had revealed some of the most traumatic events in her life. One was so shocking that the doctor, despite doctor- patient confidentiality, contacted the police. The patient related how 20 years earlier she had been in the backseat of her father's station wagon when they were stopped by police. She recalled how her father walked back toward the single officer and shot him in the stomach area. She said there was no traffic, and she remembers the officer's hat landing near the curb.

In 1984 when she married, she told her husband of the event. In a subsequent interview, the husband confirmed the story. As Champaign officers pressed their investigation with the woman, she repeatedly turned out to be wrong about specifics of the case. Eventually, her story was thought not to be plausible, and detectives moved on. To this day, no arrest has been made, and the case remains unsolved.

In 2016, approaching the 50th anniversary of the murder of Tatman, Zane Ziegler, a retired Champaign police officer and president of the Campaign Police Historical Society, initiated an idea to recognize the sacrifice of Officer Tatman. First, all police vehicles would display a memorial decal featuring Tatman's service badge and his 1967 squad car. Additionally, a silver-plated commemorative "challenge" coin was produced featuring Robert Tatman's name, his badge number and his "end of watch" date.

"I think that you remind the community, and you also remind the officers that are working today, what can happen out there," said Ziegler. "And for the family. They've gone for a long time without a father. He had four children at the time. So it's been rough on them." Although the killer is still out there, Champaign's police family will never forget his sacrifice.

SOURCES:

- http://www.odmp.org/officer/13103-patrolman-robert-l-tatman
- http://champaignil.gov/2016/11/23/champaign-police-officer-robert-l-tatman-honored-in-50-year-anniversary-line-of-duty-death/
- https://will.illinois.edu/news/story/champaign-officers-sacrifice-remembered
- http://www.news-gazette.com/news/local/2013-05-17/longtime-champaign-officer-recalls-colleagues-death.html

CHAPTER 56

The TSU Riot

THE OFFICER:

Police Officer Louis R. Kuba
Houston (Texas) Police Department
End of Watch: Wednesday, May 17, 1967
Age: 24

As the nation struggled with race relations and the emergence of the Civil Rights Movement in the 1960s, Houston, Texas, was no exception. Chief Herman Short was a proactive administrator who believed in a two-fisted approach to reducing crime. Some in the black community thought his aggressive tactics were not justified. Combine this with the changes that were taking place on college campuses in the South, and you had a 1960s recipe for conflict.

In the normally peaceful black colleges throughout the South, there were issues that were simmering in the background that needed attention. Unrest and resentment were coming to the boiling point against white school administrators, local officials, and the police, who appeared slow to accept black equality. The only ingredient missing in Houston for civil unrest was a spark, an incident, to set off the powder keg of repressed anger.

At Texas Southern University, which had a 95 percent black enrollment, the catalyst was a rumor that a black six-year-old had been shot by a white police officer. The anger was so pronounced that the real truth would not be heard. In reality, it was a six-year-old white child who was accidently shot and wounded by another white boy. As the rumor reverberated through campus, hundreds of students took to the streets, demanding justice. They were quickly met by Chief Short's officers, who were deployed to maintain order. About the same time, a police cruiser was driving through campus when a large object struck the car (later reported to be a watermelon). The affected unit asked for backup and additional units raced to TSU. As the police officers got out of their cars, they were struck by rocks and bottles raining down on them from the multistory dorms. As officers were ducking for cover, a gunshot rang out, and a Houston police officer went down with a bullet to his leg. Like a lightning bolt exploding through a tree, a full-blown riot erupted. Numerous shots were fired by gunmen in Lanier Hall. Police took cover and fired back with 3,000 rounds of shotgun and carbine fire into the dormitory for men.

After two hours of intense shooting, police formed a squad of 60 armed officers with rifles. Using tactics learned on the battlefields of Vietnam, the squad tactically advanced toward Lanier Hall. As they reached their objective, officers smashed down doors using fire axes, shot locks off doors and stormed into the dorm. In support of the advance group was a smaller squad of officers who provided cover fire. One of these men was Louis Kuba, a 24-year-old rookie just out of the academy. Kuba was positioned near a wall 100 yards from the building when he was struck in the head by a bullet. Kneeling next to Kuba was Ronnie Bird, a classmate of Kuba's. Bird became distraught when his buddy went down. Minutes after being shot, Kuba was taken away on a stretcher and died a few hours later. A large pool of blood remained on the sidewalk as a stark reminder of where he fell.

Officer Bird, while trying to hold it together, approached his lieutenant. "Look, lieutenant. Look what Louis gave me." He showed him Kuba's .38 revolver. He told his boss how Kuba handed him his gun as he lay mortally wounded. The circumstances were too much for Bird. The shooting of his classmate, the noise, the war-like conditions caused the rookie officer to go into shock, and he had to be taken from the scene in an ambulance. A policeman asked the lieutenant, "What's wrong with him?" The lieutenant replied, "He's just a kid, that's all. He was next to Kuba when he got it."

Officers eventually took over the dorm and put 480 students in the felony prone position on the grass while awaiting transportation. The students were taken away in buses and paddy wagons for booking. The next day, all but five students were released. The five remaining students stood trial for allegedly instigating the riot that led to the death of Kuba. The charges were dismissed after a jury could not reach a verdict. There was no second trial, and no student was ever charged in the shooting death of Officer Kuba. The case remains unsolved.

SOURCES:

- http://www.houstonpress.com/news/houston-101-an-earlier-time-when-shots-rang-out-at-tsu-6722963
- https://www.newspapers.com/image/?spot=12484457
- http://www.odmp.org/officer/7763-police-officer-louis-r-kuba
- http://www.houstonarchitecture.com/haif/topic/10563-infamous-riots-in-our-city/
- http://www.chron.com/news/houston-texas/article/50-years-later-what-does-the-TSU-riot-mean-for-11153675.php

CHAPTER 57

The Recreation Building

THE OFFICER:

Detective Raymond Gonser
Michigan State Police
End of Watch: Thursday, August 8, 1968
Age: 33

As the Civil Rights Movement gained momentum across the United States during the late 1960s, violent confrontations took place between predominantly African American communities and law enforcement. In 1967 and 1968, there were more than 150 riots or major disturbances in the nation. In 1967 alone, 83 people were killed and 1,800 were injured—most of them African Americans. The violence left many buildings destroyed or looted, resulting in more that $100 million in damage. Michigan State Police Detective Raymond Gonser became one of the fatalities, a victim of civil unrest in Inkster, Michigan.

The city of Inkster is one of the few Metro Detroit suburbs whose population are predominantly African American. In the summer of 1968, the city was still feeling the effects of the 1967 Detroit riots that killed 43 people and burned 1,400 buildings. With racial unrest pervasive in many black communities, it took only one small incident to ignite the kindling of despair.

In a nondescript building in Inkster was the city's recreation center. In August of 1968, a group of black youths received permission to run a recreational and cultural program at the center. But on Wednesday, August 7, city officials received complaints that a large homemade sign was displayed, renaming the center after the late Malcolm X. Officials removed the sign, which left many in the black community agitated.

That night at 10:45, two Inkster police officers were investigating a shots-fired call near the recreation center. As they drove past, they were hit by a shotgun blast from a concealed gunman. Both officers were struck with several shotgun pellets. Officer John Knight, an African American, was hit in the right arm, right side and stomach by fragments of flying metal. His partner, Tom Freeman, white, was hit in the face and shoulder. The Inkster Police Department was pleased to be one of the few integrated police agencies in the area, but not everyone agreed with the policy.

Because of the shooting and civil disobedience, other law enforcement officers from the surrounding area were sent in. Detective Robert Gonser, an intelligence officer with the Michigan State Police, and his partner, Frederick Prysby, both white, were patrolling in an unmarked police vehicle near where the Inkster officers were attacked. At 2:45 a.m. on Thursday, the troopers saw a vehicle pull from a side street and attempt to block them in. Detective Gonser alertly drove around the car. As the two vehicles passed, the officers heard the four black occupants shout obscene threats, and they ordered the officers to stop.

Gonser saw a rifle in the suspects' car and attempted to evade them. It was too late. A volley of shots erupted from the vehicle, and Gonser was hit by a bullet that entered the police car through the taillight, striking him in the back, where it splintered, killing him. The suspects sped away.

About 15 minutes after Gonser was killed, a 14-year-old African American was shot and killed as he ran from police who suspected him of being one of the shooting suspects. It was determined that he'd had nothing to do with the shooting. The officers were later cleared. The shooting was determined to be "mistaken identity," and there was no evidence of criminal action by the officers.

A few months after the shooting, two Inkster men were arrested in the shooting of Gonser. Darnell Summers, 23, and Carl James, also 23, were charged with murder. They, along with a alleged female accomplice, Gale Simmons, 22, were identified as being in the car. The key witness who testified, Milford Scott, 22, stated he had seen Summers and James fire at the unmarked State Police car that Gonser was driving. The witness said he also took part in the shooting and that he, the two men and Simmons were all in the car together. But when the defense lawyer provided an earlier written statement by Scott stating that he was not in the car the night Gonser was shot, charges against Simmons, Summers and James, were all dismissed. The case was never refiled, and the shooting remains unsolved.

Detective Gonser was the son of Dr. Ivan Gonser, pastor of the First Methodist Church in Owosso, Michigan. Gonser joined the Michigan State Police in 1956. He was a Marine Corps veteran and was survived by his widow, Maria, a son and two daughters ranging in age from three to eight. In 2006, one of his daughters wrote her reflections on the *Officer Down Memorial Page*.

> *I am very proud of my dad. We all know about the ultimate sacrifice a police officer makes; his family, in a way, makes the same sacrifice because we no longer have our loved one. I wish he could have seen his children grow up and, now, see his great-grandchildren and great-great-children. How proud he would be to see how his family has flourished. To know that his murderer is walking free is gut wrenching. His murderer has had to live with himself/herself for all their living days with his death on their conscience. I live with it as a reality. There will always be a hole in my heart for my dad no matter how long it has been since he's been gone. He will never be forgotten. He is always in my thoughts. Thanks for keeping us in your prayers. I love you Dad!!!!*

SOURCES:

- http://www.odmp.org/officer/reflections/5539-detective-robert-raymond-gonser
- http://www.mspta.net/fallen-troopers/detective-robert-r-gonser/
- In the Line of Duty by Isaiah McKinnon, Ph.D., pages 122-123. Turner Publishing Company, Paducah, Kentucky.
- Newspapers.com

CHAPTER 58

The Black Panthers

THE OFFICER:

Officer Ronald Tsugio Tsukamoto
Berkeley (California) Police Department
End of Watch: Thursday, August 20, 1970
Age: 28

The primary duty of law enforcement officers in the United States is to serve and protect the citizens of their community, county or state. But through the years, officers have unwittingly faced social and political movements that threaten their very existence and their sworn duty.

In 1966, Huey Newton and Bobby Seale formed the Black Panther Party, a self-proclaimed American revolutionary party for self-defense against what they perceived as acts of police brutality against African Americans. The group eventually called for the arming of all blacks in their war against law enforcement. From 1967 through the end of 1970, nine police officers were killed and 56 were wounded across the nation by violence attributed to the Black Panthers. "Off the pig" was their battle cry, and the slogan appeared on all their publications. The assassination of Officer Ronald Tsukamoto had all the hallmarks of a Black Panther murder.

Just before 1 a.m. on Thursday, August 20, 1970, Officer Tsukamoto stopped a motorcyclist for making an illegal U-turn. Rather than issue a citation, Tsukamoto struck up a casual conversation with the man. It was during this encounter that an African American man wearing a long, black flannel coat walked up and joined the conversation. The three men talked peacefully about the Vietnam War. Changing the course of the discussion, and the life of Tsukamoto, the black man stated how things seemed quiet—"no riots" in Berkeley. With that, he quickly pulled out a pistol and fired two shots, hitting Tsukamoto in the head. One round went through the officer's right eye and exited out his left ear, killing him.

As the suspect jumped into the passenger seat of a light-colored 1959 Studebaker to make his escape, the young motorcyclist ran to the officer's car and, using the police radio, exclaimed, "I ain't lying; one of your officers has been shot twice in the head." Officers swarmed the area but were unable to locate the suspects or recover the car.

Police released a sketch of the suspect and described him as a young, tall black man with a 2-inch-high natural haircut wearing a long coat and blue jeans. A $10,000 reward was posted. The murder was quickly labeled as political. "When you consistently reinforce in unstable people the idea of killing police officers, someone will do it," then-Chief Bruce Baker said. "Assassination has been a technique consistently advocated in the underground press," Baker further stated at a news conference the day of the shooting: "There have been comments by Tom Hayden and Huey Newton, among others, advocating violence on policemen. They're going to reap the harvest of this type of talk."

A group of whites who sympathized with black militants by forming the National Committee to Combat Fascism replied in a national publication that it was the police who were "reaping the harvest of years of oppressive brutality and murder in ghetto communities."

As with many unsolved police homicides, months turned to years as leads faded away, witnesses died and the case went from front burner to cold case. Soon, three decades had passed, still with no arrest. Then a retired Berkeley police detective, Russ Lopes, came out of retirement to give new life to a case long in deep freeze. Lt. Lopes, a highly respected investigator who spent 31 years putting bad guys in jail, had been forced to retire in 2001 for health reasons. Overcoming his health concerns, the avid outdoorsman was "climbing the walls" without the everyday challenge he had faced as a detective. In 2002, the bored investigator was back at work looking over unsolved homicides. His first challenge was the murder of Officer Tsukamoto, whose death was just four months before Lopes pinned on his badge.

Looking at everything with fresh eyes and reinterviewing witnesses, the detective was soon on the trail of several suspects. Leading the list was a retired Oakland schoolteacher, Styles Price, 56, whom Lopes identified as the triggerman. Next up was former Black Panther Don Juan Warren Graphenreed, 56, whom allegedly drove the getaway car. Graphenreed had been living on the streets in San Francisco before being convicted of drug charges and sent to prison. Lopes reasoned that the two men committed the murder to impress the Panthers.

In 2004, 34 years after the murder of Officer Tsukamoto, police arrested both men along with twin sisters Joyce Gaskin and Joy Hall, whom Lopes accused of being accessories. Lopes and officials from the Berkeley Police Department were convinced they were bringing those responsible for the murder of Tsukamoto to trial.

Shortly after the arrests, the Alameda County District Attorney's Office stated there was a lack of evidence to charge the suspects arrested by the Berkeley Police Department. All the arrestees were promptly released. Lt. Lopes responded by stating, "We strongly disagree with that statement." He went on, "To get the warrants, you have to determine to a judge's satisfaction that a crime was committed and that there is probable cause for the arrest, and a well-qualified judge of the Alameda County Superior Court said there was reasonable cause to issue the warrant."

Later, the determined Lopes reluctantly acknowledged that prosecutors needed more evidence to bring a case to trial. "We'll go back and get what they need," he said. "We will not be deterred on this case." Regrettably, now approaching 50 years since the murder of Officer Tsukamoto, there have been no arrests, and the case remains unsolved.

Ronald Tsukamoto, on the force for 11 months, grew up in a World War II internment camp and was a newlywed when he joined the force. He was the first Japanese-American police officer in Berkeley, and his death was the first ever for the department. From his untimely death came the Northern California Asian Peace Officers' Association that today represents every Asian-American officer in Northern California.

SOURCES:

- http://www.sfgate.com/bayarea/article/BERKELEY-1970-killing-still-haunts-Berkeley-2616535.php
- http://articles.latimes.com/2004/may/26/local/me-tsukamoto26
- http://www.odmp.org/officer/13472-officer-ronald-tsugio-tsukamoto
- http://www.nleomf.org/officers/search/search-results/ronald-tsugio-tsukamoto.html?referrer=https://www.google.com/
- http://www.ci.berkeley.ca.us/police/history/memorial.html

CHAPTER 59

The Chief Who Fought a Town Gang

THE OFFICER:

Chief of Police Robert Hamrick
Rock Creek (Ohio) Police Department
Date of Incident: Tuesday, March 10, 1970
End of Watch: Friday, March 20, 1970
Age: 29

In the late 1960s when the Black Panthers and other radical organizations were terrorizing larger cities, smaller towns had their own unique problems. In Rock Creek, Ohio, population 731, a sizable group of mostly younger men formed themselves into the "redneck" Rock Creek Gang. They threatened citizens, were involved in thefts and apparently were stealing cars.

The job of challenging these thugs fell to the Ashtabula County Sherriff's Department, which patrolled Rock Creek. These were challenging times for the undermanned department. According to the chief of police from neighboring Jefferson Village, "They [Rock Creek Gang members] were involved in fights, they were involved in threats and they had the entire village under their thumb. When they spoke, the village pretty much listened."

Doubting the resolve of the sheriff's department, the citizens of Rock Creek did something significant: They dumped the sheriff in favor of forming their own police department consisting of a chief of police and two officers. In the formation year of 1969, the town went through two chiefs of police within months after the chiefs received threats against themselves and their families. The third man hired was Robert Hamrick, a 29-year-old with no previous law enforcement experience. He made his objectives clear from the moment he was sworn in. As related by his wife, Myrtle Hamrick: "He wanted it to be a nice, friendly town, and he wanted, you know, to get this gang off the streets so that people wouldn't have to be afraid of them."

Several times while the chief was relaxing at home, gang members would commit criminal acts to aggravate him. His wife said that more than once, he "took off after them." Five months after being sworn in, Chief Hamrick got a break. While on patrol, he discovered an expensive sports car that had been stolen from Cleveland and tucked away in an old building on the edge of town. Officer Gary Martin assisted the chief in the investigation. "We came across it, fingerprinted it, and we bugged the building because we didn't know who was there. We put a radio in our car and just drove around and listened until the guys came back. Bob was hiding in the office, and when they showed up, we jumped out and busted them."

But keeping the alleged gang members in jail was another matter. Soon after being booked, they were out on bail and immediately fought back against the lawman. The threatening calls began in earnest. On one occasion, the chief's wife answered the phone. "There was a man on the other end, and he said, 'Tell your husband to leave things alone, and get him out of town, or he's going to be hurt. And he's going to be hurt bad.'"

Within a month of his arrest of the alleged gang members, Hamrick was on patrol and radioed in that he was in pursuit of a car on the west side of town. That was Chief Hamrick's last transmission. An hour and a half went by as the dispatcher tried in vain to reach the chief. Nothing. Calls for help went out to the Ashtabula County Sheriff's Department. Four hours later, Chief Deputy Dennis Chapman found Hamrick's patrol car smashed against a tree. "He had head and facial injuries. I was surprised to find him moving when I got there."

The deputy kept Hamrick still while he called for additional help. During his initial investigation, Chapman noticed that there was a large amount of blood in the back seat of the patrol vehicle and that Hamrick's sidearm and baton were missing. The ignition and lights were switched off, even though the pursuit took place at night.

Chief Hamrick never regained consciousness and died 10 days later. Soon after, officials ruled his death accidental, the result of a traffic accident occurring while in a vehicle pursuit. Most in law enforcement were shocked. "I still don't believe to this day that all the injuries that Bob received were the result of that car accident," Chapman later said. Other officers felt that the accident was a coverup. Many believed he had been beaten with his own baton after the crash and put back into the car. His skull was completely crushed from the front to the back.

Six hours after the crash, the vehicle Hamrick had been chasing was found at a local gas station. It had a damaged tire and mud splatters. When the owner was interviewed, she revealed that she had taken the car in for repair the previous day. She said the car was clean when she left it. It was known to the police that one of the station workers was a member of the Rock Creek Gang. One other witness claimed that she had overheard several gang members boasting how they had killed Hamrick. "We killed us a cop, and we got away with it." She overheard them describe how they set up the accident, took the chief out of his car and beat him with his baton before putting him back in the car.

Although to this day there is confusion about whether this is an ongoing investigation or just a traffic accident, the current attorney general for the state of Ohio, Mike DeWine, leaves little doubt on his website:

> *On the evening of March 10, 1970, Chief Hamrick became involved in a pursuit of unknown individuals. The pursuit ended on Callender Road in the Village of Rock Creek when Chief Hamrick slid off of the icy dirt road and struck a tree, causing moderate damage to his vehicle. The events that unfolded immediately following the accident are unknown at this time. At some point, Chief Hamrick exited his patrol vehicle and was beaten severely on the side of his head with a tire iron. Somehow his unconscious body was placed across the seat of his marked police vehicle. He was not discovered for*

hours and was transported to the Cleveland Clinic where he died 10 days later, never regaining consciousness. The suspects are unknown at this time.

An Army veteran, Chief Hamrick was survived by his wife, two sons and a daughter. No arrest has been made in the case. In 2009, Roaming Shores Police Department was formed to replace the Rock Creek Police Department.

SOURCES:

- https://unsolved.com/gallery/robert-hamrick/
- https://www.odmp.org/officer/6001-chief-of-police-robert-hamrick
- http://www.ohioattorneygeneral.gov/Files/Law-Enforcement/Investigator/Cold-Case/Homicides/Hamrick
- http://unsolvedmysteries.wikia.com/wiki/Robert_Hamrick

CHAPTER 60

"We will never give up"

THE OFFICER:

Police Officer Frederick J. Cione, Jr.
Philadelphia (Pennsylvania) Police Department
End of Watch: Friday, January 30, 1970
Age: 25

For the living, the loss of a partner, friend, son, brother, loved one is a memory that never fades—never. So it was for a 24-year-old Nick Cione on that early Friday morning in 1970. Nick was sound asleep in his parents' home when he was awakened by his mother scrambling up the steps, anxiously calling out for her husband. Nick quickly got dressed and went downstairs with his parents. They were met by a uniformed Philadelphia police officer and a detective. They were standing in the doorway looking distraught.

They said there'd been an accident, Nick remembers. They were asked to come down to St. Joseph's Hospital. The family arrived and was taken into a small private room. There the Ciones were met by the head of the Philadelphia Police Department, Commissioner Frank Rizzo. He gently told the family that Officer Frederick Cione was killed in the line of duty. "I was in shock. I couldn't believe it," Nick recalled of hearing about his brother's death. "I thought they were going to tell us it was an auto accident. I never dreamed he was dead."

Over the next 47 years, the facts of what happened that night have been studied and analyzed by scores of detectives. At 1:10 a.m., Officer Cione had stopped his police car and called out to three young men, all black, 18 to 20 years old, walking in the 1700 block of West Oxford Street. A witness saw Cione get out of the car and start walking toward the men.

The 1700 block of West Oxford Street as it looks today. This was the location where Officer Frederick Cione was gunned down by three suspects in 1970. Google maps.

The witness looked away and heard a shot. She turned back and saw Cione staggering backward, his gun still in its holster. The gunman fired two more rounds from his .22-caliber pistol, striking the young officer in the chest and abdomen. Police found him lying in a gutter, 10 feet from his patrol car. Cione would die on the operating table a few hours later.

Over the years, detectives have filled 27 boxes with files, interviews and evidence they have gathered in their efforts to solve Cione' murder. The department's cold-case unit has a lieutenant, sergeant and eight detectives working this case and other unsolved murders. Officer Cione's murder is one of five unsolved police homicides in Philadelphia. Capt. John Clark, head of the homicide unit, described the "nagging feeling" of knowing that they have not been able to solve the case. He made it clear what they have been up against: "With this case, we really didn't have any witnesses.

Detectives did their best to check on them, but they always hit an impasse or a dead spot." Another question that never gets answered is why was Cione killed?

A clipping from the Philadelphia Daily News making clear to everyone that no one was giving up their efforts to find those responsible for the murder of Officer Cione.

A sociology professor from La Salle University believes it was a racially motivated "assassination." Professor Charles Gallagher was specific: "So it's 1970. Six years prior, we have one of the worst race riots we ever had in Philadelphia." The riots were just blocks from where the killing took place. It was a time when relations between the community and the police were tense. "The times of the moment were that police officers were targets. If you were a white police officer in a black neighborhood, you could be singled out," said Gallagher. "This is one theory. Just the attitudes and the way things were at the time, and I believe that that had a lot to do with why this unfortunately happened."

Nick Cione, who was told the tragic news of his brother's killing, went on to become a Philadelphia police officer (as did two of his sons). He believes his brother's killer was alone and wanted on a warrant. So when Cione approached, he pulled a gun and shot the officer. Nick Cione also blames the weather, pointing out that it was a cold night, so few people were out. As Capt. Clark had said, "it's extremely hard to solve a case without solid witnesses."

To show their respect for the memory of Officer Cione, members of the community came together and raised money for a mural in a playground in Northeast Philadelphia. Hundreds of local kids have grown up playing in the park named in Officer Ciones' honor and have kept his story alive. Consequently, there is always hope that one day, someone will come forward with information to solve the case. As Capt. Clark proclaimed, "We will never give up." Officer Cione was survived by his brother and parents. Cione was engaged at the time of his death.

The playground and mural named in honor of Officer Cione.

SOURCES:

- http://www.odmp.org/officer/3070-police-officer-frederick-j-cione-jr
- http://guncrisis.org/2014/01/30/40000-reward-offered-in-case-of-philadelphia-police-officer-frederick-cione-killed-44-years-ago-today/
- http://philadelphia.cbslocal.com/2014/01/16/reward-in-cold-case-murder-of-philly-cop-increased-to-40000/
- https://www.findagrave.com/cgi-bin/fg.cgi?page=gr&GRid=36658146
- http://philadelphia.cbslocal.com/2017/02/03/frederick-cione-cold-case/
- Newspapers.com

CHAPTER 61

A Case for the President

THE OFFICER:

Patrolman Robert Rosenbloom
New Mexico State Police
End of Watch: Monday, November 8, 1971
Age: 28

The killing of a law enforcement officer usually does not involve the president of the United States, unless the alleged killers hijack an airliner and escape to Cuba—then it becomes an international issue. The 1970s were one of the most violent times in the history of policing. So many radical groups existed that it was difficult to separate them. On a Monday night, November 8, 1971, one of these radical groups would make headlines. Needlessly, it cost the life of a New Mexico State Police officer.

Patrolman Robert Rosenbloom was on Interstate 40 west of Albuquerque when he radioed in that he was stopping a car with California license plate 824 EDH. He asked the dispatcher for a check on the plate to see if it was stolen. When radio operator Ray Jaramillo radioed back to tell Rosenbloom that it was a "negative reading," Rosenbloom did not answer. Ten minutes went by until a passing motorist came on the police radio, "One of your policemen has been injured. Send an ambulance and some help."

Dennis Arnold from Greeley, Colorado, told police he had passed the patrol car, which was parked behind a green sedan, and he had seen what looked like "a body flying through the air." A short time later, the same green car sped past him at a high rate of speed. Arnold returned to the police car, where he found Rosenbloom's body.

The county coroner, Dr. James Franklin, said the officer bled to death after a main artery was struck by a bullet. The fatal bullet entered about two inches below the chin. The

The three suspects in the killing of Patrolman Robert Rosenbloom. Of the three, Charlie Hill is the only person still living and remains under the protection of the Cuban government after being granted political asylum.

wound indicated that a "high-energy weapon," was used.

Alerted to the shooting, Deputy Sheriff Chuck DuBois, from the Bernalillo County Sheriff's Department, saw a light-colored car speed past him. He activated his reds and went into pursuit at speeds topping 120 miles an hour. The deputy lost sight of the car at Coors Boulevard Southwest and Gun Club Road Southwest. At 6:30 a.m., the car, a 1972 Ford Galaxie, was found abandoned in a vacant lot near San Ygnacio Road Southwest and Tapia Boulevard Southwest. The car was full of evidence.

The suspects' vehicle was traced through a rental receipt to a person in San Francisco who said the car was stolen on Sunday. In the car, investigators found military rifles, dynamite, grenades, sleeping bags, food, a mess kit, canteens, backpacks, a first aid kit, a library of revolutionary publications and more than 300 rounds of ammunition. The literature included revolutionary writings of Mao Tse-tung, then-chairman of the Chinese Communist Party; Che Guevara, a deceased Latin American revolutionary; and the Republic of New Afrika, a recently formed cult of black militants who sought to break off several southern states into a separate nation for African Americans.

Through subsequent investigations, three suspects were identified, all belonging to the Republic of New Afrika separatist group. They were Michael Finney, Charlie Hill and Ralph Goodwin. Despite having all the evidence come together in the investigation, officials were unable to locate the three men who, unbeknownst to police, were hiding at a friend's house in Albuquerque.

With 250 law enforcement officers closing in on them, the trio carjacked a tow truck at gunpoint in the Southeast Heights of Albuquerque. They forced the driver, Vic Dugger, to take them to the tarmac of the Albuquerque International Airport. Early that morning of November 27, they hijacked Trans World Airlines Flight 106. The Boeing 727 flew to Tampa, where the passengers were allowed to deplane, and then the airliner flew to Cuba with the three men. The Cuban government under the rule of President Fidel Castro gave the suspected cop killers political asylum. Today, Hill is the last living member of the trio of murderers. Goodwin drowned in 1973, and Finney died of cancer in 2005.

When then-President Barack Obama ordered the restoration of full diplomatic relations with Cuba in conjunction with the opening of a U.S. embassy in Havana for the first time in over a half-century, officials in New Mexico saw an opportunity. The savvy governor of New Mexico, Susana Martinez, with the insight of a former district attorney, wrote to Secretary of State John Kerry and Attorney General Eric Holder, asking that the Obama administration push for Hill's return to stand trial for the murder of Officer Rosenbloom. "New Mexicans need your help to bring closure to the family of a New Mexico State Police officer gunned down by fugitives who have used Cuba as a sanctuary from justice for 43 years," Martinez wrote. "With your help, we may finally be able to bring a cop killer to justice." Lastly, the governor made it clear that "murder and federal hijacking charges against Hill are active, remain pending and will be pursued by both federal and state authorities."

Hill proved just what a hideous person he is in a 1999 interview with investigative reporter Larry Barker from Albuquerque's KRQE, who traveled to Cuba to interview Hill. Asked point-blank by Barker if he killed Rosenbloom, "He admitted killing Robert Rosenbloom. I asked him, 'Do you feel remorseful about it?' He said, 'No, he got what he deserved.' Chilling." In another interview in 2016, as quoted by Carlos Alvarez Rodriguez, when asked why Rosenbloom was murdered, Hill replied in short snippets: "It wasn't a decision. It was inevitable. We couldn't talk to him. He already had a gun in his hand. He wanted to make himself a hero like John Wayne. Another racist policeman. It wasn't murder."

In late 2016, the Black Lives Matter movement praised Cuba for harboring Charles Hill. As of this writing, Hill remains in Cuba, living life as a free man while the wife and two children of Officer Rosenbloom are reminded each day of his senseless death at the hands of a group of radicals.

Note: In 2017, President Donald Trump demanded that Cuba return fugitive New Jersey cop killer, Joanne Chesimard, along with 50 other U.S. fugitives (including Hill) taking refuge in Cuba. Also on the list is Cheri Dalton, who reportedly helped Chesimard break out of prison in 1979 and later drove the getaway car in the 1981 robbery of a Brinks truck in New York, in which two police officers and a Brinks guard were killed. Others include Victor Manuel Gerena, who is linked to the robbery of $7 million from an armored car in Connecticut. And the list goes on.

SOURCES:

- https://bluelivesmatter.blue/black-lives-matter-fidel-castro/
- https://www.abqjournal.com/516872/nm-state-police-officers-killer-is-still-in-cuba-2.html
- http://www.koat.com/article/lawyer-defends-man-suspected-of-killing-police-officer/5062576

- http://krqe.com/2014/12/18/gov-martinez-demands-cuban-fugitive-nmsp-murder-suspect/
- http://www.cnn.com/2015/04/09/americas/us-cuba-fugitive-charlie-hill/index.html
- http://www.huckmagazine.com/art-and-culture/long-read-story-charlie-hill-fbi-fugitive-havana/
- http://www.northjersey.com/story/news/columnists/mike-kelly/2017/06/17/ber-0617-kelly/404380001/
- http://www.nationalreview.com/corner/442711/peaceful-group-black-lives-matter-sure-does-love-cop-killers-and-murderous-dictators
- Newspapers.com

CHAPTER 62

Ambush

THE OFFICERS:

Policeman Leonard A. Christiansen
Riverside (California) Police Department
End of Watch: Friday, April 2, 1971
Age: 30

Policeman Paul Teel
Riverside (California) Police Department
End of Watch: Friday, April 2, 1971
Age: 30

A radio call of a burglary with no suspects in the area is a low-priority call. It comes down to meeting the victim, investigating and taking a report. As the officers approach the home, one takes along a notebook, not a shotgun. Riverside, California, Policeman Leonard Christiansen and his partner, Paul Teel, received just such a call on Friday, April 2, 1971. The call came out as a burglary investigation at 4792 Ottawa Ave.

As the two officers arrived at the address, they would have noted that it was so dark in the area that it was difficult to see anything. There were no streetlights and no moon to light their way. The officers might have observed the thick shrubbery around the house and driveway and that no one came out to meet them. Their suspicions were probably heightened as there were no lights on in the home, and it appeared to be vacant. Officer Teel, driving the marked police car, turned on the

The shot-up police car that Policeman Leonard Christiansen and Paul Teel were driving the night of their murders.

spotlight mounted on the front of the driver's door and shined it around the home, but he couldn't see any activity. Both officers took their time as they waited for the radio traffic to clear to report their arrival. Teel turned on the dome light, grabbed his clipboard and flashlight and started to get out of the car. Officer Christiansen followed suit and began to exit his side of the car.

Just as both officers got out, all hell broke loose. Up to three hidden suspects opened up with multiple shotgun blasts. The blinding muzzle flashes and the extreme concussion of three shotguns being fired simultaneously would have been deafening.

Officer Paul Teel was immediately struck with multiple pellets in the chest, one piercing his badge. He was blown backward, and the clipboard and flashlight went flying from his hands. Teel never had an opportunity to draw his sidearm and was dead by the time he hit the ground.

Christiansen was hit with a similar broadside as he stepped out of the car. He too was blown backward and was severely wounded. But Christiansen was resilient and refused to give up as his partner lay dead on the other side of the car. Christiansen grabbed for his gun and returned fire in the direction of the muzzle flashes. He then partially fell or stumbled back into the police car and screamed into the mic: "I need help!" The suspects were relentless in their attack. Several more rounds hit Christiansen, knocking him to the pavement next to the police car.

Responding units flooded the area from all parts of the city and surrounding area. They found Teel dead, lying on his stomach with his head facing the street. Christiansen was on the ground, unconscious, with his shooting arm outstretched, still gripping his gun. He was immediately transported but died before arriving at the hospital. The suspects had disappeared into the night.

Not long after the shootings, detectives filed charges against three men, accusing two of them in the slayings of the officers and one for making a false burglary report. Over a four-year period, prosecutors spent over $1 million on three jury trials. In the end, all three trials ended without convictions, the first two having ended with hung juries. One of those accused was Gary W. Lawton. He was thought to be the mastermind behind the killings, but he was acquitted in his last trial in 1975. He left Riverside for the Bay Area, along with his wife and two children. He died of natural causes in 2002.

It was apparent to most observers that the publicity around the trials seemed to shift focus from the black suspects' guilt or innocence to a trial of black versus white. There were demonstrations in support of the defendants, with some protesters arrested. Fights erupted around the courthouse. Black Panther Party chairman Bobby Seale traveled to Riverside in support of Lawton, whom he referred to as a "political prisoner." Other radicals joined him. Anthony Russo from the Pentagon Papers fiasco and Angela Davis, leader of the Communist Party USA, both vocally supported the defendant.

Police have always believed they had the right man, said Jim Tennell, who arrested Lawton about two months after the murders. "A lot of people know what happened," Tennell said of the double homicide. "People didn't talk out of fright, or didn't care or were happy that some white cops got killed. A lot of people didn't open their mouths."

After the ambush, Riverside police reexamined their training and tactics and made changes. No longer would officers park a patrol car in a driveway of a radio call. Dispatchers were instructed to call back homes from which crimes were reported to make sure someone inside the house had made the call.

The son of Officer Christiansen, Steve, joined the Riverside police force and later became a detective. "I would want him to be proud of me as a man," he said. "And what better way to make him proud than to be a police officer." There have been no further arrests in the case, and it remains unsolved.

SOURCES:

- http://www.pe.com/2011/04/02/40-years-on-police-pay-homage/
- https://www.newspapers.com/image/119817799/
- http://www.nytimes.com/1971/04/04/archives/2-policemen-slain-in-coast-ambush-after-false-alarm.html
- https://www.riversideca.gov/rpd/Memorial/Chrstn_Teel.htm

CHAPTER 63

Tragedy Inspires Success for Daughter

THE OFFICER:

Officer Ulysses Brown
Detroit (Michigan) Police Department
End of Watch: Friday, August 20, 1971
Age: 27

There are times when the tragedy of a law enforcement officer's death in the line of duty drives a child of the officer to change his or her life goals. The unsolved murder of Officer Ulysses Brown would inspire his daughter to become a police officer and rise through the ranks to become a chief of police in a major U.S. city. It's a bright spot in the tragedy of the shooting death of Officer Brown.

Working undercover, whether it's in narcotics, stakeouts, vice or scores of other similar assignments, is inherently

Contemporary photo of 10800 E. Jefferson St., where Officer Ulysses Brown was found shot to death. Google maps.

dangerous. Without the visibility and protection of a uniform, and many times without a weapon, the plainclothes officer can easily become a victim of violent crime. On too many occasions, these undercover officers are robbed, beaten and shot while attempting to bring a criminal to justice. It's a thankless job, with long hours, and much less time spent with the family. For the 27-year-old Brown, working a vice assignment on the night of August 20, 1971, brought all these issues home.

Brown was investigating prostitution complaints near East Jefferson Street and Lemay Street. Brown had specific information that a prostitute was setting up her customers to be robbed. There was even a report that there might have been a murder associated with the streetwalker. Other than this limited information, nothing is known about the circumstances of Brown's death.

After Brown had failed to call in for 12 hours, officers from the Detroit Police Department were alerted and began a search. Simultaneously, a call was received of a man shot in the parking lot of 10800 E. Jefferson. When officers arrived, they found Brown shot once in the chest. The pockets of his trousers were inside out and had been emptied. Police found his weapon inside his car, which was parked nearby. He was dead.

The daughter of Officer Ulysses Brown, Renee Hall, became the chief of the Dallas Police Department in 2016.

A young female prostitute was arrested for his murder, and police were looking for two male accomplices. There is little information as to the disposition of the case, but no convictions have been made, and it remains unsolved.

Officer Brown was survived by his wife and two daughters. Renee was six months old at the time of her father's death. She recalls how her mother instilled in the children the value of an education. Renee took her mother's advice and earned a master's degree. From the beginning, she thought she would become a lawyer. But it was a mentor in graduate school who encouraged Hall to become a police officer.

Twenty years later, she was a deputy chief on the same department that her father had served. In September of 2016, she became the first female chief in Dallas Police Department history. "I believe I'm finishing what my dad started," she said.

SOURCES:

- http://dfw.cbslocal.com/2017/07/19/new-dpd-deputy-chief-driven-by-personal-tragedy-to-fight-crime/
- https://www.odmp.org/officer/2370-police-officer-ulysses-brown
- Newspapers.com

CHAPTER 64

Ambushed at Home

THE OFFICER:

Trooper William Harrell Barrett
Kentucky State Police
End of Watch: Sunday, December 19, 1971
Age: 35

In researching *Unsolved*, I noted how several law enforcement officers were ambushed as they returned home after working a shift, in uniform and driving a marked police vehicle. The suspects usually are hidden near the garage or have concealment close to where the officer parks. With no witnesses, no video, many suspects get away and are never apprehended. The case of Trooper William Barrett is just such an incident.

It was just after midnight on December 19, 1971, when Trooper Barrett returned home after working the 4 p.m. to midnight shift. He was in uniform and driving a marked police car. As he always did, he backed his vehicle into his allotted parking space at the Morehead Trailer Park, off Russellville Road in Rockfield, Kentucky. He got out of the car and locked it. As he took the first few steps toward his home, a suspect emerged from around a structure next to Barrett's home and shot the trooper twice with a shotgun: once in the upper chest and once in the abdomen. Although mortally wounded, Barrett returned fire, hitting the building where the suspect had been waiting. Trooper Barrett died in his driveway.

Several individuals were investigated in the early stages, but the leads dried up quickly, and no arrests were made. "There was no one specific person that stuck out at the time that was after him," said Tim Adams, the Kentucky State Police detective who was still investigating the case in 2010. It was clear that this was not a random act of violence, but the act of a person who was intent on killing Barrett. Investigators went so far as to examine a year's worth of gun sales in the county to try to identify the murder weapon.

Shotgun wadding recovered at the crime scene and Barrett's uniform are some of the pieces of physical evidence on file. As time went on, most of Barrett's relatives moved away, and two members of the original homicide team died in the line of duty. The mobile home where Barrett lived is also gone, leaving very little for the new generation of investigators to work with. "It takes quite a bit more effort just to locate people and develop new people to interview," Detective Adams said. "A lot of times, though, you'll learn a little bit from somebody who might be able to tell you about someone else to talk to, if nothing else than just for background information."

Adams kept looking at different theories about Barrett's murder, allowing him to focus on details regarding the shooting that might need more scrutiny. In 2010, Adams said his department still was getting calls about the case. This "trickle" of information is what keeps the case moving forward, even after so many years. Detective Adams even hesitated to refer to the case as "cold," as he was working it very hard. "The ambush murder of Trooper Barrett is a high priority for the department, and no one has given up," he said. Trooper Barrett was married with two sons who loved baseball. Their father was their coach. The case remains unsolved.

SOURCES:

- http://www.bgdailynews.com/news/nearly-years-later-ksp-still-hunts-for-trooper-s-killer/article_e9215668-8050-534e-bd88-2af63363ab5c.html
- http://www.kentuckystatepolice.org/cold_case/post3coldcase_william_barrett.html
- Newspapers.com

CHAPTER 65

"Fred"

THE OFFICER:

Policeman Fred H. Early
Los Angeles Police Department
Date of Innocent: Saturday, September 9, 1972
End of Watch: Friday, March 23, 1973

This one is personal. As a young rookie police officer, I worked West Los Angeles (WLA) division of the LAPD, on the same watch as Fred Early. Although we never worked together, we were on a lot of the same calls. I had heard of his reputation as a solid cop who had been in several "good" shootings in the south end of the city where several suspects were killed. Perhaps that is why he was transferred to one of the less active areas, WLA, which borders Beverly Hills.

I learned much from Early, just watching how he handled "hot" calls with the utmost professionalism, but primarily observing his officer survival skills. You knew if Early was on your call, you never had to look over your back—he had your "6." His nickname was "Crazy Fred," and he lived up to that moniker. I recall one night after work, Early dangerously climbed a six-story tower next to the station and waved to us disbelievers down below—that was Early. After his death, many of us began calling each other "Fred" as a gesture of what he meant to us. I even named my dog after him. So how could an officer who survived so much be taken down by some burglary suspects while off duty? That is the story.

On Saturday, September 9, 1972, at 4:30 in the morning, Policeman Fred Early of the Los Angeles Police Department was on his way home after spending time with some friends. He was off duty, driving his personal vehicle near the northwest corner of National and Sawtelle boulevards, just off the 405 Freeway. Always attuned to his surroundings, no matter whether he was at work, Early observed a possible burglary suspect acting suspiciously near the closed Thrifty Drug Store.

Stopping his vehicle, he watched the suspect for several minutes. Believing this was indeed a burglary going down, he circled and parked his car at a service station at the southwest corner of the intersection to better keep the man under surveillance.

In an era with no cell phones, Early left his vehicle and went to a pay phone to request assistance. As he was talking to the operator, the suspect spooked and ran. At 4:30 in morning, the city is just beginning to stir, and there would have been very few cars moving. It appears the suspect realized this and, seeing Early's car stop, started running southbound across National. Early dropped the phone receiver in midsentence and pursued the fleeing suspect. He chased him west to an extremely dark parking lot at the rear of 11316 National Blvd. As he reached the parking lot, he was attacked from behind by one or more additional suspects and was shot twice through the left leg. The assailants beat Early, kicking him in the head and body until he lost consciousness. Leaving him for dead, the suspects escaped.

When he came to, he fired his revolver into a block wall to summon help. For the next several months, Early was in and out of the hospital for treatment of his numerous wounds. He suffered from blackouts and severe headaches. While undergoing treatment at UCLA Medical Center, he sustained irreversible brain damage and never recovered. He died from his injuries six months after the shooting. He was just 31.

Just after his murder, then-Governor Ronald Reagan took the unprecedented step of offering $10,000 in state money to find the killers who had shot and beaten Early. Twenty-five years later, in 1998, city officials met to say they would offer additional rewards. The Police Protective League, which had offered $10,000 in 1973, once again offered that money. The Los Angeles City Council offered an additional $25,000 for information leading to the arrest of the suspects. It was a positive move to crack the case, but no suspects have been arrested, and the case remains unsolved.

During his short life, Early often talked about his love for his four girls. At the time of his death, the kids were between the ages of 5 and 12. A quarter of a century after his murder, the four attended a ceremony to honor their father with LAPD's highest measure of bravery, the police Medal of Valor. A tearful Michelle Bonnee, Early's youngest daughter, said at a news conference "I have the burden of looking into my own 5-year-old daughter's eyes and trying to answer the questions she has of her grandfather—a man I remember well but barely knew and whom she will never know."

"We have nothing to lose is the way we feel about it," Hollie Ashworth, one of Early's daughters, said of the new round of rewards. "Not that [an arrest] would ever make up for my father. But there would be justice in finding the person who did this and some closure for the family. That's the hardest part, knowing there is somebody out there that got away with this at the expense of four little girls."

LAPD detective Roseanne Parino (now retired) summed up why the hunt must continue for the perpetrators of Early's murder and all the suspects out there who have gotten away with the murder of a police officer. "People become more mature, have more of a sense of mortality. I think just the time and distance from the act may bring people out who at the time were reticent, for whatever reasons, to speak." To give peace to Early and all the other victims of the 708 unsolved police murders, we can only hope and pray this happens often.

SOURCES:

- http://articles.latimes.com/1998/mar/24/local/me-32234
- https://www.odmp.org/officer/reflections/4441-policeman-fred-h-early
- http://assets.lapdonline.org/assets/pdf/Early.pdf
- http://www.lapdonline.org/officers_killed_in_the_line_of_duty/comm_bio_view/57561

CHAPTER 66

The Black Liberation Army

THE OFFICERS:

Police Officer Rocco W. Laurie
New York Police Department
End of Watch: January 27, 1972
Age: 23

Police Officer Gregory P. Foster
New York Police Department
End of Watch: January 27, 1972
Age: 22

The Black Liberation Army (BLA) came to prominence just as the Black Panther Party was in decline. The BLA was an underground black nationalist militant organization that operated against the United States, especially in larger cities. The Black Panthers members who had avoided lengthy jail sentences or death formed the foundation of the BLA. Their sworn mission was to take up arms against law enforcement—to kill cops. The BLA carried out numerous bombings, murders and robberies. The Justice Department attributed more than 70 violent incidents between 1970 and 1976 to the BLA. Members were responsible for at least 13 murders of police officers, including Officers Rocco Laurie and Gregory Foster.

In May 1971, the BLA made its violent presence known when members gunned down two NYPD officers. Following those assassinations, they struck police in San Francisco and Atlanta. But of all their cowardly attacks, the one against Officers Foster and Laurie shocked the nation and struck at the heart of every NYPD officer.

On that freezing night of January 27, 1972, the two young patrolmen were walking their beat in East Village. The area was notorious for violent crime and drug use. Greg Foster was 22 and an African American. Rocco Laurie was one year older and white. These two men were more than just partners—they were best friends, having fought in the jungles of Vietnam as Marines. They had received special permission to work together.

At 10:30 p.m., Officers Laurie and Foster were walking south on Avenue B when they noticed a car parked in front of a fire hydrant. They asked the store owner if he knew who owned the car. No, came the reply. Back on the street, the patrolmen went north, where three black men were walking toward them, going south. As the five came together, the three men calmly parted to allow the officers to walk between them.

As soon as the three passed, they spun around and opened fire on the unsuspecting officers. One suspect used a .38 automatic while the other two used 9-millimeter automatics. The gunfire was intense. Just a few feet away from the officers, the three assassins couldn't miss. They fired their weapons at the backs of the officers. Foster went down quickly after being struck with six rounds. Laurie was struck in the arms and legs with five bullets, but the sixth hit his neck. Grabbing for his wound, Laurie staggered forward, dropped to his knees and slowly fell over on his side. As blood flowed everywhere, the three killers strolled up and fired two rounds directly into Foster's eyes. They fired two more bullets into Laurie's groin.

After ripping the officers guns from their holsters, two of the suspects ran to a waiting Chrysler, while the third was so busy doing a victory dance and firing his gun over the fallen officers that he missed his ride. He ran down the street to get away.

Fellow officers were quick to arrive. What they saw would haunt them for the rest of their lives. Foster's head had been blown apart, and Laurie had literally been shot to pieces. Foster was dead at the scene, and Laurie died soon after at the hospital. Detectives were quick to identify this double homicide as a straight-out assassination not unlike the shooting eight months earlier of two NYPD officers that was attributed to the BLA. It took only a short time to attribute these killings to the radical group as the fingerprints recovered from the Chrysler were linked to Ronald Carter, Twymon Meyers, both devoted members of the BLA's Cleveland cell, and a third unidentified individual. The Black Librarian Army confirmed that finding a few days later when police received a scribbled note. In it, the BLA said it was against "salt-and-pepper" interracial teams of police officers.

Not long after the murders of Laurie and Foster, Ronald Carter, one of the probable gunman in that shooting, was killed in a wild shootout with members of the Metropolitan Police of St. Louis. Henry Brown, who was traveling with Carter, was arrested and later charged with the murders of Laurie and Foster. Officers had discovered the gun stolen from Officer Laurie in the vehicle the suspects were driving. After an eight-week trial in Manhattan, Brown was acquitted.

Twymon Meyers, the second suspect in the killings of the two officers, was later killed by NYPD detectives on a Bronx sidewalk in yet another gun battle. That left one suspect outstanding. In 2016, Robert Vickers, a probable gunman in the Laurie and Foster murders,

Robert Vickers, who police were convinced was one of three gunmen who killed Officers Rocco Laurie and Gregory Foster. The photograph is from 2016, when he was convicted for dealing heroin.

was sentenced to 21 years in prison. His conviction was not for the murders of Laurie and Foster, but for dealing heroin. Although NYPD detectives had worked Vickers hard in the decades following the murders, in an effort to get him to confess, it never happened.

The one surviving widow, Adelaide Laurie, was ecstatic. "Great! Oh my God, that's good news. This is not the crime we were looking for, but he'll be off the street, and he'll not be able to hurt anybody anymore."

The judge made it clear that although Vickers had never been charged in the Foster and Laurie murders, those assassinations permeated the heroin trial. At one point, taped evidence revealed Vickers talking with a confidential informant describing specific information about the corner where the officers were killed. Prosecutor Jasper Mills told the judge that Vickers expressed "a willingness to kill someone for financial gain. He says it's easy to kill someone. The hard part is getting away with it."

As none of the suspects ever stood trial for the murders, the case remains open. But for many, there is some semblance of peace, as two of the three primary suspects in the murders died in shootouts with the police, and the last one is in prison.

Twenty-three-year old Rocco Laurie, a native Staten Islander, was a champion shot-putter in high school before enlisting in the Marines, where he saw combat during the Vietnam War. Just back from the war, Laurie joined NYPD on July 1, 1970.

Twenty-two-year-old Queens native Gregory Foster was also a veteran of the Vietnam War where he served as a machine gunner. He was awarded the Silver Star for risking his life to save his fellow Marines while pinned down by enemy fire.

Over 10,000 people turned out for the funerals which were held within a few hours of each other. In 1975, their story was told in a TV movie, "Foster and Laurie." Two schools were later named after the officers.

SOURCES:

- http://www.odmp.org/officer/5032-police-officer-gregory-p-foster
- http://www.odmp.org/officer/7946-police-officer-rocco-w-laurie
- http://www.silive.com/news/2014/12/widow_of_slain_nypd_officer_ro.html
- http://www.politico.com/magazine/story/2015/04/the-untold-story-behind-new-yorks-most-brutal-cop-killing-117207?o=3
- http://www.nydailynews.com/new-york/nypd-embarrassment-44-years-no-arrests-article-1.2507296
- http://evhp.blogspot.com/2012/01/40-years-later-remembering-rocco-laurie.html
- https://www.quora.com/Are-there-any-unsolved-murders-of-NYPD-officers
- http://nypost.com/2016/01/07/final-suspect-in-infamous-cop-killing-heads-to-jail-for-dealing-heroin/

CHAPTER 67

Kidnapped

THE OFFICER:

Patrolman Thomas Ray Carpenter
Colorado State Patrol
End of Watch: Thursday, December 27, 1973
Age: 31

A law enforcement officer being abducted is rare. However, one does not have to look further than the well-publicized 1963 kidnapping of LAPD officer Ian Campbell and his partner, Karl Hettinger. Their kidnapping and the shooting death of Campbell was the subject of a popular movie, "The Onion Field." Through the film, a national audience saw the first accurate portrayal of the dangers of police traffic stops. Patrolman Thomas Carpenter of the Colorado State Patrol found himself facing a similar situation on Thursday, December 27, 1973. Carpenter was assigned to the Broomfield district, patrolling along the Interstate 25 corridor in Denver, Colorado.

To this day it is not clear why, but sometime before 10 a.m., Carpenter pulled his patrol car to the shoulder of U.S. 36 near Broadway. There was a car stopped, and Carpenter was going to give aid, or possibly he spotted something that was suspicious. Either way, he did not call it in. Moments later, witnesses saw the patrolman pull away with two men in the back seat. At 9:58, he received a call from dispatch directing him to an accident at East 58th Avenue and I-25. He radioed back and said he was at Interstate 70 and Havana. This was unusual, as it was eight miles from his assigned area.

At 10:04, a dispatcher again radioed Carpenter to clarify that he was en route to the accident. "10-4, I'm on my way," he said in a tense voice. Minutes later, a Denver police officer noticed the patrol car parked behind the Lakes apartment complex at 13870 Albrook Drive, in northeast Denver. The passing officer thought the patrolman was writing a ticket, as there were two youths in the back seat. The Denver officer continued on.

At 10:20, just a few minutes later, the same Denver officer drove past the parked CSP car. This time there was no one in the back seat, and the trooper's head was slumped over the steering wheel. The officer stopped and found Carpenter shot in the back of the head. He was dead. His .357 Magnum was missing. Witnesses said they saw two young men running from the snow-covered parking lot.

Detectives found what they believed to be a .308-caliber shell casing on the floor of the car. They took fingerprints from the spent round. Carpenter had been shot four times in the back of the head from the rear seat of the police car. It appeared he was still driving, as the car was in drive and had rolled 20 yards until stopping against a snowbank. The kidnapping and murder of Trooper Carpenter sparked one of the largest manhunts in Colorado history. Included in the dragnet were scores of off-duty officers who volunteered to assist in the search for the killers.

Police determined that the two young men kidnapped Carpenter at gunpoint after he made contact with them. The suspects most likely ordered Carpenter to drive to an area they were familiar with—the Lakes apartments, located next to a shopping center. Police put together a description of the suspects. One was described as a white male between the ages of 16 and 20 with shoulder-length blond hair and a short coat. The second suspect was a black male, 16 to 20, who was about 5-foot-10. He had a short haircut and was wearing a dark sheepskin coat. Two men matching their description were observed at the mall. Searching the area around U.S. 36 near Broadway, police found a stolen car with its engine still running. The car was stolen from West 14th Avenue and

Mariposa Street in Denver. Several arrests were made, but none of the arrestees were booked for the murder of Patrolman Carpenter.

Three years went by with no arrest. Then in January of 1977, an off-duty Denver police officer, James T. Myers, was patrolling the parking lot of the St. James Catholic Church, 1250 Newport Street, where he was employed to provide security for the churches' bingo games. He noticed a man who appeared to be getting ready to burglarize or steal a car. As Myers approached the man, he took off running. Myers went into foot pursuit and caught the suspect at 6801 E. Colfax Ave. As he attempted to handcuff the man, the suspect began to fight violently. During the altercation, Myers' gun went off. The bullet struck the suspect in the back, and he died from the injury. Police later found a .32-caliber handgun in the same parking lot and deducted that the suspect had thrown it as he was being chased.

Detectives determined that the man was Herbert Dixon, 23, who had been identified as a suspect in the killing of Carpenter. He had a rap sheet for major felonies and had served time for robbery and assault in 1974. Although several internet sites mention a second suspect in the murder of Carpenter being killed by police, I couldn't find any documentation to confirm this. To date, the case remains unsolved. State Trooper Carpenter was survived by his wife, daughter, and two sons. Carpenter had been with the Colorado State Patrol for five years.

SOURCES:

- http://blogs.denverpost.com/coldcases/2014/11/01/denver-state-trooper-gunned/9499/
- http://blogs.denverpost.com/coldcases/tag/thomas-ray-carpenter/
- http://www.odmp.org/officer/2820-patrolman-thomas-ray-carpenter
- http://www.dreamindemon.com/community/threads/trooper-thomas-carpenter-31-kidnapped-shot-in-the-head-dec-27-1973.73790/
- Newspapers.com

CHAPTER 68

"Who executed Mike?"

THE OFFICER:

Policeman Michael Lee Edwards
Los Angeles Police Department
End of Watch: Saturday, May 11, 1974
Age: 26

Tobie Edwards, an innocent 6-year-old, was playing in her grandma's backyard after her father, Michael Edwards, dropped her off one Friday. It would be the last day they were ever together. On the next day, her play was interrupted by two uniformed Los Angeles Police officers who were dressed just like her daddy. As she later learned from her grandparents, the news was devastating. Tobie's father, Officer Edwards, had been found shot to death, execution style. There were no suspects in custody, and 42 years later, there still aren't. The motives and theories for the murder of Edwards are as plentiful as evidence markers at a crime scene.

The 26-year-old officer was last seen alive on May 10, 1974, enjoying some buddy time with other cops at the LAPD Police Academy bar in Elysian Park. It was Friday night, and Edwards was celebrating his final stint on the anti-gang unit, CRASH, and looking forward to his upcoming vacation to Hawaii.

At 10:30 p.m., Edwards said goodbye to his friends, telling them he had a date in Long Beach. The guard at the entrance to the Police Academy substantiated the time as he watched Edwards' gold Ford Pinto drive past the guard shack. From there, he drove to 77th Street Station, where he was assigned. Afterwards he was observed at a nearby hospital. After leaving the hospital, Edwards was never seen alive again. From here, the mystery begins. It is a whodunit in epic proportions and

has haunted detectives, friends and loved ones for over four decades.

Through the years, scores of detectives have worked the Edwards case. Many are deceased, most are retired. Today, one active detective, Daryn DuPree, of Robbery/Homicide Division, has the cold case file on Edwards and says he is actively investigating it. His examination of the case adds to the generations of LAPD's elite detectives who have preceded him. Here is what is known.

A little more than a month after Officer Michael Edwards' murder, LAPD detectives issued this police bulletin seeking the public's help in locating the people responsible for his death. They are still looking four decades later.

In some way, after leaving the hospital, Edwards was forced or was transported to an abandoned, burned-out apartment building at 122 W. 89th Street, in South-Central Los Angeles. It was here that he was shot six times, execution-style, with a 9-millimeter handgun, which for identification purposes has six lands and grooves with a right-hand twist. His underwear (some have stated it was not his) was pulled over his face, and he was handcuffed. His car, his personal .38- caliber Smith & Wesson Airweight revolver, and some money were missing.

Fifteen hours after his body was discovered, police located his Pinto about 10 miles from the murder scene at 1034 W. 186th Street in Los Angeles. The location was near the old Ascot Raceway, a frequent drop spot for stolen vehicles. Divorce papers from his wife were on the passenger seat. The keys were in the ignition. A handkerchief was found in the car, but no suspect prints were uncovered. No one has come forward who witnessed the actual shooting.

In 1981, Edwards' revolver was found, and detectives were hoping this would provide the one clue to blow the case wide open. In Las Vegas, the police department had been broadcasting PSAs to encourage citizens to turn in their firearms. A woman and her friend surrendered a revolver that turned out to be the gun that Edwards was carrying on the night of his murder. LAPD was promptly notified. After an in-depth interview, the two were cleared of any wrongdoing. "We tried just about everything we could do at that time," said Tom McGuine, one of the original detectives on the case. "We had the people power, we had the time, we had everything going for us. But sometimes you get to a point where you just don't get the answer."

The 1970s were turbulent times in the nation. Not since the 1920s have so many officers been killed. Radical groups such as the SLA (Symbionese Liberation Army) committed bank robberies, murders, planted bombs under LAPD cars and kidnapped newspaper heiress Patricia Hearst. Just days after Edwards' body was discovered, six SLA members died in a firefight with the LAPD SWAT team. Some thought there might be a connection between the execution killing of Edwards and the SLA. Investigators tested the weapons used by the SLA but could not connect them to the Edwards murder. The SLA was subsequently ruled out.

In 1999, detectives from LAPD and Los Angeles County Sheriff's Department established a team to reexamine unsolved slayings of LAPD officers and sheriff's deputies. Included on the LAPD team were detectives Dennis Kilcoyne, Rosemary Sanchez and Paul Coulter. After solving a sheriff's cold case homicide, they turned their attention to the Edwards case. As a starting point, detectives reexamined prior evidence and what the prior detectives had done. They looked over possible suspects and witness statements. They established a $15,000 reward and even went so far as to send out press releases while posting billboards that read, "Who Executed Mike?"

The joint detective task force sent out letters to officers, both retired and active, who might somehow reveal evidence they missed the first time. They had the FBI retest fingerprints, with no luck. They revisited the crime scene and interviewed friends and family members. Although they received numerous calls and clues, nothing substantial was added to the case files. The cold case remained just that. It was at this point that detectives began to focus on Edwards as a man, rather than as a police officer. "It's usually not the Sunday night mystery," Kilcoyne said. "It's usually something blatant right in front of you. You just overlook it."

It was just a few days after the murder that investigators learned that Edwards may have been involved with an African American woman who worked near 77th Street station. In an interview with the *Los Angeles Times* in 2002, Detective Kilcoyne pointed out that former detectives on the case believed Edwards would have not dated a black woman. "That's hard to swallow now, but in 1974, the mind-set of society was totally different." At that time, detectives thought that tip might be the key to solving the case. As it turned out, it was another dead end.

Another individual who thought the murder of Edwards was personal and not related to his position as an LAPD officer is his daughter, Tobie Edwards—the little girl who was playing in the backyard so many years ago. Over the ensuing 40-plus years, Tobie has worked tirelessly in her personal attempt to find the killer of her dad. Much of the following information comes from an interview conducted by this author in December 2016.

She believes to the core of her being that it was a "love triangle" that got her father murdered. Mike Edwards was then separated from her mother, Penny Sue, and was dating a woman from Long Beach who wishes to remain anonymous out of fear for her life. This woman had previously dated another LAPD cop by the name of Bill Pearson before she started dating Edwards. It was this woman that Edwards was on his way to visit the night he was killed.

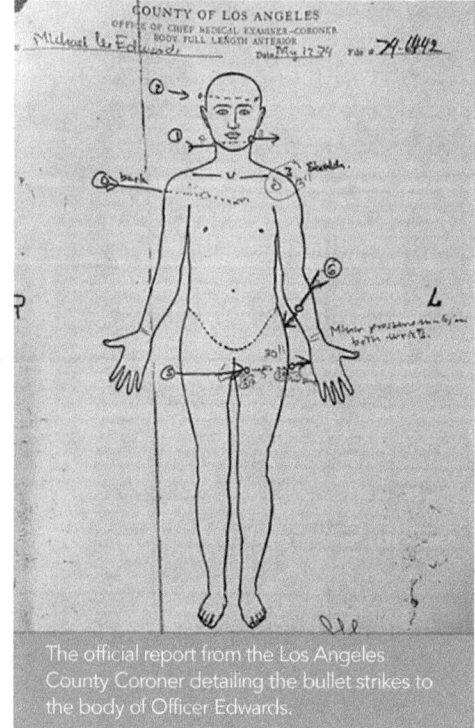

The official report from the Los Angeles County Coroner detailing the bullet strikes to the body of Officer Edwards.

The other slant to the triangle was Pearson, a disgraced cop who had been fired by the LAPD one year earlier, in 1973. Those who knew him saw his collapse exactly one year after the death of Edwards when Pearson was arrested for felony vehicular manslaughter. He was found guilty of DUI and speeding and causing an accident that killed a 16-month-old boy and seriously injured the parents. He was sentenced to one year in jail.

LAPD detectives questioned Pearson at length over "the possible love triangle." He told investigators he had been "experiencing blackout spells" on the night of the murder and "could not state whether or not he had been involved," blaming it on his memory lapses. Police conducted lengthy interviews with those associated with him but were never able to account for his whereabouts around the time of the murder.

During the subsequent years, officials have repeatedly interviewed Pearson about the Edwards murder but have not gotten anywhere. "Honestly, right now we're still at ground zero on this case," said the current detective on the case, Daryn DuPree. Regarding Pearson, "What he remembers I'm not going to say," commented DuPree, but he made it clear that officials are still looking at him as a suspect in the murder of Officer Edwards.

Tobie Edwards just wants peace and closure, not unlike what her mother and grandparents wished for—all who have since passed and never gotten an answer. "I have heard that Pearson is very sick, and when he dies, then what?" She went on, "My only wish is to know why and who killed my father." You are not alone, Tobie; you have a family of LAPD officers who want to know the same thing. No brother left behind.

SOURCES:

- http://abc7.com/news/search-for-lapd-officer-mike-edwards-killer-continues-40-years-later/690099/
- http://articles.latimes.com/2002/may/11/local/me-edwards11
- https://www.reddit.com/r/UnresolvedMysteries/comments/296rxl/michael_lee_edwards_fallen_lapd_officer/
- Interview with Tobie Edwards, December, 2016
- Interview with LAPD Detective Daryn DuPree in November, 2016

CHAPTER 69

An Off-Duty Barbecue Turns Tragic

THE OFFICER:

Patrolman William Thomas Cribb
Charleston County (South Carolina) Police Department
End of Watch: Friday, November 15, 1974
Age: 29

It was supposed to be a fun evening. Off-duty Patrolman William "Bill" Cribb, his pregnant wife and three-year-old daughter were entertaining his best friend and police partner, Grover Thompkins at their home in James Island, South Carolina, that Friday night, November 15, 1974. When the time came to light the barbecue, Cribb noticed they were out of charcoal. No problem. The two friends drove off to the nearby Sam's Red & White Grocery store. Cribb, a three- year veteran of the Charleston County Police Department, carried his weapon while off-duty, but on this day, Thompkins did not.

Inside the store, the two off-duty officers gathered up the charcoal and headed to the front of the store. As they passed a small office, they happened to see a man with a gun aimed at the manager, who it appeared was being forced to open the store's safe. Cribb immediately pulled out his weapon and approached the suspect from behind. He ordered the suspect not to move. As he got closer to the gunman, a second suspect snuck up from behind and shot Cribb in the neck. Blood splattered everywhere as Cribb went down to his knees—but he was still in the fight. Hearing the gunshot, a third suspect who had been acting as the lookout came running into the store and shot Cribb in the chest. The officer went down. The suspects quickly gathered up the money, which was now soaked in Cribb's blood, and ran out the front door. As they did so, Thompkins picked up Cribb's gun and fired at the fleeing suspects, missing them. Cribb died a short time later at the hospital.

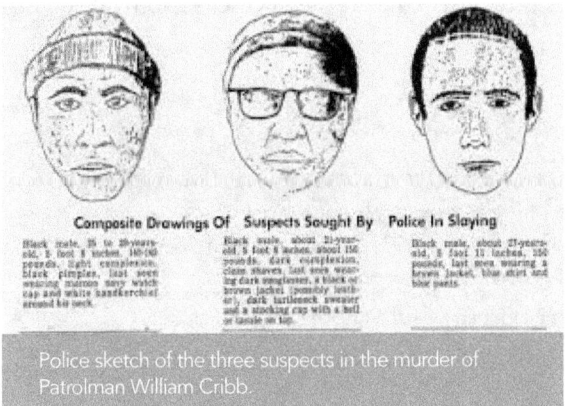

Police sketch of the three suspects in the murder of Patrolman William Cribb.

After an extensive search for the suspects, and despite the release of composite sketches of the three men, no arrest was made. One line of thought was that perhaps the three men might have been part of a gang from New York and were just passing through. That would help explain why no one recognized the men from the sketches or had any idea who the three assailants were.

In 2010, 36 years after Cribb's murder, a new generation of detectives dived into the depths of the cold file, encouraged by a private detective, Howie Comen. The

PI had personal knowledge of the case and wanted to help Charleston detectives solve it. When news got out, one 86-year-old woman could not have been happier—Mrs. Winifred Cribb, the mother of the slain officer. The night of her son's death was still burning in her soul—36 years later. "I will never forget that night. It was the most awful night of my life when that child got killed. I'll always remember him."

The job to tell her son's three-year-old daughter fell to Mrs. Cribb. "She was standing right there on those steps and cried for Bill." Shaking as she recalled the day, the grandmother went on, "Oh, that broke my heart because I knew he was gone." The elderly Cribb died shortly after the interview, having never gotten closure to her son's murder.

Private investigator Comen hoped that somehow the clergy might help solve the case. "Thirty-six years these people have had this on their conscience, that they shot this man and killed him," said Comen. "If a minister started praying about it and offered salvation, the person might jump at it and might go ahead and confess." To date, the prayers have gone unanswered, as there has been no arrest and the case remains unsolved.

SOURCES:

(Note: All three sources give varying accounts of the robbery and murder. I have used all three to write this story.)
- http://www.wistv.com/story/12408543/police-pi-reopen-36-year-old-cold-case-of-murdered-cop?clienttype=printable
- https://scfop3.org/remembering-william-cribb/
- http://www.odmp.org/officer/3621-patrolman-william-thomas-cribb
- Ancestry.com

CHAPTER 70

Three Paths to the Killing of a Police Officer

THE OFFICER:

Police Officer Franke Neal Lewis
Long Beach (California) Police Department
End of Watch: Saturday, December 13, 1975
Age: 28

Three distinct paths led to the murder of a police officer. One an officer, one a schoolteacher and the last a killer. Fate would bring these three individuals to a bloody encounter on a Saturday night, December 13, 1975. When it was over, two paths were left exposed, while the third, that of the suspect, disappeared into history. Over the next 43 years, two generations of detectives would come and go, all attempting to pull a suspect from his path of deception.

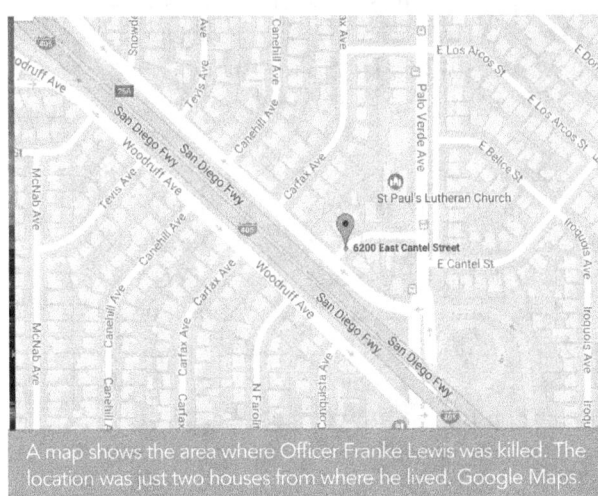

A map shows the area where Officer Franke Lewis was killed. The location was just two houses from where he lived. Google Maps.

The route of Denis Gitschier was innocent enough. He had been to a late-night party and while driving to his home in Torrance, became drowsy and thought it best to pull off the freeway and get some sleep in his car. Gitschier

PUBLIC INFORMATION BULLETIN
LONG BEACH POLICE DEPARTMENT
400 W. BROADWAY, LONG BEACH, CA 90802
(562) 570-7260

Robert G. Luna
Chief of Police

2015 - 004   DATE: November 2015

L.B.P.D. NEEDS YOUR HELP WITH MURDER INVESTIGATION

$50,000 REWARD OFFERED

Long Beach Police Officer Franke Lewis Murdered in 1975

The Long Beach Police Homicide Detail is asking for your help with the murder investigation of a Long Beach police officer nearly 40 years ago. Anyone who may have lived in the area and saw anything out the ordinary, or knows anyone who may have been involved, is urged to call L.B.P.D.

Officer Lewis

In the early hours of December 13, 1975, Officer Franke Neal Lewis was returning home after his patrol shift when he saw suspicious activity and tried to stop a violent crime in progress in the 6200 block of Cantel Street. Detectives believe, as Officer Lewis approached the suspect(s) who had violently beaten Mr. Gitschier, the suspect(s) shot Officer Lewis and fled.

Detectives are taking a fresh look at the case and believe one or possibly two suspicious vehicles with multiple occupants were in the area that night. It's possible those occupants were involved.

On March 12, 1976, Officer Lewis' police badge, badge holder, and police ID were recovered at 915 S. Acacia, Compton. These items were taken from Officer Lewis' person on the night he was murdered.

Potential suspect vehicles are described as a mid 70's, black top, blue body 4-door Fleetwood Cadillac, and an early 60's white 4-door Fleetwood Cadillac (stock photos shown)

Anyone with information regarding the murder of Officer Lewis, is urged to contact Long Beach Homicide Detectives T. Johnson, S. Robertson, or M. Bigel at (562) 570-7244. Anyone wishing to remain anonymous may call 1-800-222-TIPS (8477), or text TIPLA plus your tip to 274637 (CRIMES), or visit www.LACrimeStoppers.org

This bulletin distributed in 2015 by the Long Beach Police Department asked for the public's help in solving the four-decades-old murder of Officer Franke Lewis.

pulled off the 405 freeway near Long Beach onto Cantel Street. The teacher was so tired that he left his doors unlocked as he fell asleep on the front seat.

As Gitschier was getting comfortable, Officer Franke Lewis had just finished a shift with the Long Beach Police Department. He arrived home around 3 a.m. As he got out of his car, he heard a loud commotion just two houses down from where he had parked. The screams came from Gitschier who was being attacked and was bleeding profusely around his face and eyes. Lewis ran to Gitschier's aid. As Lewis approached, he was shot in the face by the attacker. The assassin moved quickly, taking Lewis' police badge, badge holder, police identification and duty weapon and fled the scene.

Hearing the shot, Linda Lewis ran from their home and found her husband lying in a pool of blood. She gently held him in her arms as he died. Neighbors, hearing her screams for help, called the police. "He didn't have much of a chance," said Long Beach Detective Sgt. John Hurlburt. "He caught it cold." Gitschier was knocked out and did not even know Lewis had saved his life until the next day while recovering in the hospital. He could not give a description of the suspect. "I can remember everything up to the time I went to sleep in the car, and the next thing I knew, I wake up and I'm covered in blood

A police sketch of "Bobby," a suspect in the shooting of Officer Lewis, and how he might have looked in 1975.

and I can't see, Gitschier said. "The surgeon at the time who put me back together said I was lucky Officer Lewis came when he did because you can only take so many blows to the head." He went on, "It's a little bit like a serviceman that... jumps on a grenade and is killed but you survived. That's how I've kind of felt for the last 40 years."

Detectives were busy during a 77-day span beginning in September 1975, when three officers were shot and killed in Long Beach. Only Lewis' murder remains unsolved. In May of 1976, five months after his death, investigators recovered Lewis' police badge and holder in a vacant home in Compton. His duty weapon was not recovered and remains missing.

Although one person was arrested and hundreds of leads were investigated, the case was at an impasse. It didn't matter; Long Beach detectives refused to give up. In the fall of 2015, investigators thawed out the cold case when they released a description of two cars and a sketch of a suspect. One name that came up many times during the investigation was that of a teenager known as "Bobby." Witnesses told police the teen had bragged about killing a police officer near the time Lewis was gunned down. The suspect would have been 17 at the time and lived in Long Beach. Police went on to name "Spider" as an additional person of interest and pointed out that the 18 to 20-year-old African American woman may have been with "Bobby" on the night of the shooting.

Detectives described a mid-1970s blue four-door Cadillac Fleetwood and an early- 1960s white four-door Cadillac Fleetwood that were seen in the area the night Lewis was killed. Each vehicle contained several male and female African Americans. Residents told police the occupants of the vehicles did not live in the neighborhood, and detectives said it is

A contemporary view of Cantel Street where Officer Lewis was killed. Google Maps.

possible "Bobby" was driving one of those cars.

Four decades later and the Lewis murder was again making headlines and generating interest, but as of this writing, no arrests have been made, and the case remains unsolved. Lewis was married with two young children.

SOURCES:

- http://www.presstelegram.com/general-news/20160118/la-county-to-renew-reward-for-information-in-1975-killing-of-lb-police-officer
- https://www.odmp.org/officer/8100-police-officer-franke-neal-lewis
- http://www.latimes.com/local/lanow/la-me-ln-long-beach-suspect-sketch-20151109-story.html
- http://documents.latimes.com/1975-long-beach-police-officer-shot-death-near-his-home/
- http://www.presstelegram.com/general-news/20151103/long-beach-police-release-new-information-in-1975-officer-killing
- http://ktla.com/2015/11/03/long-beach-police-offer-50000-reward-for-information-in-officers-1975-killing/

CHAPTER 71

The Off-Duty Job

THE OFFICER:

Officer Alfred Morris Johnson, Jr.
Atlanta (Georgia) Police Department
End of Watch: Saturday, February 16, 1980
Age: 31

Over the years, most law enforcement salaries have been so inadequate that many officers have had to work second jobs to help pay the bills. It's not something an officer wants to do; it is something he has to do. Most agencies allow officers to work outside the department and wear their duty uniforms. Off-duty jobs run the gamut. They include providing security at bars, restaurants, sporting events, retail stores, construction sites, almost anywhere that the employer feels an officer's presence is necessary to operate his or her business safely and to deter crime.

Officer Alfred Johnson was an Atlanta police officer working the now closed Big Buy supermarket at 470 Flat Shoals Ave., in his regulation uniform but off-duty. The Marine Corps veteran needed the extra cash for his family. It was Saturday, February 16, 1980, when two armed men entered the store. One was wearing a long trench coat and was armed with a shotgun. The second suspect was wearing a mask pulled over his face and was armed with a .38-caliber handgun. Waiting out front was a getaway driver.

As the suspects stormed in, Johnson met them head-on. Without hesitation, Johnson confronted the man with the shotgun and attempted to wrestle the weapon away from him. As they were fighting over control of the weapon, a blast from the gun struck Johnson in the abdomen. He went down, seriously wounded. As Johnson was lying there, his will to survive was strong. He went for his own weapon, hoping to shoot his attacker. But as Johnson did so, the hooded suspect shot Johnson in the abdomen with his .38. Still fighting for his life, the 31-year-old officer got his gun out and fired several shots at the two robbery suspects but missed.

The now-closed Big Buy supermarket where Officer Alfred Johnson faced down two robbery suspects and was killed attempting to disarm them.

With the officer down, the bandits cleaned out the cash registers and scooped up a batch of food stamps. The two men ran from the store to the waiting getaway car and sped off. Officer Johnson died just as he arrived at the hospital.

Atlanta Police Department Detective Ponce Harris was the lead investigator at the time of Johnson's murder. Through meticulous police work, he and his colleagues, identified three suspects they believed were responsible for the murder of Officer Johnson. But Fulton County District Attorney Lewis Slaton had issues. He pointed to the fact that none of the store patrons could identify the gunmen. There was more.

Detective Harris worked up a case using the statements of a convicted bank robber, Sam Carroll, who happened to be sharing a cell at Rutledge State Prison with one of the alleged robbers. Carroll's cellmate divulged certain aspects of the murder that only the perpetrator could have known.

Carroll cooperated with the police and went so far as to wear a hidden microphone to record their conversations. He also captured information that allowed police to recover the handgun used in the murder. The slug taken from Johnson's body matched the pistol that police had confiscated from one of the robbery suspects during an unrelated arrest.

Harris sought to get Carroll a reduction of his 20-year sentence for an earlier robbery, but DA Slaton balked. He pointed out that the killing happened in DeKalb County, which was not in Slaton's jurisdiction. Additionally, one of Carroll's partners had threatened a prosecutor in Carroll's case, to which Slaton took exception. With Slaton on the sidelines, the DeKalb County prosecutor did not want to move forward with the case. As Detective Harris made it clear later, the case "was solved back then. We just needed somebody to take it to the next level." No one would step up.

In 2010, Detective Vince Velazquez pulled the case from the freezer, motivated by the fact that it was the only unsolved murder of an Atlanta police officer still open. "This was pretty brazen because these robberies hardly ever occur when an officer is working," Velazquez pointed out. "They had to know an officer was there because they would have cased the place and...they were definitely prepared to shoot him." Jack Mallard, a former senior prosecutor for Slaton, summed up how decades later, officials never forget. "The murder of a police officer, it never gets cold. You might call it a cold case, but you never forget it."

Johnson left behind a wife (who has since died) and two daughters who have made it clear, that they will never give up hope that the killers will be brought to justice.

SOURCES:

- https://www.youtube.com/watch?v=2iVM8t0QAXI
- https://www.youtube.com/watch?v=fmlwVv8tLR0
- http://amwfans.com/thread/4268/unknown-officer-alfred-johnson-georgia
- https://patch.com/georgia/eastatlanta/americas-most-wanted-to-feature-1980-east-atlanta-mur06602c87a0
- http://www.ajc.com/news/local/cold-case-murdered-policeman-warms/6WBCqmtgq8rkIxwEpNIBKJ/

CHAPTER 72

A Mysterious Death

THE OFFICER:

Corporal Robert Glen Owen
Erie (Pennsylvania) Police Department
Date of Incident: Sunday, December 28, 1980
End of Watch: Monday, December 29, 1980
Age: 40

A native of Erie, Pennsylvania, Robert Owen was working as an ironworker, but his best friends were local police officers. One was future chief of police Charles Bowers, and the other was Dennis Tobin. The group shared many a cup of coffee, and Owen found himself doing ride-alongs with his buddies. He liked what he saw. The officers liked what they saw. Owen was a big, tough guy who knew the streets of Erie as well as any veteran officer. So, in 1971, Owen threw down his factory tools and holstered a gun for the Erie Police Department.

Quickly, Owen gained a reputation as a strict enforcer of the law. "Owen never took a back seat to anybody," Tobin said, "and brought his assertive, no-nonsense style with him to the job. If he knew he was in the right and you were wrong, he would enforce the law. Some people could consider that hard. I consider that good police work."

Owen became a motorcycle officer, soon was promoted to corporal, and six years later became the supervisor of the unit. On Monday, December 29, 1980, at approximately 1:40 in the morning, David Cambra was out walking his two dogs when he noticed an unattended police car and a flashlight lying on the ground. Cambra called the police.

Answering Cambra's phone call on the night of the murder, responding units found Owen 75 feet from his patrol car with a single bullet wound to the chest. The murder weapon was his own Colt Trooper Mark III .357 with a 6-inch barrel. Owen's police car was parked in a secluded industrial area known as a location where Erie police officers often gathered. The engine was idling, the driver's door was open, and the lights were turned off. His police radio was switched to Channel 3, which was used for communication between officers.

During a subsequent interview with Cambra, the witness confessed to taking the gun and later throwing it by some railroad tracks. Cambra led officers to the location, and the weapon was recovered. Despite the 11 day time lapse, experts found traces of Owen's blood in and on the barrel, indicating the gun was fired at close range. Cambra became a suspect in the murder and was subjected to several polygraph exams, which he passed.

The condition of Owen's jacket and shirt indicated that he was possibly involved in an altercation before he was shot. Officers followed a blood trail just north of the patrol car. There they recovered his keys and set of handcuffs with one cuff partially open. It led investigators to believe that either he was attempting to crawl to his car or was dragged.

Owen was reported to have attended a card game at a friend's house while on duty near the location where he was found dead a short time later. Before leaving the game, Owen called his wife and then a fellow police officer. A third call was made, but investigators were unable to determine the identity of the person. Just 15 minutes after Owen left his friend's house, two witnesses driving a truck observed the idling police car. They reported they had seen three people near the warehouse where the murder took place. The witnesses thought that one of the three men appeared to be a police officer.

As with almost any police department, lapses in proper crime scene management can be a problem. In this instance, the crime scene was demolished by numerous police officers and first responders who rushed in after hearing the report of an officer down. With no one taking overall charge of the scene, critical evidence was lost. The fire department was ordered to wash away the blood; consequently, footprints and tire track evidence were lost. One important piece of evidence the police recovered was a lighter. It was immediately bagged but somehow disappeared before being booked in at the station. Also recovered were butts of two different brands of cigarettes.

To further complicate the case, Owen and several other police officers were under investigation over the possible theft of a diamond ring that disappeared during a burglary investigation. Two officers and Owen were given polygraph tests. The two officers came back inconclusive, while it was reported that Owen failed. The two officers were later given another test, which they both passed. Owen was due to be tested again on the day he was found dead. Interestingly, the case of the missing ring has since been solved, with no police criminality involvement. The case of Corporal Owen remains unsolved. Owen is survived by his wife and son.

SOURCES:

- https://www.facebook.com/ErieHistoryMemorabilia/posts/1004184299621896:0
- http://www.odmp.org/officer/10273-corporal-robert-glen-owen
- http://www.topix.com/forum/city/erie-pa/TM991HK9078FQPTDV/who-killed-robert-owen-fess-up
- Newspapers.com

CHAPTER 73

An Unsolved Homicide Solved?

THE OFFICER:

Chief of Police Gregory B. Adams
Saxonburg Borough (Pennsylvania) Police Department
End of Watch: Thursday, December 4, 1980
Age: 31

Normally to solve a homicide you need an arrestee and a trial with a conviction. There are times a murder case can be cleared by a suspect's MO and circumstantial evidence, but these are less common. The murder of Police Chief Gregory Adams remained unsolved for nearly four decades and technically still is. But in a startling discovery, the prime suspect in Adams' murder was discovered buried in the backyard of his ex-wife. The history-making case begins in a small town of 1,300. The Saxonburg Borough Police Department consisted of Chief Adams, one other full-time officer and several part-time employees.

Adams began his police career on the busy streets of our nation's capital in the early 1970s. But that all changed after the brutal murder of his partner. It was too much for Adams, so he resigned and exchanged the big city for a small town. His hope was for a simpler life without the challenges of the big city, but to remain a cop.

Adams had just started the night shift around 3 p.m. on December 4, 1980, when he saw a white Mercury Cougar run a stop sign. Adams stopped the car in the Agway Supermarket parking lot. A few moments later, witnesses reported hearing several gunshots and seeing the Cougar leaving the scene.

First responders were shocked to see that Adams was so badly beaten that he was hardly recognizable—except for his voice. The dying chief kept muttering: "This shouldn't be, this

Photograph taken in 1979   Age-enhanced Photograph

Top: Photographs of Eugene Webb. Above: The suspect in the killing of Chief Gregory Adams, Donald Eugene Webb, who remained on the FBI's 10 Most Wanted list for 26 years. He was found buried in his ex-wife's backyard in 2017.

shouldn't be." He died a few moments later. The subsequent investigation revealed that the suspect, armed with a .25-caliber handgun, had shot the chief twice: once in the chest and once in the arm. Adams refused to give up and fought back bravely. After he was shot, he and the suspect became involved in a violent struggle. Adams somehow managed to shoot the suspect in the leg and rip his lower lip off before being overpowered and severely beaten on the head with his own gun. The suspect tore out the police radio and took the chief's gun but left behind his .25. He also made a critical mistake by leaving behind a fake driver's license with the name of Stanley Porta, a dead man. Detectives would determine the suspect they were searching for was Donald Eugene Webb. The driver's license left behind belonged to Webb's then-wife's deceased husband. Blood at the scene matched Adams and Webb.

Three weeks after the murder of Chief Adams, a warrant for murder, attempted burglary and unlawful flight to avoid prosecution was issued for Donald Webb. The FBI said Webb was a career criminal and master of assumed identities who specialized in robbing jewelry stores. At the time of the traffic stop, Webb had a warrant out for burglary and was most likely casing the town's jewelry store.

After five months, the FBI placed Webb on its 10 Most Wanted list for the murder of Adams. For the next 26 years, Webb escaped detection and remained atop the list. The alleged killer would have the distinction of remaining a top 10 fugitive for the longest period of any wanted person in the history of the FBI. During that same time, 450 fugitives had been located after making the Most Wanted list. In 2007, the FBI reluctantly removed Webb from the list, theorizing he was probably deceased.

But a break in the case came in 2017, nearly 37 years after the murder of Adams. Agents working on an unrelated gambling investigation were searching the home of Lillian Webb, who happened to be the ex-wife of the fugitive. In the course of their investigation, FBI agents discovered a hidden room that locked only from the inside. Sitting in the corner was a well-worn cane—a perfect implement for a man who had once been shot in the leg.

According to the affidavit for a search warrant, Webb's ex-wife, Lillian, told investigators that her ex-husband was living with her and suffered a stroke in 1997. Consequently he was no longer able to care for himself. Before he died of a second stroke, Webb had told her to dig a hole in the backyard and bury him when he died. She did so in 1999. In the summer of 2017, the FBI recovered the body and verified it was indeed Donald Webb, the suspected killer of Chief Adams. As there was no foul play involved, no charges were brought against Lillian Webb. For all of the 708 unsolved police murders to date, very few give a clue as to what happened to the suspects after fleeing the crime scene.

The murder of Chief Adams now has a plausible ending. "The biggest question in the history of Saxonburg has been answered," said the current police chief, Joseph Beachem. "While the hurt will continue, at least doubt about what happened that day has been eliminated."

But without a trial to remove all uncertainty as to who killed Chief Adams, the word "alleged" still creeps into the conversation. The FBI made one telling final comment in the Adams case: "As this remains an ongoing investigation, no additional information or comment will be provided at this time." Chief Adams was survived by his wife and two small children, both under the age of three.

SOURCES:

- http://www.mcall.com/news/nationworld/pennsylvania/mc-pa-police-chiefs-killer-still-on-the-loose-after-35-years-20151204-story.html
- http://www.foxnews.com/story/2008/10/27/wanted-donald-eugene-webb-for-murder-pennsylvania-police-chief.html
- http://boston.cbslocal.com/2017/07/20/donald-eugene-webb-saxonburg-police-chief-gregory-adams-murder/
- https://www.washingtonpost.com/news/morning-mix/wp/2017/07/17/fbi-spent-decades-searching-for-mobster-wanted-in-cop-killing-then-they-found-his-secret-room/?utm_term=.06cfaf678ab6
- https://www.fbi.gov/contact-us/field-offices/boston/news/press-releases/former-ten-most-wanted-fugitive-donald-eugene-webb-located
- https://www.odmp.org/officer/1052-chief-of-police-gregory-b-adams

CHAPTER 74

The Neighbor

THE OFFICER:

Patrolwoman Kathleen Garcia
Denver (Colorado) Police Department
End of Watch: Saturday, March 28, 1981
Age: 24

February 6, 1981, was one of the happiest days in Kathleen Garcia's short life, when the 24-year-old graduated from the Denver Police Academy. According to friends, she had always wanted to become a police officer and give back to her community in south Denver. In just six short weeks, Officer Garcia was dead, murdered in front of her mother's home, a promising career snuffed out.

Garcia was assigned to the District 1 police station at 2195 Decatur St., working the swing shift from 7 p.m. to 3 a.m., unless she was working overtime, as she was on Saturday, March 28, 1981. In her short time with the department, Garcia had already received positive rating reports that complimented her for getting along with fellow officers, performing solid police work and not complaining about working the late-night shift.

After leaving the station at 4:09 a.m., Garcia, still in uniform, drove home in her red 1981 Mercury Capri to her mother's home at 2398 S. Galapago St., where she was staying. Garcia parked on the West Wesley Avenue side of the house, near the front gate. It was 4:26 a.m. Out of nowhere, a person ran up to her car and began yelling. A loud, but brief, argument ensued. Garcia yelled out, "No, no, you don't have to do that." She then fought to get out of the car, when the suspect fired a shot. The bullet struck Garcia in the shoulder and exited out the right side of the windshield. Garcia ran 20 feet to the side gate of her mother's house with the shooter following her. From a very close range her attacker fired again, striking her in the back of the neck. The slug exited out the front of Garcia's head and struck the house, breaking a window.

A contemporary image of 2398 S. Galapago St. shows where Officer Kathleen Garcia parked after her shift ended with the Denver Police Department. She was attacked and shot with her own weapon. Google Maps.

Garcia's mother and a neighbor both heard two loud gunshots, glass shattering and then an engine starting from a truck that was parked near the Garcia home. As Kathryn Garcia ran from her house, the truck sped away. Kathryn cradled her dying daughter in her arms while blood poured from the wound. Garcia was transported to Denver General Hospital, where she died 10 hours later.

Denver detectives began their investigation immediately. Wearing black bands over their badges, officers scoured the neighborhood, interviewing anyone who might have seen or heard anything. They listened to all the radio transmissions that Garcia and her training partner had made during their shift. Investigators found powder residue on her hand, suggesting that the officer was struggling for control of her duty weapon when it went off.

The killer escaped with her weapon, but ballistics determined that the fatal bullet appeared to be from her .38-caliber gun. Officials interviewed a neighbor who lived directly across the street, 27-year-old Steven C. Warren, who met police when they first arrived. By coincidence, Warren's brother was a Denver police officer who was a classmate of Garcia. Police received conflicting statements from Warren, and he soon became a suspect in Garcia's murder.

Police were also looking at other suspects, including William James Otto, who was arrested and then released after he passed a lie director test. The investigation appeared to stall for 11 months, but inside detective headquarters, officers were preparing a case against Warren. They arrested him in early 1982 for the murder of Officer Garcia. Warren's rap sheet included an arrest for carrying a concealed weapon—a knife and a 1979 disturbance.

An opening in the Garcia case came when detectives interviewed Warren's close friend, Raymond "Ray" Gardino. Several clues suggested the involvement of Gardino. First, he owned an older-model gray pickup that matched the description of the vehicle speeding from the scene. That was only the beginning. Gardino told police how he picked up Warren that Saturday morning at 1:30 a.m. They went cruising through town, drinking heavily and smoking pot.

At approximately 4 a.m., Gardino parked near an alley, within sight of where Garcia was murdered. Gardino said they were sitting there smoking and drinking when Officer Garcia pulled up. Warren got out of the truck and walked toward Garcia's car. He would later state that he was going to hit on her. According to Gardino, he was tired, so he put his head down on the steering wheel. He was immediately startled by two gunshots and sped off, believing he was being shot at, leaving Warren behind.

When the two next talked, Gardino said he flat-out asked Warren if he had killed Garcia, to which Warren replied, "Yes." When asked why, Warren said, "Just for the hell of it." A second witness, Tom Ramirez, was in a bar when he heard a man, reported to be Warren, brag how he "killed a damn cop."

In May of 1982, Warren had his preliminary hearing. On the witness stand, Gardino suddenly could not remember anything and recanted most of his earlier incriminating statements. Gardino claimed the Denver police had pressured him to testify against his friend. He did not have any idea what happened that early morning. Another key witness, Ramirez, also developed a short memory and could not identify Warren as the man he overheard in the bar boasting how he had killed a cop. He said he hadn't seen Warren in eight years and that the man he heard talking in the bar had a beard.

Despite the recanted testimony, the case was held over for trial. In September 1982, 40 prosecution witnesses testified, including Ramirez. In one cynical statement, Ramirez testified, "If he [Warren] gained weight and put his beard back on, I bet he's the same guy" he saw in the bar. In closing arguments, defense attorney Scott Robinson told jurors that his client was not too bright, with a functional IQ of only 74, and was not capable of murder. Robinson implied that it was probably Gardino who killed Garcia.

The jury deliberated for 6½ hours before voting unanimously to acquit Warren. One juror said the prosecution witnesses were not credible. No other arrests have been made, and the case remains unsolved. Garcia was survived by her mother.

SOURCES:

- https://www.odmp.org/officer/5270-patrolwoman-kathleen-garcia
- http://blogs.denverpost.com/coldcases/2013/07/27/denver-rookie-policewoman-murdered-after-graveyard-shift/7095/4/
- Email correspondence with retired Lt. Bill Finch of the Denver Police Department in October 2017.
- Newspapers.com

CHAPTER 75

Protecting Our Nation's Buildings

THE OFFICER:

Officer Robert W. Yesucevitz
United States General Services Administration-
Federal Protection Service
End of Watch: Tuesday, July 20, 1982
Age: 24

Criminals exist around every corner. To combat this threat, there are scores of diverse agencies that make it their job to put lawbreakers behind bars. One of these is the Federal Protection Service (FPS), which is a division of the General Services Administration (GSA). It employs over 900 law enforcement officers. FPS provides security services to U.S. federal buildings, courthouses and other properties administered by the GSA. One of these FPS officers was Robert Yesucevitz. He would become the first officer killed in the 47-year history of FPS.

On the night of Tuesday, July 20, 1982, Officer Yesucevitz was patrolling the area around the John F. Kennedy Library in Dorchester, Massachusetts. Yesucevitz had received information from a University of Massachusetts police officer, at the adjoining Harbor Campus, of an intruder in the area. Around 11 p.m., Yesucevitz radioed in that he was going to investigate a suspicious person near the service road near the ocean at the rear of the library. A few minutes later, dispatch received a duress alarm from Yesucevitz's radio, indicating he could be in trouble. That was the last communication received.

Quickly, officers assigned to the interior of the library responded to search for Officer Yesucevitz. Approximately five minutes later, they discovered him behind the library, on the lawn near the loading dock, 30 feet from his patrol car. Yesucevitz was lying face down in the grass with a single bullet wound to the back of his head. It appeared the officer had been shot with his own gun, which was later discovered under his body.

The FBI, Boston Police Department and UMass police all responded to search the area. A prime area of interest was the partially boarded-up Columbia Point housing project. But no suspect was found, and the case remains unsolved.

Yesucevitz was a four-year veteran of the FPS and had served most of his tenure in the New England area. In the weeks leading up to the shooting, Yesucevitz had told family members that he was unhappy with staff cutbacks and was planning to leave his job in four days to go back to college. Yesucevitz was survived by his parents, two older brothers and a sister.

SOURCES:

- http://www.odmp.org/officer/14594-officer-robert-w-yesucevitz
- http://www.upi.com/Archives/1982/07/22/A-Federal-Protective-Service-officer-killed-while-patrolling-the/5575396158400/
- http://the-puzzle-palace.com/files/Guard_shot.txt
- https://www.newspapers.com/newspage/14271212/
- https://en.wikipedia.org/wiki/Federal_Protective_Service_(United_States)

CHAPTER 76

"I've always wanted the death penalty. He needs to die"

THE OFFICER:

Officer Lowell Clayton "L.C." Tribble
Farmers Branch (Texas) Police Department
End of Watch: Saturday, August 27, 1983
Age: 38

What were the chances? Officer Lowell Clayton "L.C." Tribble took just a minute from patrolling Farmers Branch on the northwest fringe of Dallas to drop off some medicine to his wife and 2-year-old son, who were both sick with the flu. A few minutes later he was dead.

It was a Saturday night in August 1983. After kissing his wife goodbye, Officer Tribble got back into his marked police vehicle and started to leave the parking lot of the 112-unit apartment complex. As he drove away, someone shot him three times. One of the rounds severed his spinal cord, and his car careened into a ditch.

It was his wife, Frances Tribble, who heard gunshots and called the police. Seeing his car in the ditch, the frightened spouse ran as fast as she could to help her husband. As she ran past the first unit arriving on location, she heard a report that an officer had been shot. Frances was shocked. She thought her husband had just been in an accident, never putting together the gunshots with the crash. Seeing him covered in blood and not moving was a sight that has haunted her ever since.

When the ambulance arrived, Frances rode in the back, holding Tribble's hand. She said "the fireman told me they were having a hard time keeping him breathing." A short time later, she received word in the hospital that her husband did not make it. "I still couldn't believe it was him. I wanted to see him. I don't know how people react to death, but I wanted to make sure it was him," she said.

There was speculation that a car with illegal drugs triggered Tribble's slaying, but no arrest was made and the case went unsolved. That is until exactly 27 years to the day after his murder. A grand jury returned an indictment naming Gary Wayne Pettigrew, a small-time drug dealer, as the murderer of Officer Tribble. He was arrested, and he immediately proclaimed that he was being framed. He had a lengthy rap sheet and convictions. In addition to drug violations, there were arrests for burglary, the unlawful carrying of a weapon and theft. "We do have evidence that we think will lead to a conviction," said Kevin Brooks, the top prosecutor in the DA's office. He added, "There was new evidence, and there were individuals we spoke to who provided that."

Sheila Tribble Shaack, who was 18 when her father was killed, gave a glimpse into the grief she felt when she said she believes the person who killed her father should die for his crime. "I've always wanted the death penalty. He needs to die," she said. "He's lived long enough to enjoy what my dad missed out on. If you'd asked me when I was younger, I would have said I wanted to kill him myself."

The night Tribble dropped off the medicine, Sheila saw her father as she was getting out of her car. She said she's so grateful for their last words to each other. "He said, 'I love you,' and I said, 'I love you,'" she remembered. "It was really good I was able to say that."

After eight months, all the excitement and relief that family members felt because officials had finally caught the man responsible for the murder of Officer Tribble went the way of a discarded newspaper. Dallas County District Attorney Craig Watkins had held a headline-grabbing news conference announcing that an arrest was made in the Tribble case. Some argued that Watkins made the announcement because he was in the throes of a contentious re-election battle, which he barely won. Less than a year later, he dismissed the charges because prosecutors did not have enough evidence to proceed.

Jamille Bradfield, a spokeswoman for the DA, stated that "after further investigation, we discovered information that is leading us to additional suspects." Five years later, no "additional suspects" have been arrested, and the case remains unsolved.

Frances Tribble, upon learning of the arrest of Pettigrew, prepared a speech for the criminal proceedings. "I've written down a speech. I will get to tell it when he goes to trial. I wrote the words down 25 years ago. I will change a few words, but I'm ready to read it to the jury." Keep that speech ready, Mrs. Tribble. The entire law enforcement family hopes and prays that someday you will get to read it. In addition to his wife, Frances, and daughter, Sheila, Tribble was survived by a son.

SOURCES:

- Dallas News reported by Jennifer Emily: http://www.dallasnews.com/news/farmers-branch/2010/08/27/Dallas-County-announces-indictment-in-1983-721 and
- Texarkana Gazette reported by Jim Williamson: http://www.texarkanagazette.com/news/texarkana/story/2010/sep/13/flood-memories-hit-widow-slaofficer/191622/
- Newspapers.com

CHAPTER 77

Ambush of a Park Police Officer

THE OFFICER:

Park Police Officer Howard Shao Wai Huang
Los Angeles County (California)
Department of Parks and Recreation Police
End of Watch: Sunday, March 11, 1984
Age: 42

Imagine for a minute that you are sitting in a marked police vehicle writing a report in the early morning hours of a Sunday morning. It's so quiet you can hear the soft creak of your leather web belt creak as you move in your seat. Suddenly the peaceful night is torn apart with the roar of an AK-47 firing an uninterrupted volley of fire. This would have been the last sounds heard by Park Police Officer Howard (Howie) Huang. One minute you are writing in your log, the next minute you are a victim of an unsolved homicide.

Officer Huang was alone the night of March 11, 1984, assigned to the graveyard shift. Working for the Los Angeles County Department of Parks and Recreation Police, a now defunct agency, Huang duties included patrolling all parks and recreational facilities in the county. On this night, he was in South Central Los Angeles patrolling a group of warehouses, the county administrative and supply buildings, all that had been the target of numerous burglaries.

At 7 a.m. when Huang did not report back to headquarters to go end of watch, a manhunt began for the missing officer. At 7:50 a.m., LAPD located Huang's police car at Link St. and Lanzit Av. In the Willowbrook area, approximately two miles from his last know patrol area. Officers noted the engine was still running. Blood coated the driver's side of the front seat and several bullet holes marked the driver's door.

At 8 a.m., park employees found Huang's bullet riddled body in an alley in the 12900 block of South Broadway, just 75 yards from police headquarters. He had been shot numerous times in the chest. His personal belongings and wallet were still on his body, but his service revolver was missing.

The motive was not clear that night nor three decades later. "We don't have any motive or suspects at this time," said Lt. Charles Elliott from the Los Angeles County Sheriffs. "It may have been that he was just killed for his gun, or maybe somebody just wanted to kill an officer. It appears as if he was just shot and dragged out of the car."

Lt. Carl Moore, Huang's immediate supervisor, said Huang was "a very alert officer who took pride in wearing his uniform. He was a people person and had a very pleasant attitude while on the job. He was respected and well-liked. He knew what as going on around him and based on the evidence, it's reasonable to assume that it may have been an ambush situation." Moore added, "It's happened before to our force but never ended in death." The subsequent investigation determined that the suspects shot from the driver's side of the vehicle using an AK-47 and discharged 20 rounds.

Officer Huang was an eight-year veteran and was the first officer murdered in the then 15-year history of the department. Huang left behind his wife and two grade-school daughters. The case remains unsolved.

SOURCES:

- https://www.newspapers.com/clip/11146268/the_los_angeles_times/
- https://www.facebook.com/permalink.php?story_fbid=960413593992163&id=875218969178293
- https://camemorial.org/honor-roll/tribute/howard-s-w-huang/
- http://www.odmp.org/officer/6769-park-police-officer-howard-shao-wai-huang

CHAPTER 78

Suicide or Murder

THE OFFICER:

Detective Garland Linwood Joyner, Jr
Portsmouth (Virginia) Police Department
End of Watch: Sunday, March 18, 1984
Age: 39

In *Unsolved*, too often I have written of law enforcement deaths that might be interpreted as a suicide as opposed to murder. My assertion is that officials must get it right, because if they don't, and classify the death of an officer as a suicide, and it isn't, the perpetrator lives out his life as a free man. Not acceptable. The death of Detective Garland Joyner in 1984 was first officially ruled a suicide, over the objections of some close to the investigation. Nearly three decades later, the finding of suicide was thrown out when new evidence emerged indicating it was a homicide. Twenty-seven years had passed, while the murderer escaped punishment for the murder of a detective. Now the hunt is on to identify the killer.

It was on Sunday, March 18, 1984, when Olivia Mundie and her husband, Keith, were awakened at 5:30 in the morning by gunshots. Olivia told investigators she heard one, two, three shots, then a pause, and then a fourth shot went off. She said it sounded like a high-powered handgun. The couple wrote it off as likely poachers. That opinion changed when numerous emergency vehicles blanketed the area around a small bridge that crossed the hollow at Warwick Swamp, off North Carolina Highway 32 at the Gates and Chowan County line.

Keith Mundie thought he had better take a look. So Mundie walked down his road, 100 yards to the swamp. As he arrived, the body of Joyner had just been found floating facedown near the bridge. Mundie paid close attention to the details as he took in the scene. "The buttons from his shirt were laying on the bridge," he said. "His wallet, his cards, all of the paperwork from his wallet, it was all floating in the creek. That weren't no suicide."

A contemporary photo of the swamp where the body of Detective Garland Joyner was found with a single gunshot wound to the chest. At first, investigators ruled his death a suicide. Twenty-seven years later, officials reopened the case as a homicide. Photo credit to David Hollingsworth of The Virginian-Pilot.

The multiagency task force investigating Joyner's death included two sheriff's departments, the Virginia State Bureau of Investigation, the Portsmouth Police Department and others. They soon concluded that Joyner had taken his own life, basing their theory on his debts from bad investments and the hefty insurance policies he had recently taken out on his own life.

Detective Joyner had been on the police force for 14 years, specializing in forensics. He was considered one of the best. He had a wife and daughter and they lived near the Norfolk Naval Shipyard. He'd lived in the same house his entire life. Joyner had spent most of the day before his death with his buddy Mike Holley, who owned a local restaurant that police frequented. Joyner was having trouble with the brakes on his car, and he asked Holley if he could borrow his spare car. Holley didn't ask any questions as he handed Joyner the keys.

What happened next is difficult to understand. None of his friends or family could say why, but at 10:30 p.m., Joyner left Portsmouth in the borrowed gray 1977 Datsun. The only hint he gave was that he was going to meet someone in Edenton, N.C., 70 miles away, regarding a gun-smuggling case he was investigating. It was an important case to Joyner as he had spent two years working it. He would often talk about it to people he hardly knew.

After leaving town, Joyner stopped in Gloucester, N.C., (approximately 2½ hours from his home) and spent considerable time talking with a convenience store worker, even going into details about the illegal gun activity. That was the last reported sighting of Joyner until he was found floating in the swamp.

Medical examiners reported that Joyner died of a close-contact wound to his left chest, and that it appeared that he used his left hand to hold the gun against his body. The question naturally arose: How he ended up in the swamp? Investigators suggested that Joyner would have had to been sitting on the railing of the bridge to end up in the position in which he was found. There is no public record speculating as to why his jacket and outer shirt were removed.

Many people familiar with the case were not buying into the suicide ruling, including his wife, Lillie Joyner. After the dust settled on the case, Lillie hired a private investigator from Virginia Beach, Billy Franklin, to examine the circumstances of her husband's death and report his findings to the insurance company. The outspoken Franklin wasted little time. "I've seen dog-biting cases that were worked better than this one. The coroner's ruling was based on statements from the Portsmouth police concerning Joyner's debt and his mental state." Lillie told police that she and her husband had never been happier, and things could not have been better. Suicide made no sense to her.

As I've stated before, in these types of cases, there is usually no formal trial or hearing to determine if an officer committed suicide or was murdered. The closest examination is a formal investigation into the incident by the victim's insurance company, which has a vested interest in the outcome. Although police investigators pointed to the recent purchase of a high-payout insurance policy as contributing to their findings of suicide, Franklin proved otherwise. In a convincing step-by-step account of what his investigation revealed (not made public), Franklin proved to insurance officials that Joyner was in fact murdered. The executives at the insurance company were convinced, and after not paying a cent to the victim's wife earlier, they awarded her $130,000 out of the $135,000 policy. As in other similar cases, the ruling had little or no effect on the official ruling that Joyner committed suicide.

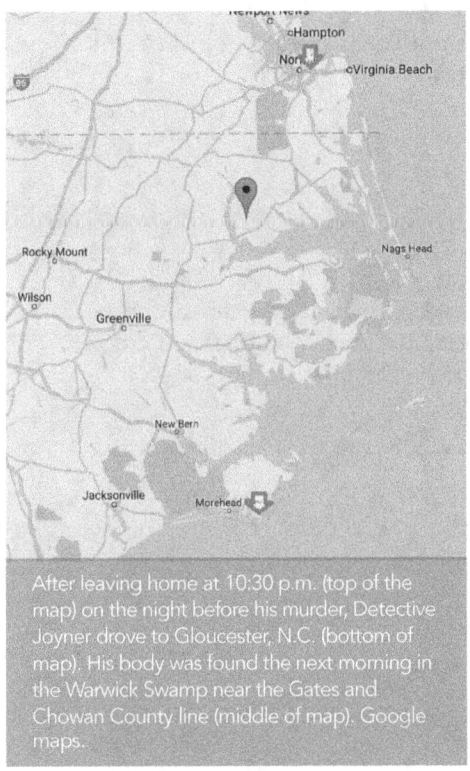

After leaving home at 10:30 p.m. (top of the map) on the night before his murder, Detective Joyner drove to Gloucester, N.C. (bottom of map). His body was found the next morning in the Warwick Swamp near the Gates and Chowan County line (middle of map). Google maps.

Time marched on.

Then it happened. Nearly 30 years later, in 2011, the Portsmouth Police Department, working in conjunction with the FBI, did something that many thought was overdue. They reopened the Joyner case. But now it was being investigated not as a suicide, but as a homicide. Robert Huntington, a police official heading the investigation, said there was new evidence in the case that caused the reversal of the initial ruling of suicide. He refused to elaborate. Immediately, fliers with the bold headline, "Homicide," with the facts of the case neatly listed, greeted customers in convenience stores from Virginia-North Carolina state line to Edenton, along N.C. 32.

Although the killer had a nearly three-decade head start before police started looking for him, one can only hope that justice will be served for the Joyner family. Detective Joyner can rest a little easier now that the real story of what happened back in 1984 has been made public. Complete closure will come with an arrest and conviction.

SOURCES:

- Much of the independent investigation into the Joyner case was done by The Virginian-Pilot, from which this story was developed. The newspaper is doing a truly commendable job in keeping this case on the lips of the readers. https://pilotonline.com/news/local/crime/decades-later-hunt-for-portsmouth-officer-s-killer-begins/article_43190b93-ed5d-5006-afe4-91e5d68de6e9.html
- http://www.odmp.org/officer/22819-detective-garland-lindwood-joyner-jr
- http://names.lawmemorial.org/officers/j/joyner41821.html

CHAPTER 79

Double Jeopardy

THE OFFICER:

Chief of Police Murray Wilson Griffin
Belle Center Village (Ohio) Police Department
End of Watch: Saturday, July 5, 1986
Age: 64

When a chief of police is killed in the line of duty (there are several in *Unsolved*), one might ask how it is possible, as chiefs are usually administrators who wield a pen, not a gun. In fact, there are numerous chiefs of police in this country who "are" the police department—there are no subordinates. Consequently, the chief works the field just as if he was a slick-sleeve police officer. In this case, Chief of Police Murray Griffin, a veteran of World War II and a 25-year veteran of the one-man department in Belle Center Village, Ohio, was killed answering an unknown-trouble call.

In my research into *Unsolved* homicides of law enforcement officers, this is the only case I found in which one of the family members, in this instance the chief's daughter, Jody Griffin, wrote in detail about the murder and subsequent trial. Jody's writing is from the heart and to the point. There is no official police phrasing, no cop jargon, just a grieving daughter writing about her murdered father.

Belle Center was a village of 900 in 1986. Nothing much ever happened. The law in town came down to one man, Chief Griffin. If you were to join him for coffee at the local restaurant, where the waitresses called everyone "honey," his simple philosophy would have been, "Someone needs to do it." And he did, for well over two decades. But he didn't do it for the money. He received only $25 per week; a teenager flipping hamburgers made more.

On Saturday night, July 5, 1986, at 11:20 p.m., the phone rang at the Griffin home. It was an anonymous caller who said he had just received a phone call from Phyllis Mullet, 37, who was screaming for help. She sounded desperate. The caller also phoned the Logan County Sheriff's Department. Chief Griffin didn't give it much thought, as he had been to the home several times for family quarrels. Griffin strapped on his gun belt, told his wife he would be right back and took off in the family sedan.

Just as Griffin drove off, the phone rang again; this time it was the sheriff's office. The deputy told Mrs. Griffin to stop her husband, that there was serious trouble at the Mullet house, and they were sending backup. It was too late—Chief Griffin had already traveled the three blocks to the Mullet home.

With sirens blaring, the sheriff's deputies raced to the residence, arriving 10 minutes later. Before rushing into the darkened home to assist Griffin, they decided to go down the street two houses and asked a man on his porch what was going on at the Mullet house. The resident gave them the runaround for several minutes before the deputies finally went to the Mullet house. At the same time, family members left behind at the Griffins' began to worry when the police scanner in their home started to come alive with anxious, fast-talking deputies. The code used for "officer down" kept repeating. This was followed by a call for search dogs and an order for all personnel to respond.

Inside the Mullet home, it was a gruesome, bloody scene. The deputies first discovered the body of Phyllis Mullet. She had been tied up, severely beaten and stabbed through the throat (and later discovered to have been raped). When the officers went upstairs, they found Chief Griffin shot in the left knee, stomach, shoulder and the middle of the back. He was dead. It appeared to the officers that Griffin was shot with his own gun. As Jody Griffin would later recall, "Thus the nightmare began for us."

Suspicion immediately focused on the ex-husband. Deputies quickly located Mr. Mullet and arrested him as he was driving toward Belle Center. With his arrest, the search and investigation went on hold, allowing valuable investigative time to tick by. When the ex-husband was released because he had an indisputable alibi, the search for the killer resumed.

The investigation into Griffin's murder progressed slowly, with no solid leads. As Jody Griffin complained, "The police knew nothing." A break in the case came from a seemingly unrelated call from a citizen in Belle Center. The caller, Raymond Lowe, told police that his son, Terry Lowe, had written a suicide note, and he feared for his son's life. The Deputies went to the home of Mr. Lowe to investigate. In the process they discovered pictures of Mrs. Mullet and her children in Terry Lowe's room, along with other evidence potentially tying him to the murders. After reading the suicide note, the deputies determined that Lowe was at a nearby lake. They asked the father if they could take the evidence they discovered with them, to which the father gave his permission. The decision not to get a search warrant before removing the property would prove detrimental to the case.

At the lake, deputies found Lowe's car with his wallet and keys locked inside. Officials spent the next three days dragging the lake with no results. Meanwhile, a phone call from the Greenville Police Department on the Indiana-Ohio border reported that they had found a credit card belonging to Raymond Lowe, the father of the suspect. Detectives went to Greenville and found Terry Lowe in a hotel room. They noticed that the young Lowe had scratches on his face and legs. They arrested him and took him back to Ohio. During questioning, Lowe denied any wrongdoing, stating that he did not commit the homicides or write the suicide note. Without enough evidence to prosecute, and unable to put Lowe at the crime scene, police were forced to release him. Lowe quickly moved to Arizona and became a maintenance worker in an apartment complex.

Four years went by. Finally, in 1990, the investigators had amassed enough evidence to charge Terry Lowe with the murders and take him to trial. According to the family, "the next nightmare began," as pretrial motion hearings dragged on. Jody Griffin said the family just "sat back and watched the whole case fall apart." The court ruled that the evidence taken from Lowe's home was obtained illegally. Additionally, an FBI expert witness was not allowed to testify. Terry Lowe did admit to "doing things" to Mullet's daughter, but the defense argued in court that "the accused was not on trial for being a pervert; he was on trial for a double murder." In the end, all charges were dropped against Lowe, and he was set free a second time.

In 1999 the family wrote how they had given up hope of seeing justice prevail in the murder of their father and had moved on. Jody Griffin wrote in her final paragraph, "I have also been determined to not let the killer take any more from me. He got away with killing Murray. We couldn't have stopped him, and we can't bring Murray back. All we can do is take what we have left in our lives and hang on to that. By trying to be kinder, more helpful people, Murray and Phyllis did not die in vain."

So, it appeared as though this was the final chapter in the murders of Chief Griffin and Phyllis Mullet. But it wasn't. Over a decade later, new DNA evidence was tested and revealed that the Logan County investigators likely charged the right man in the double-murder case—Terry Lowe. A spokesman for the sheriff's office said, "DNA testing confirmed the presence of the previously charged individual [Terry Lowe] at the residence and on the physical evidence used in the crime."

With heightened hopes that Lowe would have to answer for allegedly killing two people, the new evidence was submitted to the Logan County Prosecutor's Office. This included Lowe's blood found on a sliding glass door and inside a knot on a rope used to bind Mullet's legs. When the prosecutor's office ruling was released, it was not what law enforcement officials were hoping to hear. Because a defendant cannot be tried twice for the same crime after it has been dismissed—double jeopardy— the murder charges against Lowe could not be filed. It was last reported in 2012 that Terry Lowe, 72, was leading a contented life in Lima, Ohio —a free man. It appears that everyone involved has moved on.

SOURCES:

- https://www.ohio.com/akron/news/suspect-in-1986-deaths-unlikely-to-be-charged-again
- http://www.murdervictims.com/voices/murray_griffin.html
- http://www.peakofohio.com/news/details.cfm?clientid=5&cid=38079#.WYYGzYjytPY

CHAPTER 80

Airport Police Killing Left Few Clues

THE OFFICER:

Officer Kenneth Stanley Baldwin
Okaloosa County (Florida) Airport Police Department
End of Watch: Friday, September 11, 1987
Age: 42

No matter the badge worn, law enforcement officers are one extended family. It doesn't matter if the officers (or by any other title) work for the railroad, hospital, airport, fish and game, state parks, a college or other agency. If they have the powers of arrest, they are represented in this book. In compiling *Unsolved,* I did not intentionally leave anyone behind. But for whatever reason, some of those law enforcement officers killed received very little acknowledgment of their sacrifice. Police Officer Kenneth Baldwin is one about whom very little has been written. A couple of paragraphs in a local paper and then nothing. By including him in *Unsolved*, I hope to get the police family talking about his cold case.

The Okaloosa County Airport, located in the Florida Panhandle, leased land from Eglin Air Force Base to build a terminal. The airlines then used the base's runways. Providing security for the airport was the Okaloosa County Airport Police Department. It was early Friday morning as Officer Baldwin patrolled the deserted airport. He was working alone, and though he always wore his bulletproof vest, he choose not to this night.

Patrolling in front of the closed terminal, Officer Baldwin spotted someone or something that caused him to get out of his patrol car. As there is no video evidence or witnesses, no one knows why he was shot four times in the chest and once in the left arm. Or why the suspects ran over his body, leaving behind a 30-foot blood trail. A newspaper delivery man found his body at 2:30 a.m. and called police. Because the crime occurred on federal property, the FBI took investigative responsibility.

Everyone was searching for a motive. Why? It was difficult to determine. One theory carried the most weight. Earlier in the year, Baldwin had assisted the county sheriff in the capture and arrest of three men on cocaine-related charges at the terminal—the very terminal where he was gunned down. It was not the only case he assisted in; there were several more. A few days after his murder, it was reported by WEAR-TV in Pensacola, that the station's source said Baldwin was on a hit list because of his involvement in the drug raid. The FBI strongly denied the theory and said that "his role in the drug bust was insubstantial." The news director for the TV station did not back down from the story, expressing that he believed in the veracity of its unnamed source.

Okaloosa Sheriff Larry Gilbert said his department had received information regarding three officers who had been targeted for death following a drug arrest during the past year, but he would not release the names. However, he did point out that "Officer Baldwin was not on that list." After these reports, Baldwin's case fades from the media, and from the internet. The case remains unsolved.

Officer Baldwin was a Vietnam veteran, having served with the Army for 20 years, retiring in 1982. He had been with the airport police for less than two years. He was survived by his wife and two children, Kenneth Jr., 15, and Sherry, 13.

SOURCES:

- http://www.odmp.org/officer/20126-officer-kenneth-stanley-baldwin
- http://www.sheriff-okaloosa.org/wp-content/pdfs/newsreleases/2011/May%206%20-%20Airport%20Officer%20Remembered%20in%20Tallahassee.pdf
- Newspapers.com

CHAPTER 81

Burglary or Setup?

THE OFFICER:

Deputy Sheriff Charles Robert Anderson
Los Angeles (California) Sheriff's Department
End of Watch: Saturday, January 24, 1987
Age: 35

For many *Unsolved* homicides of law enforcement officers, it's the lack of evidence and witnesses that causes detectives sleepless nights. When there is very little to go on, speculation on what happened often sneaks into the equation. The shooting death of Deputy Sheriff Charles Anderson is just such a situation.

At just past midnight on January 24, 1987, Charlie (as he liked to be called) Anderson, along with his wife, Beth, and two young sons, returned home from an outing. Mrs. Anderson was interviewed by Detective Roger Mason of the Burbank Police Department, who reported on the events of that night:

> *They arrived home, and because Mrs. Anderson was suffering from a back injury, her husband offered to go inside the house with their oldest boy first. He asked her to wait in the car, and she did so. Charlie Anderson went in the house with the oldest son and, we believe, took him upstairs. A few moments later, Mrs. Anderson heard what sounded like backfires from where she was parked in the driveway. She was still seated in the car. Because the sound was unusual, she walked to the house and called in to see if there was anything wrong.*

Mrs. Anderson then rushed upstairs, found her husband dead, scooped up their 5-year-old from the bedroom and with their 11-month-old son, Ricky, ran to the neighbor's house. At no time did Mrs. Anderson see a suspect. The initial investigation pointed to a burglar in the home when the family returned. Just after Anderson put his son into bed, he was shot dead by the intruder. According to another police theory, Anderson confronted the burglary suspect and announced he was a deputy and then was shot. But quickly the investigation looked at the possibility of a staged burglary to cover up the murder of Anderson. Detective Mason substantiated the speculation:

While they [the intruders] had selected certain items, and placed them together to be taken from the house, they had overlooked other items that were much more valuable that were in plain sight. This led to a second theory that this might have been someone that perhaps knew Deputy Anderson that confronted him and shot him.

Inside the home, there were few clues. There were no fingerprints and no evidence of any consequence. Investigators had a murdered deputy with essentially no leads to identify the killer. A day after the murder, Detective Mason said investigators received a phone call from a man who sounded very nervous and said he had information on the Anderson murder. He said he did not want his voice recorded or traced. The detective suggested he call back on a number that did not record conversations. The mysterious caller agreed but never called back.

Police have said they believe someone close to the family was involved in Anderson's murder, but they have been unable to make any arrest. In 1999, investigators presented what evidence they did have to the Los Angeles district attorney, but prosecutors said there was insufficient evidence to charge any suspect(s). According to the very limited information released about the case, Anderson's wife, Beth, was considered a person of interest, based mostly on the fact that she has refused to be interviewed by detectives since the night of the murder. It should be noted that Mrs. Anderson has never been named a suspect.

Now 31 years later, the case remains unsolved. A new generation of detectives is searching for the murderer of Deputy Anderson. But for those loved ones left behind, optimism has all but faded away. "We all like to see justice done, don't we?" said Trish Belisle, Anderson's sister. "It's difficult to go on thinking that will never happen. Every now and then we have a little ray of hope that the person will be brought to justice. As every day goes by, you become a little less excited about that happening, less optimistic."

Charlie Anderson was the youngest of four children and was born in Duluth, Minnesota. The family later moved to Southern California. He attended the University of Southern California, where he earned a bachelor's and master's degree. Anderson was a 14-year veteran of the sheriff's department.

SOURCES:

- https://unsolved.com/gallery/charlie-anderson/
- https:www.thefreelibrary.com/15+YEARS+OF+MYSTERY+DEPUTY'S+SLAYING+STILL+HAUNTS+BURBANK+POLICE,...-a082115104
- http://articles.latimes.com/1987-01-25/local/me-5763_1_deputy-killed
- https://www.odmp.org/officer/1192-deputy-sheriff-charles-robert-anderson
- http://unsolvedmysteries.wikia.com/wiki/Charlie_Anderson
- http://www.dailynews.com/2007/01/29/probe-ongoing-in-cops-slaying/

CHAPTER 82

"Inconclusive"

THE OFFICER:

Patrolman Stephen A. Sandlin
Mountainair (New Mexico) Police Department
End of Watch: Saturday, May 7, 1988

When a law enforcement officer is killed while on duty with his or her own service weapon, the investigation into the death must look at the possibility that the officer took his own life. The statistics bear this out. Officer suicides took more lives (108) than gunfire and traffic accidents combined (97) in 2016. Taken in context, the current suicide rate for law enforcement is comparable to the incidence in the general public. Officers commit suicide at a rate of 12 per 100,000, compared with a rate for the public of 13 per 100,000. These are the facts, but statistics can be a two-edged sword. Investigators must be certain before they list an officer's death as suicide. Because if they make the wrong call, and the death was a murder, the suspect has a "Get Out of Jail Free" card for the rest of his life.

Patrolman Steve Sandlin's death from a single gunshot to the head by his own service weapon while in the police station had all the earmarks of a suicide. But like so many others, it was not convincing to all those involved.

Sandlin had the genes to become a police officer. His father was a career law enforcement officer, and the young boy never wavered from his decision to follow in his father's footsteps. But just two months into his chosen profession, things went terribly wrong. For the rookie officer, it began with a solo meeting with the chief of police, David Carson. It was not unlike a rookie football player being called into the coach's office and told to bring his playbook. "What I told Steve was, Steve, slow down some; you can't catch everybody. That's not your role," the chief explained. "Just take it easy. And he seemed a little down about that. He wasn't chewed out. It was just a conversation."

Alone in the small police station—containing a force of just three officers, Sandlin talked with his girlfriend, Michelle Sturtevant. It was 7 p.m., May 7, 1988. As reported by "Unsolved Mysteries," Sturtevant said, "We were making plans for the next day." She went on that:

Chief Carson yelled at him to go back into the station. And so he was kind of mad about that. And he said if they want him to be a security guard that he would sit up in the station and be a security guard. And while I was talking to him, a lady's voice came in. He muffled the phone. I couldn't hear what was said, but it sounded like he was getting loud and like she was yelling at him. And he said it was no big deal and he said he had to go."

Forty-five minutes later, Sandlin was found dead in the station. According to Chief Carson, "I saw no evidence of any confrontation, no shots fired, nothing. And from an average person's point of view, it was apparently a suicide." The chief also had an explanation if it was not a suicide. "There was information that came to us that he was prone to play with his gun. I can see the possibility that perhaps he was playing with his gun, and I think that that probably is the strongest possibility in Steve Sandlin's death. The possibility of it going off is tremendous."

The autopsy results came back "inconclusive." Several officials publicly stated that Sandlin was shot from at least two feet away from his body. Additionally, the powder residue on Sandlin's hands was rather insignificant for the hands of someone who had shot himself with a gun. However, the New Mexico Attorney General's Office refused to rule out suicide. The family vehemently disagreed and began its own investigation.

About three weeks before his death, Sandlin had stopped a Manzano, N.M., man named Melvin King for DUI and arrested him. During a search of the car, Officer Sandlin recovered marijuana. This led to a search of King's home, where police seized 54 pounds of marijuana worth more than $100,000—big money for a town of only 1,180. But incredibly, the confiscated marijuana mysteriously disappeared from the nearby Torrance County Sheriff's Office evidence room. King was never prosecuted.

Tom Gillespie, head of the state attorney general's investigation unit, looked into the theft. Evidence emerged that the seized marijuana disappeared from the sheriff's custody before Sandlin was shot. After Sandlin's death, several packages of marijuana were discovered in Sandlin's rental house. Investigators believed this was an attempt to cast doubt on Sandlin. Also recordings of his traffic stops and arrests that he kept at his house went missing.

Immediately after the arrest, Sandlin had received death threats. For the family, this was the smoking gun, proof they wanted investigators to follow up on. But the Attorney General's Office was following another lead.

Spending thousands of hours interviewing witnesses and pursuing leads in the case, agents finally thought their efforts were being rewarded. Attorney general's office investigators were interviewing a person on an unrelated topic when suddenly Sandlin's name came up. The unnamed person related a conversation in which a law enforcement officer from an unnamed agency said he'd killed Sandlin. According to statements, the officer said Sandlin had been walking around the station and sat down to complete some paperwork. As Sandlin turned around to face his attacker, he was shot. The report continued, quoting the unnamed officer as saying "that if he had kept his nose out of things (he'd) be better off. (Sandlin) wouldn't have died."

Within days of the startling revelation, then-Assistant Attorney General James Carnation, who led the investigation, was abruptly fired. Two other agents reassigned. It has yet to be published what became of the interview. Officials said they won't comment on the investigation because it is still active. They added that the firing had nothing to do with the Sandlin case.

Along with former Assistant Attorney General James Yontz, the fired Carnation shot back, issuing a public statement stating that evidence in the attorney general's files showed "people engaged in illegal drug trafficking conspired to kill Officer Sandlin," just as the parents of Sandlin had alleged. The attorneys said they were driven off the case and out of their jobs for pursuing the investigation too aggressively, charges denied by officials.

Questions remain. Did Sandlin discover that the marijuana had been stolen from the evidence room? Was he about to report the missing dope to the AG's Office? Could this be why he was murdered?

The fourth state attorney to consider the death of Sandlin made a pledge in 2013, "I don't think that I can tell you today what the truth is, but it's something that we continue to work on. I have agents that continue to work on this case, and we hope that one day we can find out what occurred to give some closure to the family. And also, if there's anybody still out there that's responsible for this, we still want to bring them to justice."

In 2013, then-Chief of Police Robert Chung, a retired NYPD sergeant, oversaw the building of a monument to honor Officer Sandlin. "Somebody who may not have come forward back then will be moved to do so," Chung said, adding, "Wouldn't it be something if someone just looking at the memorial would be moved to maybe provide the little piece so the attorney general can put it all together?" While the case is still being investigated, it remains unsolved. Officer Sandlin had served with the Mountainair Police Department for just two months. He is survived by his son and girlfriend.

SOURCES:

- http://www.officer.com/article/12293261/police-suicides-in-2016
- https://www.abqjournal.com/201338/officers-death-still-a-mystery-after-25-years-2.html
- http://unsolvedmysteries.wikia.com/wiki/Steve_Sandlin
- http://unsolved.com/archives/steve-sandlin
- https://www.newspapers.com/image/157701140/

CHAPTER 83

One That Got Away

THE OFFICER:

Master Officer Howard Ellsworth Dallies, Jr.
Garden Grove (California) Police Department
End of Watch: Tuesday, March 9, 1993
Age: 36

Unsolved homicides of law enforcement officers, in a profession rife with death, hurts deep down—into one's soul. Knowing the perpetrator is free from having to pay for his or her crime causes untold suffering for those who care. But the worst is when a suspect is arrested for the crime, and it appears like a sure conviction, but then the defendant walks—on a technicality. The disappointment is devastating. Regrettably, this is exactly what happened in the murder of Master Officer Howard Dallies Jr.

At 2:45 a.m., in the 10100 block of Aldgate Avenue, a comfortable middle-class neighborhood of single-family homes, just 3 miles away from Disneyland, everything was quiet, as it should have been. Charles North was reading in bed when he heard, "Pop pop pop, pop pop pop." The sound was so close he thought he was being shot at. Others also heard the gunshots and ran outside to see about the commotion. What they found was Officer Dallies lying in the street with a large pool of blood outlining his body. In a situation like this, people just want to help. One witness gently held Dallies' head in his arms while another used his police radio to call for help

Officer Dallies was working alone, as did all the officers on the Garden Grove Police Department, when he stopped a motorcyclist for reasons that are unknown because he didn't radio in the incident. As the officer stepped from his vehicle, events happened suddenly and without warning. The suspect fired six rounds from a semiautomatic handgun so fast that Dallies never had an opportunity to draw his weapon. He was struck multiple times. One bullet grazed his face, one lodged in his bulletproof vest and the fatal round struck Dallies in the abdomen, just under his vest. As he lay there mortally wounded, he whispered to witnesses that the suspect was a male white, 5-foot-10, 30-35 years old wearing a black leather jacket. Dallies was taken by ambulance to the University of California, Irvine Medical Center, where he died three hours later. The gunman fled on a stolen gray Kawasaki that was later recovered.

After the shooting of Officer Dallies, every available detective from the Garden Grove PD scoured the streets, interviewing informants, drug dealers and the behind-the-scenes scum that attach themselves to communities. But it was a cab driver who was interviewed about a ride he gave a man the night of the shooting that got the investigators pumped. The person identified was John J. Stephens. Although he had a questionable alibi for the night of the shooting, police officials were very interested in him as the man on the motorcycle. Stephens had a lengthy violent criminal record including convictions for assault and battery and brandishing a weapon during a drug deal. In 1993, just days after Dallies was killed, Stephens was arrested for thrashing a man with a hammer. He was later convicted of burglary and shooting a man in an unrelated crime. It was off to prison for Mr. Stephens.

As time passed, detectives, some of whom were retired, kept the case alive and active. They worked thousands of leads and recorded 80,000 pages of investigative notes. They also had time on their side. As four years had passed since the killing of Officer Dallies, many of Stephens, so-called friends began to talk. Police had concluded that Stephens, shot Dallies when he was pulled over on a stolen motorcycle and feared Dallies would arrest him.

A fresh lead in the case came just weeks before Stephens was to be released from prison. Lola Duvall, a former drug addict and girlfriend, broke down and told detectives she would testify against Stephens. She said he had persuaded her to lie by saying he was with her the night of the murder. Duvall further stated that Stephens had gone out that Monday night, and returned the following morning with dyed hair, offering no explanation.

Culminating four years of arduous investigative work, the detectives had all they needed. Just days before he was to be released from prison, investigators traveled to the supermax prison in Tehachapi, went to his cell and arrested Stephens. He was swiftly transported back to Orange County and booked for the murder of Officer Dallies. From this high point of the case, things quickly spiraled downward.

During the preliminary hearing in the summer of 1999, it was alleged that a detective from the Garden Grove Police Department had coerced or even abused two key witnesses. The allegations included that he slapped Duvall, the defendant's girlfriend, and threatened a second witness with having her children taken away if she failed to cooperate.

Although most in the police department, including the future chief of police, thought the detective was innocent, the district attorney's office determined the accusations were too damaging and the case could not be saved. The charges against Stephens were dropped. The accused killer who came into court in restraints left the court by the front door, a free man.

In 2003, Stephens was again arrested for another crime and sentenced to 25 years to life. A fitting end to the murder of Officer Dallies? Difficult to say, but at least the man was in prison—again.

Dallies is survived by his wife, Mary, and their two sons, Christopher and Scott. Dallies began his police career at the age of 17 in the Army's military police. He joined the Garden Grove Police Department in 1984.

SOURCES:

- The Orange County Register as reported by Frank Mickadeit. http://www.ocregister.com/articles/stephens-498646-dallies-police.html
- http://www.ocregister.com/articles/stephens-498838-raney-dallies.html
- https://camemorial.org/honor-roll/tribute/howard-e-dallies-jr/
- http://articles.latimes.com/1993-03-10/news/mn-1033_1_garden-grove-police-department

CHAPTER 84

"Don't move or I'll bust a cap in you"

THE OFFICER:

Detective Lonnie C. Miller Sr.
Jacksonville (Florida) Sheriff's Office
End of Watch: Saturday, May 6, 1995
Age: 62

Veteran Detective Lonnie Miller was not your typical cop. It was probably his black eyepatch that attracted people's attention. It seemed everyone knew the outgoing detective. Celebrities who came to town would often call him for their security needs. Off-duty, Miller was active in his community of Jacksonville, Florida. He was a member of several groups such as the Democratic Executive Committee and the National Council of Negro Women. But more than that, he loved helping the children of the community. In the end, the dedicated cop's desire to do a favor for a friend got him killed.

The fateful call was one that street cops get every shift—a burglary alarm at a local business. Detective Lonnie Miller was just heading home after working the night shift at the Jacksonville Sheriff's Office. As the call came out, Miller recognized the address as a friend's business. He immediately turned around and responded. When he arrived, several patrol cars were already at the scene, along with the owner, Abdullah Shah. Officers quickly determined that it was, as it is most times, a false alarm. As the patrol officers drove off, Miller got out of his car to talk with his good friend Shah.

Miller and Shah had conversed for about 20 minutes when suddenly an African American man walked up and warned them, "Don't move or I'll bust a cap in you!" Without provocation, the suspect fired two rounds into Shah and shot

Miller in the chest before running away. Shah told investigators that he checked on Miller and found that his friend was dead, so he left the scene without calling for help. He drove to University Medical Center for treatment.

Early in the investigation Shah became a suspect in Miller's death, but was soon cleared. However, Miller's friend did raise a question. "If it was a robbery, why didn't they take my money?" said Shah. He had more than $400 in his pockets. "If it was me they were after, they could have made sure they killed me. Maybe if I didn't show up, maybe Lonnie still would have gotten hit." He went on, "It's a helluva psychological thing. You get shot, the man got killed. It's like I couldn't get it back together. This is something you live with the rest of your life."

Over the years, detectives focused on one man as the murderer of Miller, Pressley Alston, a death row inmate who confessed to killing Miller, but later recanted and blamed others for the murder. Detectives weren't buying it. Alston knew facts only the killer could have known. High on the list is a signet ring found at the crime scene belonging to Miller. During one interview, Alston gave detectives a precise description. When investigators checked the ring that was in evidence, a detective said, "We pulled it out and daggone if he ain't right."

While sheriff detectives were convinced they had their man, the DA's office wasn't. Prosecutor Angela Corey questioned whether Alston could even have been at the crime scene. "He has accused everybody in the universe of every crime and has no credibility." She went on, "Pressley has recanted, retracted, re-everything'd on this case. The scary thing is if we had put that murder on him and cleared it and found out he was like he is, where would we be now?" The DA wanted more evidence. Retired Detective Bob Fagan, who was certain it was Alston, wished he could get another chance. "I know one day I'm going to look Lonnie in the eye, give the man a big hug and tell him I did the best I could." The case remains unsolved. Miller was survived by his wife, four sons and a daughter.

SOURCES:

- https://www.odmp.org/officer/823-detective-lonnie-c-miller-sr
- http://www.firstcoastnews.com/news/cold-case-the-murder-of-a-jso-detective/188343400
- http://jacksonville.com/tu-online/stories/100404/met_16808946.shtml#.WWKoVYjytPa
- http://crimefeed.com/2016/05/who-murdered-jacksonville-sheriffs-detective-lonnie-miller/

CHAPTER 85

The Sniper Shooting of a Chief of Police

THE OFFICER:

Chief of Police Bobby Spencer
Shannon (Mississippi) Police Department
End of Watch: Saturday, January 18, 1997
Age: 58

The murder of small-town police chief, an officer who believed the bullet was meant for him and a deathbed confession from a Marine sniper all contribute to a case that remains unsolved.

Officer Steve Whitehead was working the early morning shift that Saturday, January 18, 1997, in the town of Shannon, Mississippi, population 1,600. But because it was so busy, he asked Chief Bobby Spencer to come in and help. Sometime between 4:15 and 4:45 a.m., Spencer drove to the front of the police station. For whatever reason, he got out of his marked police car, leaving the door open and the engine running. As he started down the sidewalk, a single shot from a high-powered rifle struck him in the back of the head. Chief Spencer was dead before he hit the ground. No one was at the station to witness or hear the shot. The other three on-duty officers were booking arrestees into the county jail in Tupelo.

Two Shannon police officers, Carl Trice and James "Stem" McPherson, were returning to the station for the change of shift at 5 a.m. They saw the chief lying on the ground. At first, they supposed he must have had a heart attack, but upon closer inspection, they saw blood. When Officer Whitehead heard the news, he was devastated. Until the day he died 20 years later, he always believed the bullet was intended for him. About six weeks earlier, Whitehead had received a telephone call from a man who said "he would kill me or someone close to

The headline from the Clarion-Ledger, Jackson, Mississippi.

me." He had no idea who the man was.

As investigators from the Mississippi Bureau of Investigation (MBI), the highway patrol and sheriff's department arrived at the scene several hours later, little evidence was discovered. They were all in agreement that the shooter was a long distance from the station and fired one round from a high-powered rifle that was never recovered.

As time passed, it was a lack of cooperation among agencies that riled Trice, the officer who discovered the body. "It just shocked me that the best investigative unit in the state of Mississippi couldn't find one clue," stated Trice. He said that none of the investigating agencies shared anything with Shannon P.D. The chief's widow agreed.

Ten years after the shooting, she said she had never been contacted by detectives about her husband's murder—nothing. "It just makes me feel like he's gone and nobody cares" she said.

During an interview in 2007 with Ashley Elkins from dJournal.com, MBI Col. David Shaw reported, "There are no new leads. To have any chance of solving it, we need someone to come forward with new evidence or new information." In January of 2017, the twenty-year anniversary of the death of Chief Spencer, MBI again declined comment, this time to William Moore, also a reporter with dJournal.com, stating that the agency doesn't discuss ongoing cases.

A revelation came in 2005 that gave substance to Officer Whitehead's statements about the threat he had received and that he was likely the intended target of the bullet that killed the chief. A man (not named as officials said he was never indicted, but that he is now dead) with a criminal record led the Mississippi Highway Patrol on a high-speed pursuit in October 2004. At the termination of the pursuit, the armed suspect shot it out with the police. The attacker was struck by several pellets from a police 12-gauge shotgun. Inside his car, officers found a second weapon and loads of crystal methamphetamine.

Paralyzed and wasting away in a hospital in Atlanta, the former Marine sniper and instructor confessed to killing Chief Spencer. Before he died in February 2005, he told authorities where the shot was taken, which was confidential information that only the police would have known. He described how he cut up the gun and disposed of it piece by piece. The brother of the suspect also said his brother told him he had done it. Jim Johnson, the sheriff from Lee County, passed this incriminating information to MBI but never heard back.

"I hope that there is still someone out there living who knows something and will come forward," the wife of the slain officer said. "Maybe they want to get it off their chest before they die." No one who ever loved the man will ever give up hope.

Chief Spencer was a 23 year veteran in law enforcement and served with the United States Air Force during the Korean War. He was survived by his wife, daughter, and granddaughter.

SOURCES:

- http://djournal.com/news/who-killed-bobby-spencer/
- http://djournal.com/news/hedtwo-years-later-police-chief-bobby-spencers-slaying-remai/
- http://djournal.com/news/bobby-spencer-killing-unsolved-two-decades-later/
- Newspapers.com
- http://www.odmp.org/officer/18722-chief-of-police-bobby-spencer

- http://www.djournal.com/news/crime-law-enforcement/bobby-spencer-killing-unsolved-two-decades-later/article_cb234cad-a9b5-5a46-a00d-001930705384.html
- http://www.clarionledger.com/story/news/local/2017/06/08/police-chief-killed-2-decades-ago-still-not-memorial-wall/101545324/

CHAPTER 86

"Show me out with three"

THE OFFICER:

Officer Davina Buff Jones
Bald Head Island (North Carolina) Police Department
End of Watch: Friday, October 22, 1999
Age: 33

Bald Head Island is a normally quiet village located on the southernmost barrier island of North Carolina, on the ease side of Cape Fear river in Brunswick County. It has a reputation as a playground for the wealthy and for sea turtles. To cops in the area, it is also known for the contentious death of Officer Davina Buff Jones. Some argue that her death was a suicide, while others maintain it was a cold-blooded murder. Jones's death was first classified as a suicide by the local district attorney. His ruling was overturned by his replacement, who changed it to "undetermined." To bury this story as a suicide is not fair to Officer Jones. And if it was a murder, calling it a suicide allows the perpetrator to live life without having to look over his or her shoulder. This case needs to be discussed and reexamined.

To reach Bald Head Island, travelers take a 20-minute ferry ride. Once on the island, you don't need a car—they aren't even allowed for tourist. You either drive a golf cart, ride a bike or walk. The houses dotting the coast are worth millions, as are their owners.

Davina Buff Jones came to work each day using the same mode of transportation as the visitors on the ferry. Jones was a nine-month rookie officer still learning her way through the intricacies of law enforcement. Like most rookie officers, she was aggressive and vigorous in the enforcement of the law, no matter which mansion you owned. There were complaints that she was too energetic—too uncompromising. The barely 5-foot, 100-pound officer didn't change her ways for anyone.

On Friday night, October 22, 1999, she was on patrol near the Old Baldy Lighthouse. Built in 1817, it was a renowned landmark in North Carolina. The area had a reputation for drug dealers peddling their poison. Just before midnight, Jones radioed in to dispatch: "C-COM, 4206. Show me out with three. Stand by, please." Then quiet. A few minutes later, another broadcast. "There ain't no reason to have a gun here on Bald Head Island, OK?" Not panicked, she said, "You wanna put down the gun. Come on, do us a favor and put down—." Then only loud, distorted feedback.

Her partner that night, Officer Keith Cain (or Cane), was at the police station. After Jones failed to respond to repeated requests for her status, Cain began a search of the island. Not knowing her whereabouts, Cain took 15 minutes to find his partner. She was on the ground next to her police vehicle. She had been shot in the back of the head and was dead.

As the investigation by the Brunswick County Sheriff's Department got underway, officials became aware that Jones had made 170 visits to a psychiatrist over a five-year period. Three days before she died, she talked about suicide with her doctor, and she was on antidepressants. For those who saw this only as a suicide, what more did they need? However, the doctor said she was at "low risk" for suicide when she left the office.

While it may be tempting to just categorize the death of Officer Jones as a suicide because she was having personal issues, it flies in the face of logic and circumstantial evidence. For starters, the crime scene was in shambles. A bloody palm print on the back of Jones's truck, drag marks and blood splatters could not be investigated properly because the fire chief ordered the crime scene hosed off. With a torrent of water, most of the evidence was washed away. When asked why, the fire chief pointed out that a prominent Bald Head Island family was hosting a wedding the next day and did not want the newlyweds to look at blood splattered on the ground. Years later, the North Carolina Industrial Commission noted that "the crime scene had been annihilated, was annihilated. It was destroyed."

Then-Chief of Police Karen Grasty was having no part of the suicide theory. She believed Jones interrupted a large drug deal. For several months, allegations of drug trafficking had been rampant in the community. At 6 a.m. the day after the murder, three men tried to sneak off the island on the ferry. They were caught and questioned briefly, but were soon allowed to continue. When Chief Grasty attempted to reinterview them on the mainland, she was told by an unnamed official to "just let it lie." After all, the source said, they were good Christians. Despite the warning, Grasty continued her investigation. She found that between two of the men, they had a 48-page rap sheet. The three were never charged in the case. Several hearings were conducted to hear testimony from experts to decide on the manner of the officer's death. On one such occasion, a commissioner wrote:

> *To self-inflict a gunshot wound to the posterior mid line of her head and accomplish a slight upwards trajectory, she would have had to have aimed the gun at the front of her face with her thumb on the trigger, then raised her arms over her head so that the gun would be in the mid line, and upside down. In this position, the Glock would have ejected the casing to the left. The casing was found to the right of her body.*

Despite the pieces that didn't line up, Brunswick District Attorney Rex Gore determined the cause of death to be suicide. He slammed the lid on the case and refused several requests to reopen the investigation. His words were, "Only God and Officer Jones know what really happened."

The family and loved ones of Officer Jones thought the ruling preposterous. They appealed the suicide verdict to North Carolina Industrial Commission which rules on police pensions. The commission had two options. Families of police officers killed in the line of duty are entitled to death benefits. Officers who take their own lives are not. To make their decision on Jones, commission members reviewed the written reports of experts who had investigated her death and presented their analysis and opinions.

On July 19, 2004, a final ruling was made. "The determination of suicide is very unlikely," the report said, "and the Commission finds that plaintiff (Jones's father) has proven by sufficient evidence that her manner of death was not suicide but rather by homicide." The family felt vindicated. But the state did not—they filed an appeal to a three-person panel for another round of examinations.

The case went through an appellate process, pushed along by District Attorney Gore. It found its way back to a second Industrial Commission. Another appeal was brought before the U.S. Department of Justice in 2006. Both rulings came down together, and both pointed to a homicide.

This time the commission reached the same verdict but doubled its previous awards to the family. The feds wrote that there was "substantial and significant doubt as to suicide." They also pointed out "the existence of some investigative biases in focus, coverage and thoroughness of activity." They continued, "there were some prime suspect leads which appear not to have been pursued...." The federal government awarded the family $147,000.

As DA Gore left office in 2010, he refused to accept the possibility of a homicide and kept the case closed to any new investigations. Newly elected District Attorney Jon David had other thoughts. "By our action today, I'm officially changing the designation by the District Attorney's Office in the death of Davina Buff Jones to undetermined," David said. "I do that because a process was put into place that called into question an earlier decision by this agency." He added, "We are able to say conclusively that the earlier determination of suicide is not appropriate in light of what we now know." He declared that the file should remain open and all new leads pursued.

Note: I could not find any listing on ODMP or the National Law Enforcement Officers Fund for Davina Buff Jones. That should be changed.

SOURCES:

- http://listverse.com/2015/12/09/10-bizarre-unsolved-mysteries-involving-police-officers/
- Portcitydaily.com reported by Caroline Curran on December 17, 2013. http://portcitydaily.com/2013/12/17/brunswick-da-changes-cause-of-death-of-bald-head-island-police-officer-from-suicide-to-undetermined/
- "11 Eyewitness News," reported by Kelli O'Hara, May 15, 2012. http://abc11.com/archive/8661279/
- Charlotte Magazine, by Adam Rhew. Published March 19, 2014. http://www.charlottemagazine.com/Charlotte-Magazine/April-2014/Shadows-by-the-Sea/
- Forbes, reported by Stacy Dittrich, June 25, 2012. https://www.forbes.com/sites/crime/2012/06/25/analysis-of-13-year-mysterious-death-of-cape-fear-police-woman/3/#2a46fa037638
- Newspapers.com

CHAPTER 87

Always on Duty

THE OFFICER:

Officer Joseph Jerome Daniels
Birmingham (Alabama) Police Department
End of Watch: Monday, November 18, 2002
Age: 31

There is an axiom in law enforcement that an officer is never off-duty. You may work for 10 hours, but the other 14 you are expected to protect yourself, your family and the community. If an unlawful event takes place, you are either an excellent witness or, depending on the circumstances, you put yourself in harm's way. That is the life of a law enforcement officer.

Off-duty Birmingham Police Officer Joseph Daniels was hungry on the night of November 18, 2002, so he decided to eat at Reno Chicken & Burgers located on Graymont Avenue, near his home. Dressed in his street clothes, Daniels was waiting to eat his dinner when a masked gunman burst into the business. He ordered everyone inside to get on the floor and fired several rounds into the ceiling. When an employee was slow to react, he shot him in the back.

Daniels had a few seconds to formulate a plan. He pulled his gun, firing at the robber. His shots missed their mark. The suspect then directed all his attention at Daniels. There was a struggle, and the crook managed to shoot Daniels several times in the chest. He then fled. But even though he was mortally wounded, Daniels chased his killer out of the store. He collapsed and died after just a few steps.

Detectives had a few suspects in mind but were not able to bring any suspects to trial. Time started to work against the investigators. Soon, eight years had passed, and still no arrest.

Current Chief of Police A.C. Roper and lead detective Jody Jacobs had enough. They wanted results and refused to give up on the case. At a press conference in 2010, exactly eight years after the murder of Officer Daniels, these dedicated officers brought renewed attention and focus to the cold case.

With a large contingent of officers in attendance, Chief Roper pleaded with the community for help. "His family deserves closure, and the city needs justice in this case. Our detectives are still actively investigating this homicide and believe strongly that the information needed to identify and prosecute the person that is responsible for the officer's death is still out there." Roper said. "Someone knows, and I am asking you to get the courage and call." Officials were able to raise $32,000 in reward money for information leading to the arrest and conviction of Daniels' killer.

After the press conference, investigators crossed their collective fingers and hoped someone would come forward with the clue they needed to break open the cold case.

No luck. But no giving up, either. The team of Detective Jacobs and his chief of police kept the case alive. A year and a half later, in 2012, the Birmingham Police Department finally thought they had their man. Adam Bradford, who was 31, was serving time in the St. Clair Correctional Facility on unrelated charges. He had a record of burglary from motor vehicles, theft and robbery. He was in prison for a robbery conviction. He was now charged with capital murder in the shooting death of Daniels and attempted murder in the shooting of the employee during the robbery. Detective Jacobs did not reveal how Bradford's name came up, but he did indicate that he had been a prime suspect since day one.

As happy as the detectives were, Daniels' mother was near speechless after suffering through a decade of grief. "I am extremely proud of our cold case unit and their efforts in this case. These detectives chased down every lead, some involving out of town travel. The citizens of Birmingham should be proud of their professionalism and dedication to duty, not just in this case but on a daily basis," Mrs. Daniels said.

In early 2014, as the case was going to trial, Jefferson County Deputy District Attorney Joe Roberts filed a motion to dismiss the case against Adam Bradford without prejudice. "At this time, the State of Alabama does not have sufficient available, credible and admissible evidence to prosecute the case," Roberts said. Alaric May, one of several attorneys for Bradford, said the dismissal came about after his team met with prosecutors. The defense attorneys claimed they had interviewed 68 witnesses in the case. Because of these interviews, the defense believed it had identified the real killer. As of this writing, no other suspect has been charged with the murder of Officer Daniels, and the case remains unsolved. Bradford was still in prison (for his earlier robbery conviction) in 2014, but his lawyers were attempting to get him released. Officer Daniels was survived by a son.

SOURCES:

- http://www.odmp.org/officer/16458-officer-joseph-jerome-daniels
  http://blog.al.com/spotnews/2010/11/birmingham_police_ask_for_help.html
- http://blog.al.com/spotnews/2012/07/birmingham_police_announce_arr_2.html
- http://www.wbrc.com/story/19124707/slain-officers-partner-jumped-for-joy-when-police-charged-suspect?clienttype=printable

CHAPTER 88

The Case of the White Van

THE OFFICER:

Deputy Sheriff Jeffrey Vaughn Mitchell
Sacramento County (California) Sheriff's Department
End of Watch: Friday, October 27, 2006

There was a lot going against Deputy Sheriff Jeffrey Mitchell that Thursday night in 2006. He was working a one-man unit. Backup was not close. It was morning watch, meaning most people were home asleep, and those that weren't could mean trouble. And he was patrolling in a rural area, implying no witnesses.

At 3:27 a.m., Deputy Mitchell was at the intersection of Meiss and Dillard roads near Highway 16, which leads to Highway 49 and Plymouth, a famous historical area near where gold was discovered. Mitchell, a nine-year veteran of the Sacramento County Sheriff's Department, had observed a white Chevrolet van that appeared to have no license plates. He contacted sheriff's dispatch from his vehicle computer, saying he was going to stop the van, and he gave his location. He stated that the van contained one person. There were no more transmissions from Mitchell. When dispatch attempted to contact the deputy, there was no reply.

Immediately, other patrol units were dispatched to the location of the traffic stop. Upon their arrival, deputies discovered Mitchell mortally wounded at the rear of his vehicle. Deputy Mitchell had been shot in the head with his own service weapon. Evidence at the scene indicated that Mitchell was involved in a violent struggle for his life. Hundreds of law enforcement officers converged on the area in the search for the white van. According to then-Sheriff John McGuinness, it appeared Mitchell had drawn his weapon and may have been trying to place the driver in custody or detain him when he was shot.

The intersection of Meiss and Dillard roads where Deputy Sheriff Jeffrey Mitchell spotted a suspicious white van. Google maps.

Just a few hours later, officers located a white Chevy van in 18 inches of water in the Cosumnes River in El Dorado County, not far from the shooting scene. The van did have a plate, but it was damaged and bent up. Inside the van, officials found the bodies of Allan Shubert and Nicole Welch, who, it was later determined, had died of carbon monoxide poisoning.

As the result of years of work, detectives do not believe Shubert and Welch were participants in the murder of Deputy Mitchell, and their deaths very well could have been an accident. But they do think the two dead bodies are connected in some way to

Mitchell's murder. One theory is that the bodies were in the van the night Mitchell stopped it and his death could perhaps have been part of a cover-up. Many think it was no coincidence that the van ended up in the river after the shooting.

"The white van is the right direction," said the lead detective, Tony Turnbull, in 2011. "I don't have a crystal ball. I wasn't there that night. Is there a chance something different happened that night? Sure, but everything we have…points to the van."

DNA recovered from the scene was not enough for testing, but authorities are hoping that in future years, it can be. It could be the glue that seals the case. A criminalist was assigned to the case full time.

With more than 4,000 tips and 200 notebooks filled with notes, officials have positive feelings that the case will be solved. A sheriff's spokesman said Mitchell's killing remains a "dark cloud" over everyone in the department. "We lost a brother, a co-worker, and justice hasn't been done." Deputy Mitchell is survived by his wife, Crystal, and a son.

SOURCES:

- http://www.sacsheriff.com/Pages/Services/MemorialPages/mitchell.aspx
- http://www.sacbee.com/news/local/crime/article2581679.html
- http://sacramento.cbslocal.com/2011/08/18/wife-of-murdered-deputy-speaks-out/
- http://www.sfgate.com/bayarea/article/SACRAMENTO-COUNTY-Search-for-shooting-suspect-2485774.php
- http://www.lawenforcementtoday.com/after-5-years-deputy-jeff-mitchells-shooting-death-remains-unsolved/

CHAPTER 89

Sacred Ground

THE OFFICER:

Police Officer Thomas T. Wood
Maywood (Illinois) Police Department
End of Watch: Monday, October 23, 2006
Age: 37

It's not the best of neighborhoods, but for Mrs. Helene Wood, that's not an issue. For her, where she stood was sacred ground. Sacred because it was where her husband of eight years, Police Officer Thomas Wood, was gunned down. Struggling to cope with his death, Helene visited the site often. It was on the first anniversary of his murder that she and her five kids lit some candles in a makeshift memorial for their dad and husband. Neighbors, on edge because of gang activity in the area, called police.

Quickly a police car showed up, then another and another. Soon, the disturbance call turned into a solemn tribute to the slain officer. From this chance meeting, an annual vigil and tradition has begun. Now, on every 23rd of October, the Maywood Police Department's third shift conducts roll call at the very spot where Wood was killed. Ten years later, there are officers who were in high school when Wood was shot, paying their respects to a man they never met.

It has been a decade since the murder of Wood, and the case remains unsolved. Ask why and be prepared to be bombarded with finger-pointing, name-calling, and assorted acquisitions. Just before 11 p.m. on October 23, 2006, Officer Wood and his K9 partner responded to an unknown problem at the parking lot of a closed business. Providing backup was Officer Robert Welch. After the two officers determined nothing was wrong, Welch headed for the station, as their shift was just ending. As he drove off, he noticed that Wood was driving toward home.

For whatever reason, Wood didn't drive home. Instead, he drove his marked SUV police vehicle to the intersection of Sixth Avenue and Erie Street, where he had responded earlier to a drug-related call. He stopped in front of 319 N. Sixth Ave. This was an area of known gang and drug activity. He talked

A contemporary photograph of the area around 319 N. Sixth Ave. at the intersection of Erie Street, where Officer Thomas Wood was gunned down by unknown assistants while he sat in his patrol car. Google Maps.

with radio dispatch two times just after 11 o'clock. Sitting in front of the house was a white Pontiac Grand Prix. Wood ran the license plate. He then phoned the girlfriend of a reputed Maywood gang member, who was the registered owner.

October 23 was an unseasonably cold night, with temperatures in the low 30s—a night when most drivers would have their windows up. Wood had his window partially down. Most investigators theorize that he either recognized someone or was talking to a person standing in the street who did not alarm him. He had his foot on the brake, and the SUV was in drive. Suddenly shots erupted. Witnesses reported hearing multiple rounds being fired. Wood was struck in the head and upper body with bullets from a likely .380 hand gun. He died at the scene.

The first witness to arrive at the scene was a former Maywood cop, Robert Novak, who lived in the area. He had left the department because of unspecified complaints against him. The former officer said he heard gunshots about 11:15 p.m., went to the scene and, seeing that Wood's SUV was still in drive, reached in and put it in park. He stated later that he was worried the car might roll forward.

Arriving Maywood officers interviewed Novak but did not remove him from the crime scene. According to Novak, "I helped them look for evidence, and made them coffee." As additional senior officers arrived, Novak quickly went from being a witness to a prime suspect in the murder of Wood.

Novak had a sordid history with Maywood PD. Police had been called to Novak's home 81 times in the previous seven years. The calls ranged from domestic complaints to neighbor disputes. Officer Wood had responded to many of these calls, and Novak made it clear that he did not like Wood. The ex-cop complained to supervisors about Wood's handling of the quarrelsome calls. Simply stated, the men did not get along.

Within hours of the shooting, former Mayfield police officer Novak was handcuffed and arrested for the murder of Wood. Investigators searched his home, interrogated him extensively and administered a polygraph test. His skin was tested for gunshot residue and his .380 handgun to see if it was the murder weapon. Although detectives told him he failed several of the tests, Novak was never charged and is no longer a person of interest in the case.

Perhaps no one outside the police department, and perhaps even within, is more familiar with the killing of Wood than reporters Dane Placko and Robert Herguth.

Beginning in 2011, motivated by what they saw as Maywood's bungling of the case, the duo spent nine months "tracking down witnesses, suspects, police and politicians connected to the case." In their 2012 *Chicago Magazine* article, the authors identified "numerous problems with the investigation."

The Maywood Police Department made errors. Officers took down the wrong house without a warrant. They allowed a suspect to wander around the crime scene. They removed wanted posters because of a mistaken belief that the reward money was no longer available. And some have questioned why they didn't interview some of the individuals Wood had been associated with around the time he was murdered.

But conceivably, the largest hurdle to overcome was the decision by then-Chief Elvia Williams to ask for the help of the West Suburban Major Crimes Task Force. WESTAF is an association of investigators from police departments in the western suburbs of Chicago. As Maywood was not part of WESTAF, many thought the group could not fully understand who the local criminals were, as did the local detectives. Meanwhile, some WESTAF members were aware of the history of corruption and reported brutality on the Maywood Police Department. The result was bickering and lack of cooperation. Both organizations pursued their own leads.

Maywood investigators questioned a reputed street gang member who lived in the area and had even once rented an apartment to Wood. Later, Wood had arrested the alleged gang thug with an illegal gun in 2005. It was this girlfriend of this suspect that Wood called just before being shot. Maywood officials thought they had broken open the case, only to be told by WESTAF, which included the county prosecutor, that the informant was not credible on any level.

While Maywood investigators were pursuing their lead, WESTAF went after Terry Gilford, the driver of the Grand Prix whom Wood had been investigating the night of his murder. But Gilford had an alibi that he was with his mistress the night of the shooting. She lived near the crime scene, and Gilford argued that was why his car was parked on North Sixth Avenue. It was reported that some among the Maywood police believed that WESTAF had the wrong guy. This is how it went between the competing agencies, with the net result of zero arrest.

In 2016, Maywood Police Chief Valdimir Talley said there would be a renewed effort to solve the case through re-examination of the evidence, DNA testing and the possibility that two TV crime shows might feature the case. "I owe it to the family to bring closure," Talley stated. "I'm definitely committed to getting this resolved."

Meanwhile, Mrs. Wood, a widow for 10 years, says she is hopeful, but not overly optimistic, that the case will be solved. She maintains that the initial investigation was not handled properly: "They don't really have anything. What are they going to do with nothing?" But one thing is for sure: On October 23 of every year, she will be at Tom's corner. "[I'll be here] every year—until I can't walk anymore."

Officer Wood was survived by his wife, five children, three brothers, one sister, his father, and a large extended family.

SOURCES:

- "Maywood Confidential: The Unsolved Murder of Police Officer Tom Wood" for Chicago Magazine, published August 14, 2012. By Robert Herguth and Dane Placko. http://www.chicagomag.com/Chicago-Magazine/September-2012/The-Unsolved-Murder-of-Maywood-Police-Officer-Tom-Wood/index.php?cparticle=4&siarticle=3#artanc
- https://www.fbi.gov/wanted/seeking-info/officer-thomas-t.-wood
- http://chicago.suntimes.com/politics/maywood-cop-tom-wood-murder-unsolved-10-years-watchdogs/
- https://thevillagefreepress.org/2014/10/24/on-eighth-year-anniversary-of-his-death-slain-maywood-cop-tom-wood-still-remembered/

CHAPTER 90

"If I get stopped, I'm gonna kill the cop"

THE OFFICER:

Sergeant Christopher Reyka
Broward County (Florida) Sheriff's Office
End of Watch: Friday, August 10, 2007
Age: 51

It happened fast and without warning. At 1:20 a.m., Sgt. Christopher Reyka was on patrol at the rear of Walgreens when he was gunned down without ever drawing his weapon. Despite a massive manhunt and an unheard-of $270,000 reward, the baffling case has never been solved. Through the ensuing 10 years, two different set of suspects have been identified as the focus of the investigation. One suspect is dead, the others are in prison.

Broward County Sheriff Sgt. Christopher Reyka was an expert at locating stolen vehicles. He just had that knack, like a slugger in baseball. He received several commendations and was twice chosen as officer of the month for his diligence in recovering stolen vehicles. On Friday, August 10, 2007, Reyka silently pulled his marked patrol vehicle behind Walgreens Pharmacy at 960 Pompano Parkway in Pompano Beach, Florida.

Sgt. Reyka was aware that over the past several months a gang of robbers had been targeting 24-hour pharmacies in the area—many of them Walgreens. The thugs were after prescription drugs, which they easily sold on the streets. As he pulled into the rear parking lot, he observed two vehicles idling, and he parked in the back of the lot, which was dimly lit. As he pulled behind the cars, he entered the first plate into his terminal as a Florida license plate, F168UJ. He was told the plate was stolen.

It was at the rear of this Walgreens that Sgt. Christopher Reyka was killed. Google Maps.

As one of the cars abruptly started to move, Reyka hit his emergency lights and exited his vehicle. As he did so, an unknown person fired 10 rounds from a 9 mm semiautomatic pistol, striking the sergeant five times in areas not protected by his vest. Deputies found Reyka slumped against his vehicle, his weapon still in its holster. A review of video evidence showed a white 1995-2004 Crown Victoria or Mercury Grand Marquis speeding off. The car has never been recovered.

Four months after his murder, 11 suspects in the drugstore robberies were arrested. Three were singled out as possible suspects in the murder of Sgt. Reyka: Timothy "Black Arms" Johnson, 24, who was convicted of robbery and weapons charges and sentenced to life; Gerald "Dread" Joshua, 28, who was awaiting trial on multiple robbery and weapons charges and had 32 arrests on his rap sheet; and Detrick "Real Deal" Johnson, 22, who also had charges pending against him.

"We think it's definitely not a coincidence that Chris [Reyka] was killed at a drugstore," Sheriff Al Lamberti said at the time. "With a rash of robberies before and robberies afterwards, then the arrests were made. Now [the robberies] have stopped. We think Chris interrupted something at that drugstore."

According to Dan Riemer, a local private investigator examining the case, he identified Gerald Joshua as the triggerman in the murder. His cohort, Timothy Johnson's siblings, Allen Johnson and Consuela Jones, allegedly disposed of four guns linked to the drugstore robberies, one of which officials reportedly believed was used to kill Reyka. Three of the guns were found in a canal, but a fourth gun—the possible murder weapon—is still missing. Deputies charged Consuela Jones with tampering with evidence.

Security cam footage of the 1995-2004 Ford Crown Victoria or Mercury Grand Marquis leaving the scene of the shooting just minutes after Sgt. Reyka was shot.

As the years rolled by, sheriff's detectives have ruled out the robbery gang as murder suspects. But ever since the shooting, one suspect keeps gaining more and more attention, Shawn LaBeet, a 25-year-old who was shot to death by police just a month after the Reyka shooting. Years later, his nephew, Jaleel Torres, provided some insight into the man as Torres sat in prison for drug convictions.

In an interview with Michael E. Miller of the *Miami New Times*, the heavily tattooed Torres made it clear he was tight with his uncle: "No bullshit, I was probably the closest person to him." He described LaBeet as a "regular" guy who had early run-ins with the law when he was a juvenile. From that point on, he had an extreme hatred for anyone wearing a badge. LaBeet, who had done hard time, told his nephew, "I'll never go to jail again."

To prove his point, he nearly always carried an AK-47 in his car and a loaded pistol in his waistband. "He'd tell you when you got in his car: 'If I get stopped, I'm gonna kill the

Jaleel Torres, the nephew of Shawn LaBeet, showing off his tattoos while in prison for drug convictions.

cop.'" Torres went on to say that LaBeet spoke to him only a few days after the murder of Sgt. Reyka. "I had a dream," his uncle allegedly said. "I had a dream about being in a shootout with police." Torres added that it seemed many of LaBeet's dreams turned out to be reality.

This pattern of hatred of cops morphed into real-life actions. Torres said LaBeet bragged about "taking a potshot" at a police car in Naranja, which was substantiated by detectives. The case was never solved, and the officer was not hit. LaBeet told how he killed a man near his Naranja apartment when the man attempted to steal his beloved bulldog.

Once again, the episode matches an unsolved murder in 2006, when a man by the name of Sasha Henderson was shot two blocks from LaBeet's house by a man in a mask with an AK-47, LaBeet's weapon of choice.

The Broward County Sheriff's Office had not focused on any one suspect until approximately two years after the shooting, when detectives uncovered new evidence that pointed to LaBeet. They obtained sworn statements from two witnesses that place LaBeet near the scene of Reyka's shooting the night the incident occurred. LaBeet was already wanted for shooting his girlfriend at the time Reyka was shot.

The department has received over 3,000 tips related to the case, with LaBeet mentioned repeatedly. Police have stressed that LaBeet is their most likely culprit because of "powerful and compelling evidence." The lead detective in the case, John Curcio, said that LaBeet is the only suspect who can be tied to the scene, to the same type of getaway car and to the type of weapon used to kill Reyka. "When you look at those three factors…Shawn LaBeet moves ahead of every other tip." But

Shawn LaBeet, the primary individual who is the focus of the investigation into the murder of Sgt. Reyka.

with no murder weapon, and the car never recovered, it has been difficult for detectives to gather enough evidence to clear the case with LaBeet as the murderer.

LaBeet continually boasted he would never go back to jail. He told relatives that if the police tried to arrest him, he "would go out in a blaze of glory" and the people "would hear about it on the news."

His blaze of glory began on the morning of September 13, 2007, just 33 days after the murder of Reyka. LaBeet was furious about a confrontation he'd had with a staff member at a veterinarian's office about the age of his dog. Storming out of the clinic in a rage, LaBeet drove like a wildman. According to his girlfriend, "He was driving kind of fast and taking the corners kind of shaky."

Miami-Dade officers Jose Somohano and Christopher Carlin, patrolling in plain clothes in an unmarked car, spotted LaBeet's maroon Buick LeSabre racing down the road. They turned around to investigate. As they did so, they saw LaBeet stop his vehicle and run into a backyard (later determined to be his). Both officers gave chase. Several large barking dogs kept the two officers from jumping the fence. At this time, LaBeet's girlfriend pulled up in a white Honda. They asked her who was at home, and she replied that it was her boyfriend. She allowed them inside.

As they entered the house, they saw LaBeet in the backyard. After they eyed each other, LaBeet took off. Once again, the officers went into a foot pursuit of the suspect. But LaBeet, who graduated from high school with a 4.0 GPA, was a crafty individual. He circled around back to the house, where he donned a bulletproof vest and grabbed his trusted AK-47.

Officer Somohano was the first to reach the house and went straight to the front door. As he reached for the doorknob, LaBeet, standing in the doorway, opened fire, spraying rounds and striking Somohano in the head. LaBeet then walked outside, stood over the dying Somohano and pumped several more rounds into him.

Officer Carlin heard the firing and ran to the front of the house, only to see his partner's lifeless body on the ground. Carlin's attention was then drawn to the white Honda, with LaBeet now sitting in the driver's seat and his girlfriend standing next to the car. Carlin commanded LaBeet to get out of the car. The cop killer answered with another fusillade of bullets, hitting Carlin in the right leg. At that moment two more officers arrived. As soon as LaBeet saw them, he opened fire. LaBeet hit officer Jody Wright in the right leg, shattering her femur. Officer Tomas Tundidor was also shot. With three officers wounded on the ground, and one dead, LaBeet sped off in the Honda.

LaBeet went to a friend's house, with his dog in the backseat. He told Lazaro Guardiola, "I just shot a cop; you got to get me out of here." LaBeet quickly ditched his Honda, his vest and the AK-47. He shaved his beard in the bathroom sink. Guardiola and two others drove him to a remote spot in north Miami-Dade County. He next called his brother Shane, yelling, "I'm in trouble, I'm in trouble!" Shane agreed to pick him up on the turnpike. After a short time, concerned about his children in the car, Shane dropped LaBeet at the home of his nephew, Jaleel Torres. Shane never notified the police.

A short time later, approximately three hours after the death of Officer Somohano, police found LaBeet's car. The dog inside was shot to death. Police located the AK-47, vest and croppings from his beard. Police also located LaBeet's nephew, Jaleel Torres, who had taken LaBeet to Pembroke Pines apartment complex. LaBeet asked Torres to bring him women's clothes. Torres refused and called police to tell them that LaBeet was hiding in a bathroom near the complex's pool.

The Miami-Dade SWAT team arrived, now 13 hours after the death of Somohano. When SWAT team members approached, LaBeet fired on them. Officers returned fire and hit LaBeet with 15 rounds. He died at the scene wearing a woman's wig and makeup. He remains the primary person of interest in the case.

Jumping ahead to July 2016, the latest class of graduates from the Broward County Sheriff's Office was proudly awaiting to be sworn in as deputies. Among its members was Autumn Reyka, daughter of Sgt. Christopher Reyka. She was chosen to address the large crowd in attendance. "I know I've shared with a few of you what it's like to be a daughter of a fallen officer," she said. "Do everything in your power not be the reason your loved ones are waking up to a knock on the door in the middle of the night and you're not standing behind it." Standing humbly alongside her, was her brother, Deputy Sean Reyka, who was there to present his sister her graduation certificate. In her closing remarks, Autumn Reyka gave her classmates sound advice: "Have your head on a swivel and watch your six." If only their dad could have been there, what a happy celebration it would have been.

Sgt. Reyka was a veteran of the U.S. Marine Corps. He'd worked for 18 years with the Broward County Sheriff's Office. He was active in his church and in his community, participating in fundraising events for Special Olympics and serving as a scoutmaster with the Boy Scouts. He left behind a wife, two sons and two daughters.

SOURCES:

- http://miami.cbslocal.com/2013/07/02/bso-announcing-new-details-in-reyka-murder-case/
- http://kidnappingmurderandmayhem.blogspot.com/2010/10/267000-reward-offered-for-slaying-of.html
- http://www.browardpalmbeach.com/news/pi-says-sgt-chris-reyka-murder-case-is-solved-6437489
- http://www.mypalmbeachpost.com/news/wellington-sgt-reyka-was-victim-cop-killer/i6205BqNNwGttFs08arHAP/
- http://www.mypalmbeachpost.com/news/crime--law/day-dallas-ambush-daughter-fallen-sgt-reyka-becomes-deputy/Jo27lDEiHEd873gM5L16lO/

- http://www.palmbeachpost.com/news/crime--law/new-evidence-murder-broward-sheriff-sgt-chris-reyka-wellington-points-man-who-died-2007-shootout/7J4ldCRtaE4mapGcDMFrsI/
- http://www.miaminewtimes.com/news/chris-reyka-killing-investigation-leads-to-polk-county-prison-and-convicted-drug-dealer-6554361

CHAPTER 91

Murder or Suicide—Which Was It?

THE OFFICER:

Sgt. Sean Thomas Drenth
Phoenix (Arizona) Police Department
End of Watch: Monday, October 18, 2010
Age: 34

As I have written too many times in *Unsolved*, when a law enforcement officer is the victim of an on-duty violent death, clues almost always provide enough evidence to determine what happened and, most times, who did it. But occasionally, evidence can be interrupted to suggest, or even prove, that the victim took his or her own life—a suicide. But even that conclusion can be exceedingly controversial. There is tremendous pressure on detectives and the coroner to make the right call. If investigators rule that a death was a suicide, and they are wrong, then a cop killer is walking free, never having to look back again. On these close ones, it is difficult to even get forensic experts to agree. The death of Sgt. Sean Drenth, a well-liked 12-year veteran of the Phoenix Police Department, has confounded police officials since he was found, sprawled on his back, dead from a shotgun blast. Did Drenth take his own life, or was the sergeant murdered?

On the evening of Monday, October 18, 2010, one of the most dreaded calls officers receive came over the radio: "All units—officer down!" The location for the call was a dirt area next to a parking lot a half-mile south of the Arizona Capitol building, near 18th Avenue and Jackson Street. A Capitol police official discovered the body of Sgt. Drenth and called Phoenix police. First responders found Drenth on his back, near his marked police vehicle. A 38-inch-long Remington 870 shotgun was lying lengthwise on Drenth's body. The muzzle of the weapon was just a few inches below the contact wound, which was just under the chin.

Adding to the developing mystery, detectives located Drenth's service pistol on the other side of a chain-link fence that bordered the area. His handcuffs, cellphone, and flashlight were found on the ground near his body, as was his backup revolver. It appeared that the revolver had been fired. The sergeant's uniform was dirty, and he had fresh cuts on both hands. Evidence suggested that a struggle took place, then a murder.

But while many supported this theory, especially those who knew him best, others were skeptical. These individuals were convinced it was a suicide made to look like a murder. Why, they exclaimed, would suspects overpower Drenth, run to the car, figure out how to remove the shotgun, place it under his chin and pull the trigger? The cynics argued that the suspects could have simply shot him with one of his two handguns.

The debate over murder or suicide began minutes after officers arrived at the crime scene and has not diminished in the ensuing eight years. A police homicide sergeant who was at the scene from the beginning was so sure it was suicide, he left a few hours later to attend a seminar. This contrasts with the views of the lead detective, a seasoned veteran homicide detective, who was convinced it was a murder made to look like a suicide.

Still others point out that Sgt. Drenth and several colleagues had been under criminal investigation for allegedly overcharging for off-duty security work. They say Drenth was so shaken by the investigation that he took his life. But friends and relatives swear that there's no way the inquiry would have bothered him, especially to cause him to take his own life. They were somewhat vindicated later when a judge threw out the overcharging case because there was a lack of proof to substantiate the charge.

A year after the sergeant's death, Phoenix pathologist Dr. Robert Lyon ruled that Sean Drenth had killed himself and that his death was a suicide. It was a "WTF" moment, said the sergeant's mother, echoing what many others felt. One of these was Dr. Vincent DiMaio, a leading pathologist from Houston who was a consultant for the Phoenix PD on the case. He told Paul Rubin, a reporter for *Phoenix New Times*: "I don't agree with the assessment that this was a suicide." He pointed out that suicide seems too obvious due to the nature of the wound. He went on, "Too many things happened out there to make this a clear-cut ruling. If you're going to commit suicide, why bother getting the shotgun out? You've got two guns on your body. If you went there to commit suicide, this is a bizarre way [to] try to make it look like murder."

Several firearms specialists point to the "recoil factor" as a key to the case. When the body was discovered, the muzzle of the powerful shotgun was just four inches from the entry wound on the chin. Ballistics experts said that if Drenth had fired the fatal round, the instantaneous loss of muscle control and the recoil of the gun would have sent the muzzle as much as a foot and a half from his chin.

Jon Colvin, a Phoenix private investigator who spent scores of hours on the case, said, "He was murdered while kneeling or standing by people he had gone out there to meet for reasons we still don't know. They placed the shotgun on his body, which is how it was found."

There has been no trial to determine what happened to Sgt. Drenth, no grand jury testimony, no formal police hearing. But what is the nearest thing to a trial occurred in front of the Phoenix Police Pension Board. After the initial ruling of suicide by the pathologist, Colleen Drenth was given less than 50 percent of her husband's pension. The amount was also taxed. Seeking vindication, Colleen and family members hired a shooting reconstruction expert, a medical investigator and a forensic psychiatrist. Their testimony was put in detailed reports that were submitted to the pension board in 2013. After the submission, the pension board was to make a final ruling on whether the death was in the line of duty (murder) or suicide.

The specialists raised substantial questions to the veracity of the medical examiner's conclusion. They highlighted the position of Drenth's body as being "inconsistent with suicide." They added that the pump-action shotgun had been prepared to fire again after the weapon had fired the fatal shot, indicating someone else would have had to have done it. They also pointed out that the shotgun could not have been positioned on the body like it was found because of the force of the recoil. The report said if he shot himself while sitting or lying down, it would have been impossible to hold the shotgun in such a position that the slugs' trajectory shows it was held.

The forensic psychiatrist wrote in the report that Drenth simply did not behave the way a person who is about to take his life does, adding that a person who interacted with Drenth just before his death said he was happy and was making plans for the immediate future. And why would a man on the day he was to take his life casually phone his wife and remind her to pick up items from the grocery store?

The pension board said the report by the subject-matter experts was very "persuasive." They in essence reversed the verdict of the city pathologist and said the death of Sgt. Drenth was in the line of duty, and the widow should receive 100 percent of the pension, untaxed. The pension board would not have made this decision if its members even remotely thought it was a suicide. Drenth's mother, Diane Drenth, made what many agreed is the conclusive assessment on an extremely controversial case. "This has really never been about the money. It's been about having Sean recognized as a fallen officer." Mission accomplished.

SOURCES:

- Phoenix New Times reported by Paul Rubin, November 8, 2012. http://www.phoenixnewtimes.com/news/the-curious-death-of-sergeant-sean-drenth-6456218
- Phoenix New Times reported by Paul Rubin, November 15, 2012. http://www.phoenixnewtimes.com/news/inside-drenth-a-look-at-what-made-a-fallen-cop-tick-6456352
- https://www.reddit.com/r/UnresolvedMysteries/comments/4tl4r9/curious_death_of_sergeant_sean_drenth/

- New York Times reported by Marc Lacey, October 20, 2011. http://www.nytimes.com/2011/10/21/us/phoenix-officers-2010-killing-confounds-colleagues.html
- https://cronkitenews.azpbs.org/2015/08/31/court-cops-can-be-ordered-to-provide-dna-in-probe-of-officers-death/
- http://www.azfamily.com/story/28343930/phoenix-police-officer-sean-drenths-death-ruled-a-suicide
- The Arizona Republic-12, June 7, 2013. http://archive.azcentral.com/community/phoenix/articles/20130607phoenix-police-drenth-granted-death-benefits-abrk.html

CHAPTER 92

"Daddy is not coming back"

THE OFFICER:

Police Officer Jason Scott Ellis
Bardstown (Kentucky) Police Department
End of Watch: Saturday, May 25, 2013
Age: 33

Law enforcement officers are trained to handle threats of all kinds. If it can kill you, you train for it. Officers spend time on the combat range, practicing with computer-generated live-action scenarios and doing almost daily exercises to keep the mind sharp and the reactions focused. But one event is difficult to train for—the assault of a hidden assassin who attacks without warning when an unsuspecting officer is concentrating on the performance of his or her duty. Many times, these cowardly attacks are so sudden that the officer doesn't even have the time to draw a weapon. In the early-morning hours of Saturday, May 25, 2013, Police Officer Jason Ellis was a victim of just such an attack.

Officer Ellis could have been the poster cop for all the things one looks for in an officer. He was a veteran officer who had seen much in his developing seven-year career with the Bardstown, Kentucky, Police Department. A decorated K9 officer, he was commended for his brave actions in a dangerous situation in 2007, and he received the ultimate award, being chosen as Police Officer of the Year.

After an uneventful shift on the night of his murder, Ellis notified communications that he was end of watch. In uniform, and driving his marked police vehicle, Ellis took the usual 15-mile route home. Pulling onto Exit 34 of the Bluegrass Parkway, the always-alert officer noticed rubbish blocking the off-ramp. At 2 a.m., off-duty, tired and ready for bed, Ellis might have driven around the blockage, but that was not his style. Instead, he immediately positioned his vehicle to block traffic, activated his emergency lights, switched on his dome light, and got out of the car.

The 33-year-old officer noticed that several tree limbs were covering the off-ramp. As soon as he collected the large branches using both hands, he pulled the load onto his chest for better leverage. Suddenly, shots rang out. Several blasts from a shotgun slammed into his torso and arms. The officer went down, unable to get to his service weapon. Gunshots continued to blast the wounded officer, and as he was struck several more times. Officer Ellis died in the roadway, still grasping the limbs.

Twenty minutes later, Chad Monroe was on his way home from work when he came across the roadblock at Exit 34. There was a Toyota Corolla stopped in front of him. Monroe pulled behind the Corolla, left his car and walked up to the police car. He looked inside; the car was empty. Monroe walked around to the front of the cruiser and saw a pile of tree limbs blocking the road. He got closer and was stunned to see a uniformed officer under the pile, outlined by a pool of blood. He ran back to the idling Corolla and ordered anyone in the car to get to the police radio and call for help while he would give first aid to the downed officer.

A woman from the Corolla sprinted to the police car and grabbed the radio. "Hello! Hello! Officer down! Officer down! Bloomfield Road." The dispatcher remained calm and asked for her location. The only reply he got was "officer down." Monroe, upon hearing the confusion as to the location, picked up Ellis's radio, "Hey, this is Chad Monroe…we're on the BG parkway. There is a police car in the middle of the road with lights on. And I…we didn't know what it was…it's a tree across the road and I, I didn't know what it was. I believe someone hit him." When asked if the officer was still breathing, Monroe answered, "No sir, he is not breathing. Body temperature is cold."

Officers Michael Meadley and Andrew Riley were the first to arrive at the scene. Meadley recalled later, "It seems like it was just yesterday. I miss him every single day. There are days or times when things come up and remind me of him instantly. I still find myself wanting to call him. I don't know if that will ever go away." Later that day, Ellis' grieving wife, Amy, told their two young sons, "Daddy is not coming back."

An investigation into the ambush killing of Officer Ellis was immediately launched by the Bardstown Police Department and the Kentucky State Police. The only evidence the police acknowledged was the discarded shotgun shells from the murder weapon (which was not recovered) and signs that the tree branches had been deliberately placed on the highway exit by the suspect. The police considered gangs and specific individuals, but no arrests were made, and the case remains unsolved.

Two years after her husband's murder, Amy Ellis opened her heart to the media: "Time cannot close our wound; we cannot heal without knowing who, and why he was taken from us by this senseless murder. We struggle with the need to understand before the healing can truly begin." Besides his wife, Ellis is survived by two young boys.

Update: In May, 2017, Major Jeremy Thompson with the Kentucky State Police updated the progress on the case: "We know a lot about who did not commit this crime because of how we've had to work this almost backwards, but I'd love to be able to say we're close to an arrest, but unfortunately at this time, we're not."

SOURCES:

- https://www.lawenforcementtoday.com/who-murdered-officer-jason-ellis/
- http://swordandscale.com/the-unsolved-murder-of-officer-jason-ellis/
- http://www.cincinnati.com/story/news/2017/05/11/ex-troopers-investigate-ambush-killing-cop-glen-este-grad/317489001/

- http://www.whas11.com/news/local/remembering-ofc-jason-ellis-4-years-later/443147455
- http://www.wdrb.com/story/35517222/bardstown-community-mourns-fourth-year-since-officer-jason-ellis-murdered

APPENDIX I

UNSOLVED HOMICIDES OF LAW ENFORCEMENT OFFICERS (CONFIRMED)

- RESEARCH NOTES
- RESEARCH SUGGESTIONS
- KEY FACTS

RESEARCH NOTES

As I have written in the Introduction, there are no agencies that you can contact and get a record of all unsolved law enforcement homicides. I know, as I tried repeatedly to find just such a list. After two years of comprehensive research, I have been able to make this compendium of the sacrifices of these heroic officers and list them together in *Unsolved*.

With the research data I have collected, I have confirmed the following list of 708 law enforcement homicides as being unsolved. I was able to accomplish this because there was information available that made it evident that the perpetrators were never captured, or in some cases, convicted. In a small percentage of these homicides, I used available documentation to determine if the case should be classified as unsolved based on the circumstances of the incident, even though there was no mention of the offenders. In compiling this data, I looked for law enforcement officers who were killed by gunfire, assault or stabbing. There may be rare occurrences in which an officer is killed by some other overt means, but because it's rare, I used the parameters listed above. All but three states, Vermont, Delaware and New Hampshire, have at least one unsolved police homicide.

Within *Unsolved*, many types of law enforcement officers are listed. The list includes any officer who has powers of arrest as a function of the job description. This includes city, county, state, federal, hospital, airport, railroad, harbor police, correctional officers, and others. If an officer is killed using his or her powers of arrest, on-duty or off, the officer is listed.

It should be noted that the list of 708 unsolved homicides will grow considerably as the second part of the project is completed. In collecting the confirmed data, I uncovered an additional 1,052 homicides where the outcome is not clear, primarily because there is no recorded disposition of the perpetrators. For example, some officers are listed as killed in the line of duty but with no additional information. Because many of these murders occurred so long ago, documentation is very difficult, if not impossible, to locate. In too many cases, the scant records state that officer so-and-so was killed outside a bar or in a fight with a drunk. And that is it—one sentence to describe the death of an officer in the line of duty. There is no mention of the circumstances or whether any suspects were taken into custody. Unacceptable.

Still other cases, including some much more recent, do note the circumstances but fail to mention the status of the suspects. All these cases can be investigated, but the time required would be too burdensome for one individual. That is why I am hopeful that each agency I have listed on my web page (www.unsolvedpolicehomicides.com) will take the time to identify a fallen comrade's case and determine exactly what happened as well as the disposition of the suspects. Were they arrested, did they escape, were they tried and found not guilty or convicted? With that completed, the information could be shared with me so I might update the master list and post the information online. I offer the following basic research suggestions as a place to start for those law enforcement officers or others, who want to be involved and help finalize the list of *Unsolved* homicides.

RESEARCH SUGGESTIONS

A solid first step is The Officer Down Memorial Page and the National Law Enforcement Officers Memorial Fund. Although many of the listings don't state what happened to the suspects, each entry does contain the date of the incident and a description of the circumstances along with pertinent information about the officer.

Next is a solid source of primary documentation. Go to your local newspaper and contact the archives section to see if they have information on the case. This is a major source for specifics in many cases, including witness statements. I used Newspapers.com, which charges a membership fee, but it is well worth it. The drawback for this site is the limited number of papers available.

The internet is of course an excellent source. Of the 708 cases I listed as being unsolved, more than 100 came from online articles written about the deceased officers. Many sites write follow-up articles on each anniversary of the officer's death, adding the latest information. Keep your search broad at first and then narrow it down. Try searching the individual without a middle name or initial and without his or her rank. Note that on Google, you can set parameters on your search. Under "Tools" you have control over how old the articles are, and you can find the newest first. If you get too many results, use the "Verbatim" tab to help narrow the search.

I also used Ancestory.com for additional information about an officer's birth, death and family information. I also found photographs of officers who before had none. Another site is Findagrave.com, which occasionally has detailed accounts of an officer's death and many times a photo of the gravestone.

Contacting your department's detectives is a must. They of course will have the case file and the specific details about the case. What they share with you might be limited but it still can be a major source. I might add that this did not work for me, as none of the detectives I contacted would share or confirm any information because they did not know who I was. But someone within their own department should get better results.

If you can determine who was present at the scene of the crime, and if these witnesses are still alive, they can be a major source of information. I did this on several cases and was surprised by how much more information I could obtain.

And lastly, if you reach a dead end, email me, and we can go over the details of the case to see where we can go from there.

Good luck.
Jim Bultema

Policehistoryjamesbultema@gmail.com
Website: www.policehistorybyjamesbultema.com
Website listing the 1,052 officers: \www.unsolvedpolicehomicides.com

Also on the website is a listing of all unsolved law enforcement homicides by state.

KEY FACTS AND DATA

- There are more than 900,000 sworn law enforcement officers serving in the United States.
- There have been over 20,000 law enforcement officers killed in the line of duty. The first recorded police death was in 1791 while the first unsolved police homicide was in 1852.
- The 1920s were the deadliest decade in law enforcement history, when 2,461 officers died. This is an average of 246 each year compared to 2017 when 129 police officers were killed. The deadliest year was in 1930 when 307 officers were killed.
- The decade of the 1920s also had the most unsolved police homicides with 133 compared to the last 10 years when only four were unsolved. The worst single year for unsolved police homicides was 1921 when there were 23. (Note that this data will change considerably as the remaining 1,052 police homicides are investigated as outlined under Research Notes).

Year/Total/Name	Agency	End of Watch

Note: Italicized names have a chapter in the book

1852-1859

Watchman Joseph Stoddard	Cincinnati (OH) P.D.	9/10/1852
Constable Jack Whellan	Los Angeles County (CA) Constable's Ofc.	12/7/1853
Officer Alexander Algeo	New Orleans (LA) P.D.	3/26/1856
Patrolman Stephen P. Hardenbrook	New York (NY) Municipal Police Force	4/15/1857

1861

Sherriff Jesse S. Harris	Brown County (TX) Sheriff's Dept.	6/6/1861

1864

Patrolman George W. Duryea	New York (NY) Metropolitan Police Force	5/16/1864
Deputy Sheriff Andrew Kriss	San Diego (CA) Sheriff's Dept.	5/25/1864
Deputy Marshal Charles Ring	Saginaw (MI) P.D.	9/14/1864
Sheriff Matthew Nolan	Nueces County (TX) Sheriff's Office	12/22/1864

1865

Officer Thomas DeVane, V	Wilmington (NC) PD	8/3/1865
Sheriff John H. Payntor	Cedar County (MO) Sheriff's Office	10/5/1865
Lieutenant William L. Harvill	Cedar County (MO) Sheriff's Office	10/5/1865

1866

Sheriff William Read McMullen	Angelina County (TX) Sheriff's Office	5/19/1866

1867

Deputy Sheriff George Frank S. Griffin	Ray County (MO) Sheriff's Dept.	5/23/1867
Jailer Barry G. Griffin	Ray County (MO) Sheriff's Dept.	5/23/1867
Sheriff Benjamin Franklin Orcutt	Kalamazoo (MI) Sheriff's Office	12/3/1867

1868

Patrolman John Gear	Memphis (TN) P.D.	3/7/1868
Constable Manuel Garcia Y. Griego	Ranchos de Albuquerque (NM) Constable's	6/24/1868
Inspector William H. Phelps	U.S. Dept. of Treasury-Custom Service	12/18/1868
Inspector George T. Hammonds	U.S. Dept. of Treasury-Custom Service	12/18/1868
Officer David S. Faulkner	Malden (MA) P.D.	12/22/1868

1869

City Marshal John T. Thompson	Covington (KY) P.D.	2/2/1869
Sheriff Orson Rodolphus Colgrove	Jones (NC) County Sheriff's Office	5/2/1869
Sheriff Thomas Wilson Napier	Lincoln (KY) County Sheriff's Office	9/18/1869

1870

Deputy John A. McClain	Colusa (CA) County Sheriff's Dept.	9/17/1870

1871

Agent Gauger Clinton Gilbert	U.S. Dept. of Treasury-Internal Revenue	7/16/1871
Deputy Sheriff Carlos B. King	Sedgwick (KS) County Sheriff's Dept.	9/23/1871

1872

Deputy U.S. Marshal Jacob G. Owens	U.S. Dept. of Justice-Marshals Service	4/15/1872
Special Deputy Marshal William Hicks	U.S. Dept. of Justice-Marshals Service	4/15/1872
Special Deputy Sam Beck	U.S. Dept. of Justice-Marshals Service	4/15/1872
Special Deputy Blacksut Beck	U.S. Dept. of Justice-Marshals Service	4/15/1872
Posseman William Beck	U.S. Dept. of Justice-Marshals Service	4/15/1872
Posseman George Selvidge	U.S. Dept. of Justice-Marshals Service	4/15/1872
Special Deputy Jim Ward	U.S. Dept. of Justice-Marshals Service	4/15/1872
Special Deputy Riley Woods	U.S. Dept. of Justice-Marshals Service	4/15/1872

1873

Deputy U.S. Marshal R.T. Dunn	U.S. Dept. of Justice-Marshals Service	8/8/1873
Sheriff George Washington Law	Callaway (MO) Sheriff's Dept.	8/14/1873

Year/Total/Name	Agency	End of Watch
1873		
Deputy U.S. Marshal John P. Fries	U.S. Dept. of Justice-Marshals Service	10/25/1873
Constable William Stewart Mettler	Kern (CA) County Sheriff's Dept.	11/6/1873
1874		
Policeman J. Peter Mooney	Rome (GA) P.D.	4/18/1874
Deputy Sheriff Richard Roach	Hillsborough (FL) County Sheriff's Dept.	8/22/1874
1875		
Patrolman John Michael Kick	Cleveland (OH) P.D.	6/15/1875
1877		
Constable Samuel Norman	Tarentum Borough (PA) P.D.	7/26/1877
1878		
Deputy Sheriff Robert Lum	Claiborne (MS) County Sheriff's Dept.	11/27/1878
1879		
Deputy Sheriff George M. Doolittle	Lampasas (TX) County Sheriff's Dept.	1/8/1879
Sheriff A. Harvey Mize	Walker (GA) County Sheriff's Dept.	2/7/1879
Patrolman Charles Printz	St. Louis Metro (MO) P.D.	6/1/1879
1880		
Constable Peter Scanlon	Dubuque (IA) County Sheriff's Dept.	7/13/1880
Patrolman Michael Walsh	St. Louis Metro (MO) P.D.	12/5/1880
1881		
Deputy U.S. Marshal Henry Seagraves	U.S. Dept. of Justice-Marshals Service	4/8/1881
Patrolman Timothy Mahoney	Chicago (IL) P.D.	6/11/1881
City Marshal William D. Patton	Fayetteville (AR) P.D.	7/2/1881
Deputy Sheriff John Isham Mount	Washington (AR) County Sheriff's Dept.	7/2/1881
Deputy Collector Thomas L. Brayton	U.S. Dept. Of the Treasury-Internal Revenue	7/20/1881
Sheriff Nimrod Johnson Miller	Burnet (TX) County Sheriff's Dept.	9/1/1881
Patrolman Habersham H. Harvey	Savannah (GA) P.D.	9/9/1881
1882		
Deputy Collector James M. Davis	U.S. Dept. Treasury-Bureau Indian Affairs	3/13/1882
Lighthorseman Joe Barnett	U.S. Dept. Treasury-Bureau Indian Affairs	7/30/1882
Captain Sam Scott	U.S. Dept. Treasury-Bureau Indian Affairs	7/30/1882
Marshal William E. Gibson	U.S. Dept. of Justice-Marshals Service	10/19/1882
Sheriff Uel Musick	Wilbarger (TX) County Sheriff's Dept.	12/7/1882
Patrolman Absalom Kyle McCarty	Denison (TX) P.D.	12/25/1882
1883		
Special Dep. Marshal Lewis Merritt	U.S. Dept. of Justice-Marshals Service	9/27/1883
Special Dep. Marshal Addison Beck	U.S. Dept. of Justice-Marshals Service	9/27/1883
Patrolman George C. Kimball	Detroit (MI) P.D.	10/5/1883
Marshal Baxter Stingley	Salida (CO) P.D.	10/28/1883
Deputy Sheriff Isaac Bosse Heffington	Lee County (TX) Sheriff's Dept.	12/1/1983
1884		
Officer John Nicholson	San Francisco (CA) P.D.	2/16/1884
Patrolman Frank Piszczek	Milwaukee (WI) P.D.	6/21/1884
Village Marshal John George Wisebaker	Willard (OH) P.D.	7/7/1884
Marshal Casper Zweifel	Central Pueblo (CO) Marshal's Office	7/25/1884
1885		
Constable William Thomas Cody	Butler (KS) County Sheriff's Dept.	6/2/1885
Deputy U.S. Marshal William Lee Miller	U.S. Dept. of Justice-Marshals Service	7/6/1885
Sheriff William Meredith King	Jack (TX) County Sheriff's Dept.	7/17/1885

Year/Total/Name	Agency	End of Watch
1885		
Deputy U.S. Marshal Miller Hurst	U.S. Dept. of Justice-Marshals Service	10/11/1885
Deputy Sheriff Wayne B. Parks	Mitchell (TX) County Sheriff's Dept.	10/29/1885
1886		
Deputy U.S. Marshal James E. Richardson	U.S. Dept. of Justice-Marshals Service	3/29/1886
Patrolman Edwin J. Osgood	San Francisco (CA) P.D.	12/13/1886
1887		
Constable Jerry M. Matthews	Matagorda (TX) County Constable 's Office	9/25/1887
Policeman William D. Johnston	Philadelphia (PA) P.D.	10/3/1887
Patrolman John Keegan	Chicago (IL) P.D.	11/4/1887
Deputy Maurice B. Moore	Travis (TX) County Sheriff's Dept.	11/10/1887
1888		
Deputy Sheriff Bill Thompson	Las Animas (CO) County Sheriff's Dept.	2/17/1888
Det. Elie D. Kreigh	Chicago & Alton (IL) Railroad Police	4/3/1888
Deputy U.S. Marshal John Phillips	U.S. Dept. of Justice-Marshals Service	6/30/1888
Marshal William Whitson	U.S. Dept. of Justice-Marshals Service	6/30/1888
Deputy U.S. Marshal Thomas Goodson	U.S. Dept. of Justice-Marshals Service	12/1/1888
Special Officer Hank Frost	Nogales (AZ) P.D.	12/30/1888
1889		
Policeman John C. Phillips	Denver (CO) P.D.	7/16/1889
1890		
Constable William W. Lowther	Bisbee (AZ) P.D.	4/10/1890
1891		
Deputy U.S. Marshal J. Locke Ezzell	U.S. Dept. of Justice-Marshals Service	5/8/1891
Policeman W.A.R. Wilson	Chester (SC) P.D.	5/8/1891
Deputy Sheriff Benjamin Stirling White	Hinds (MS) County Sheriff's Dept.	11/10/1891
1892		
Deputy U.S. Marshal John S. Hamilton	U.S. Dept. of Justice-Marshals Service	4/28/1892
Sheriff Abraham G. Byler	Baxter (AR) County Sheriff's Dept.	6/15/1892
Policeman William F. Jordan	Butte (MT) P.D.	6/24/1892
Special Deputy Marshal James Ballenger	U.S. Dept. of Justice-Marshals Service	7/21/1892
Sheriff Santiago A. Brito	Cameron (TX) County Sheriff's Dept.	8/21/1892
Deputy Sheriff Henry Barganier	Butler (KS) County Sheriff's Dept.	12/10/1892
1893		
Patrolman Albert Turregano	New Orleans (LA) P.D.	2/9/1893
Constable Shadrick R. Heslep	Trinity County (TX) Constable's Ofc. Prec. 1	4/22/1893
Policeman Lee A. Boone	St. Louis Metro (MO) P.D.	5/16/1893
Private J.W. Woods	Texas Rangers (TX)	7/1/1893
Deputy City Marshal Louis W. Ahlers	Victoria (TX) P.D.	8/7/1893
Special Agent William E. Ransom	Union Pacific Railroad Police (NE)	12/22/1893
1894		
Sheriff Hamilton Bass Dickson	Wharton (TX) County Sheriff's Dept.	2/7/1894
Policeman John W. Flynn	Helena (MT) P.D.	4/11/1894
Policeman Dennis W. Daly	Butte (MT) P.D.	7/4/1894
Patrolman Nicolas Sheehan	Cleveland (OH) P.D.	9/5/1894
Sheriff James Christopher Burns	Sanpete (UT) County Sheriff's Dept.	9/26/1894
Deputy U.S. Marshal John M. Beard	U.S. Dept. of Justice-Marshals Service	12/9/1894
1895		
Night Watchman William Lewis	Pennsylvania Railroad Police (OH)	6/28/1895
Deputy Sheriff Alfred Werner	Crittenden (AR) County Sheriff's Dept.	8/6/1895

Year/Total/Name	Agency	End of Watch
1896		
Patrolman Jacob Neibert	Muscatine (IA) P.D.	6/12/1896
1897		
Night Watchman John Wesley Alford	Watsonville (CA) P.D.	2/7/1897
Deputy Constable James Green	Union County (KY) Constable's Office	4/14/1897
Patrolman Pitt McClellan Doxsie	Independence (IA) P.D.	10/26/1897
1898		
Marshal George Leonard	Cameron (MO) P.D.	3/16/1898
Policeman Robert D. Austin	Richmond (VA) P.D.	4/11/1898
Village Marshal James Weiss	East Alton (IL) P.D.	7/6/1898
Constable Larkin Secrest Hope	Colorado County (TX) Constable's Ofc. Prc.1	8/3/1898
Constable Silas A. Gamble, Sr.	Williamson County (TX) Constable's Ofc.6	8/29/1898
Det. D.H. Kiley	Chicago & Alton (IL) Railroad Police	10/12/1898
Chief of Police John T. Sisemore	Ruston (LA) P.D.	11/17/1898
Policeman William Christian Prinslow	Fond du Lac (WI) P.D.	11/18/1898
Constable John E. Rhodes	Henderson (TX) County Constable's Ofc. PG	12/22/1898
1899		
Deputy Sheriff James Stubblefield	Clay (KY) County Sheriff's Dept.	7/6/1899
Officer William E. Griffiths	Denver (CO) P.D.	8/13/1899
Officer Thomas C. Clifford	Denver (CO) P.D.	8/13/1899
Constable Samuel Thomas Tobias	Clarendon (SC) County Magistrate's Ofc.	8/26/1899
Officer Robert A. Dickerson	Atchison (KS) P.D.	10/20/1899
Constable William L. Smith	New Haven (OH) Township P.D.	11/27/1899
1900		
Sheriff George W. Wall	San Augustine (TX) Sheriff's Dept.	4/21/1900
Constable Zeb B. Lancaster	Pikeville (NC) P.D.	6/13/1900
Patrolman James Golden	Dunmore (PA) Borough P.D.	8/15/1900
Sheriff George T. Young	Park (MT) County Sheriff's Office	11/19/1900
1901		
Deputy Sheriff James Vernon Fish	Kent (RI) County Sheriff's Office	1/13/1901
Deputy Sheriff William Rainbolt	Chaves (MN) County Sheriff's Dept.	2/8/1901
Patrolman Bert Brannon	Joplin (MO) P.D.	4/23/1901
Deputy Sheriff Cub Burney	U.S. Dept. of Int.-Bureau of Indian Affairs	7/17/1901
Private Leander Brown	U.S. Dept. Treasury-Bureau Indian Affairs	7/17/1901
Chief of Police Sheldon Jones	Shelby (NC) P.D.	8/4/1901
Deputy Sheriff George M. Leftwich	Jack (TX) County Sheriff's Dept.	8/10/1901
Ranger Carlos Tafolla	Arizona Rangers (AZ)	10/7/1901
Deputy Sheriff William Thomas Maxwell	Apache (AZ) County Sheriff's Dept.	10/7/1901
Marshal Rolland P. Smith	Chelsea (IA) P.D.	12/5/1901
1902		
Patrolman Charles Mayer	St. Paul (MN) P.D.	2/1/1902
1903		
Town Marshal Everett Smith	Olla (LA) P.D.	1/1/1903
Officer Paul Mendelssohn	Waterbury (CT) P.D.	3/10/1903
Marshal James C.A. Parsons	Centralia (WA) P.D.	6/3/1903
Patrolman John Ledbetter	Joplin (MO) PD	6/7/1903
Special Agent Andrew Creason	Chicago, Rock Island & Pacific RR Police (IL)	9/9/1903
Patrolman James H. Mullin	Birmingham (AL) P.D.	9/27/1903
Sheriff Bill Miller	Weston (WY) County Sheriff's Dept.	11/5/1903
Deputy Sheriff Louis Falkenburg	Weston (WY) County Sheriff's Dept.	11/5/1903
Night Marshall Jeff Jones	Starke (FL) P.D.	11/20/1903
Patrolman Charles Haggerty	Mobile (AL) P.D.	12/30/1903

Year/Total/Name	Agency	End of Watch
1904		
Sheriff W. M. Russell	U.S. Dept of Justice-Bureau of Indian Affairs	12/24/1904
1905		
Truant Officer Claude R. Ball	Calhoun (WV) County	1905
Posseman John Carver	U.S. Dept. of Treasury-Internal Rev.	1/10/1905
Det. Sgt. James Higgins	Erie (PA) P.D.	5/14/1905
Deputy Sheriff Julian E. Howard	Wood (TX) County Sheriff's Dept.	7/10/1905
Patrolman Nicholas Bernard Smith	Buffalo (NY) P.D.	9/7/1905
Private Thomas Jefferson Goff	Texas Rangers (TX)	9/13/1905
Constable Thomas E. Hardy	Washington (MD) County Sheriff's Office	10/10/1905
Deputy Constable Johnnie Harris	Hardin (TX) County Constable's Ofc. P-6	12/24/1905
1906		
Chief of Police Denver B. Pore	Mount Pleasant (PA) Borough P.D.	4/7/1906
Patrolman Daniel Passage	Andover (SD) P.D.	7/29/1906
Patrolman Herman M Personius	Valley City (ND) P.D.	8/28/1906
Town Marshal John C. Dickinson	Trenton (KY) P.D.	9/10/1906
Patrolman Joseph A. Freshman	Butte (MT) P.D.	9/23/1906
1907		
Special Agent Ramsey D. Blackburn	Louisville & Nashville Railroad P.D. (AL)	1/2/1907
Dep. Game Warden G. E. Eldredge	Illinois Dept. of Conservation Div. of L.E. (IL)	2/14/1907
Officer Harry S. Van Meter	Freson (CA) P.D.	2/21/1907
Deputy Sheriff Joe D. Price	Fresno (CA) County Sheriff's Office	3/13/1907
Patrolman Lemuel R. Boyce	St. Louis Metropolitan (MO) P.D.	3/31/1907
Deputy Sheriff John Roderick	Bibb (AL) County Sheriff's Dept.	4/8/1907
Deputy Sheriff John Boykin	Orange (TX) County Sheriff's Office	5/6/1907
Patrolman Joseph N. Allen	Fort Collins (CO) PD	7/3/1907
Constable Thomas J. O'Sullivan	Pennsylvania State Constable (PA)	7/12/1907
Constable John O'Brien	Pennsylvania State Constable (PA)	7/12/1907
Special Officer Marcus M. Martin	Gracey (KY) P.D.	8/13/1907
Patrolman Clarence Shockley	Niles (MI) P.D.	8/18/1907
Sheriff D.W. "Doc" Tyus	Grady (GA) County Sheriff's Office	8/21/1907
Patrolman George H. Wilson	Detroit (MI) P.D.	11/13/1907
Special Ofcr. George "Merkel" White	Oakland (CA) P.D.	11/25/1907
1908		
Deputy Sheriff Charles Edwards	Gila (AZ) P.D.	1/10/1908
Patrolman William Alvah Clyde	Sumter (SC) P.D.	1/21/1908
Marshal John Thompson Hamilton	Hope (AR) P.D.	1/22/1908
Deputy US Marshal John C. Mullins	U.S. Dept. of Justice-Marshals Service	2/25/1908
Patrolman Willis A. Smith	Birmingham (AL) P.D.	3/10/1908
Patrolman Pat Sweeney	Tiffin (OH) P.D.	3/29/1908
Patrolman Charles Miller	Salem (OH) P.D.	4/8/1908
Patrolman August Lind	Danville (IL) P.D.	4/10/1908
Patrolman William H. Beck	Denver (CO) P.D.	5/2/1908
Sheriff Alfred Henry Bath	Albany (WY) County Sheriff's Office	5/29/1908
Constable Thomas D. Conger	Ellis County (TX) Constable's Office Prec. 4	6/6/1908
Patrolman Frank Duncan	Latonia (KY) P.D.	6/19/1908
Detective Daniel F. McCrea	Buffalo, Rochester & Pitt. Railroad (NY)	6/20/1908
Patrolman Michael McCormick	Niagara Falls (NY) P.D.	7/23/1908
Patrolman Francis McDermott	Methuen (MA) P.D.	8/8/1908
Patrolman Charles H. Emerson	Methuen (MA) P.D.	8/8/1908

Year/Total/Name	Agency	End of Watch
1908		
Detective Charles L. Stewart	Atchison, Topeka & Santa Fe RR Police (TX)	8/13/1908
Chief of Detectives Patrick Gill	East St. Louis (IL) P.D.	9/6/1908
Warden L. Pressley Reeves	South Carolina (SC) Dept. of Natural Res.	9/22/1908
Patrolman Friedrich "Fred" P. Widman	Waterloo (IA) P.D.	10/11/1908
Chief Deputy Seymore L. Clark	Weber (UT) County Sheriff's Dept.	11/27/1908
1909		
Patrolman Frederick Barner	Pueblo (CO) P.D.	3/21/1909
Constable Jesse Simon Long	Bug Hill (NC) Township Constable's Office	4/5/1909
Deputy Sheriff Sheldon S. Nicks	Paco (FL) County Sheriff's Dept.	5/8/1909
Deputy Sheriff Harry H. Exley	Allegheny (PA) County Sheriff's Office	8/22/1909
Private John L. Williams	Pennsylvania (PA) State Police	8/22/1909
Private John Curtis Smith	Pennsylvania (PA) State Police	8/23/1909
Patrolman Clifford A. Hawley	Huron (SD) P.D.	9/7/1909
1910		
Patrolman David Brooks	Los Angeles (CA) P.D.	4/8/1910
Merchant Policeman Ambrose Donahue	Leavenworth (KS) P.D.	7/2/1910
Chief of Police John Albert Struble	Clinton (IL) P.D.	7/14/1910
Ranger Quirl Bailey Carnes	Texas Rangers (TX)	7/31/1910
Special Deputy Henry B. Lawrence	Cameron (TX) County Sheriff's Office	7/31/1910
Deputy Sheriff Ben F. Pearson	Atoka (OK) County Sheriff's Office	10/14/1910
Chief of Police William C. Temple	Anadarko (OK) P.D.	11/12/1910
1911		
Patrolman H.B. Patridge	Bessemer (AL) P.D.	1/6/1911
Captain John T. Sullivan	Spokane (WA) P.D.	1/7/1911
Patrolman Herman Reimer	Cleveland (OH) P.D.	1/28/1911
Game Warden Charles W. Estes	Oklahoma (OK) Dept. Wildlife Conservation	2/26/1911
Deputy Sheriff H.M. Holloway	Pulaski (KY) County Sheriff's Office	3/12/1911
Deputy Sheriff J.T. Lovett	Pulaski (KY) County Sheriff's Office	3/12/1911
Marshal Joseph Kaschmitter	Alton (IA) P.D.	3/27/1911
Patrolman Joseph Raimo	Kansas City (MO) P.D.	3/28/1911
Patrolman John F. Brennan	Providence (RI) P.D.	4/2/1911
Patrolman William H. Cunliffe	Seattle (WA) P.D.	6/17/1911
Patrolman Henry Lee Harris	Seattle (WA) P.D.	7/4/1911
Patrolman Thomas Schweig	Chicago (IL) P.D.	7/15/1911
Patrolman Walter G. McQuarry	Warwick (RI) P.D.	7/27/1911
Patrolman Walter Chapman	Cleveland (OH) P.D.	8/22/1911
Marshal J. Henry Clemens	Maryville (TN) P.D.	8/25/1911
Patrolman Alfred Evans	Youngstown (OH) P.D.	11/5/1911
1912		
Patrolman Charles Berry	Scranton (PA) P.D.	2/1/1912
Village Marshal George Claude Kloster	Wyoming (OH) P.D.	5/3/1912
Patrolman Edward Parker	Cleveland (OH) P.D.	6/19/1912
Patrolman John M. Taylor	Memphis (TN) P.D.	6/22/1912
Special Agent Robert F. Stringer	White Oak (WV) Railway Police	7/25/1912
Special Agent Lloyd James Spaur	Union Pacific (WY) Railroad Police	8/4/1912
Patrolman Fred C. Griffin	Owen (WI) P.D.	8/14/1912
Deputy Marshal William H. Loud	Cassville (WI) P.D.	8/19/1912
Patrolman Clarence Livingston	Chattanooga (TN) P.D.	9/1/1912
Patrolman W. R. Roberts	Monroe (LA) P.D.	9/2/1912

Year/Total/Name	Agency	End of Watch
1912		
Deputy Sheriff Albert Munguia	Graham (AZ) County Sheriff's Office	9/24/1912
Deputy Sheriff Tom "Jack" Campbell	Graham (AZ) County Sheriff's Office	9/24/1912
Patrolman Albert R. Peterson	Boston (MA) P.D.	10/29/1912
Patrolman John J. Gaffney	Newark (NJ) P.D.	12/6/1912
1913		
Deputy Sheriff Joe W. Meeks	Pima (AZ) County Sheriff's Dept.	1/21/1913
Deputy Sheriff J. Davis	Allegheny (PA) County Sheriff's Office	1/28/1913
Game Warden Bert Blanchard	California (CA) Dept. Of Fish & Wildlife	2/2/1913
Inspector John S.H. "Jack" Howard	U.S. Department Treasury-Custom Service	2/12/1913
Patrolman John Robert Estridge	Charlotte (NC) P.D.	3/29/1913
Patrolman Charles W. Schoof	Detroit (MI) P.D.	7/19/1913
Night Policeman Harry Floyd Hooker	Jacksonville (TX) P.D.	7/22/1913
Patrolman Red Holwedel	Detroit (MI) P.D.	8/22/1913
Patrolman James W. Witcher	High Point (NC) P.D	9/15/1913
Patrolman Willie W. Heath	Salisbury (MA) P.D.	10/9/1913
Constable Samuel L. Queen	Hume (MO) Constable's Office	11/23/1913
City Marshal Henry N. Norman	Santa Paula (CA) P.D.	11/25/1913
1914		
City Marshal William Easley Blakemore	Humboldt (TN) P.D.	2/10/1914
Town Marshal John Clifton	Dania (FL) P.D.	3/7/1914
Game Protector Samuel S. Taylor	NY Environmental Conservation Police (NY)	4/5/1914
Chief of Police Samuel Henderson Smith	LaFollette (TN) P.D.	5/13/1914
Det. Cleveland Kemp	Chesapeake & Ohio Railroad Police (KY)	6/7/1914
Deputy Game Warden Ernest G. Berry	Utah Division Wildlife Resources Police (UT)	9/27/1914
Sgt. Hans Gilbert Aamold	St. Paul (MN) P.D.	9/27/1914
Det. Sgt. Frank Dealy	Chicago (IL) P.D.	10/5/1914
County Ranger James A. Mercer	Pima (AZ) County Sheriff's Dept.	12/2/1914
1915		
Sgt. Michael F. Gibbons	St. Louis (MO) Metropolitan P.D.	1/9/1915
Town Marshal John N. Harris	Sellersburg (IN) P.D.	1/14/1915
Patrolman Frank McKinsey	North Vernon (IN) P.D.	1/16/1915
Posse Member Joseph Carl Akin	U.S. Dept. of Justice-Marshals Service	2/21/1915
Det. Lt. Elijah Newton Boileau	Baltimore & Ohio Railroad Police (OH)	2/24/1915
Deputy U.S. Marshal Robert Logan	U.S. Dept. of Justice-Marshals Service	3/9/1915
Det. Leslie D. Johnson	Chesapeake & Ohio Railroad Police (KY)	3/25/1915
Patrolman Ivan W. Lincoln	Butte (MT) P.D.	3/30/1915
Patrolman James O'Neill	Cincinnati (OH) P.D.	4/18/1915
Sheriff John Henry Franks	Caldwell (TX) County Sheriff's Office	5/12/1915
Customs Agent Joseph Russell Sitter	U.S. Department Treasury-Custom Service	5/24/1915
Night Marshal Charles Schram	El Dorado (KS) PD	6/28/1915
Marshal Frank Peak	Loveland (CO) P.D.	7/13/1915
Assistant Marshal Victor Helburg	Louisville (CO) P.D.	10/28/1915
Patrolman Lawrence E. Kost	Seattle (WA) P.D.	12/12/1915
Det. William Francis Mertz	Bloomfield (NJ) P.D.	12/15/1915
Det. Robert J. Shannon	Bloomfield (NJ) P.D.	12/15/1915
1916		
Patrolman Robert E. Beasley	Petersburg (VA) PD	2/6/1916
Town Marshal Ernest E. Buckley	Selah (WA) P.D.	3/1/1916
Patrolman Henry Schwartz	New York (NY) Police Department	5/29/1916

Year/Total/Name	Agency	End of Watch
1916		
Deputy Sheriff Henry Voiers	Kanawha (WV) County Sheriff's Office	6/13/1916
Patrolman James M. Karr, Jr.	Rosedale (KS) P.D.	7/10/1916
Sheriff Martin Moore	Morton (KS) County Sheriff's Dept.	7/22/1916
Patrolman Daniel Passage	Andover (SD) P.D.	7/29/1916
Patrolman John Laufhutte	Columbus (OH) Division of Police	8/22/1916
Deputy Night Watchman Fred French	Kingsburg (CA) P.D.	11/2/1916
1917		
Det. Otto Mosholder	Cleveland (OH) P.D.	2/3/1917
Patrolman John Fow	Louisville (KY) P.D.	2/17/1917
Patrolman Sidney J. Benson	El Paso (TX) P.D.	6/28/1917
Patrolman Del Macintyre	Riverside (CA) P.D.	7/1/1917
Patrolman Noah Roll	Springfield (IL) P.D.	8/7/1917
Patrolman George William Mattern	Des Moines (IA) P.D.	8/7/1917
Constable Valmore De Rosier	Marysville (MT) P.D.	9/13/1917
Det. Albert W. Wegener	Cincinnati (OH) P.D.	11/12/1917
Det. Frank Caswin	Milwaukee (WI) P.D.	11/27/1917
Det. Frederick Kaiser	Milwaukee (WI) P.D.	11/27/1917
Det. David J. O'Brien	Milwaukee (WI) P.D.	11/27/1917
Det. Charles Seehawer	Milwaukee (WI) P.D.	11/27/1917
Operator Edward Spindler	Milwaukee (WI) P.D.	11/27/1917
Det. Stephen Stecker	Milwaukee (WI) P.D.	11/27/1917
Det. Albert Templin	Milwaukee (WI) P.D.	11/27/1917
Station Keeper Henry Deckert	Milwaukee (WI) P.D.	11/27/1917
Det. Paul Weiler	Milwaukee (WI) P.D.	11/27/1917
Deputy Sheriff Frank Martin, Sr.	Cameron (TX) County Sheriff's Dept.	11/25/1917
Night Watchman M.E. "Mote" Witt	Lorena (TX) P.D.	12/11/1917
1918		
Patrolman Thomas Patrick Farrell	Pittsburgh (PA) P.D.	3/2/1918
Patrolman James F. Looney	Chicago (IL) P.D.	4/18/1918
Patrolman Charles Rajchinetz	East Chicago (IL) P.D.	8/1/1918
Patrolman John Friel	Nashville City (TN) P.D.	9/23/1918
Patrolman J.C. Sherrod	Pocatello (ID) P.D.	10/14/1918
Det. Alfred Olin	Aurora (IL) P.D.	10/29/1918
Special Policeman Panfilo Di Rossi	Chicago-Terre Haute & Southeastern RR (IL)	11/5/1918
Private T.E.P. Ellzey Perkins	Texas Rangers (TX)	11/7/1918
1919		
Patrolman John F. Schuetz	Chicago (IL) P.D.	1/23/1919
Patrolman William Armstrong	Cleveland (OH) P.D.	3/9/1919
Deputy Sheriff George J. Dorminey	Ben Hill (GA) County Sheriff's Office	4/6/1919
Patrolman A.L. White	Memphis (TN) P.D.	4/13/1919
Deputy Walter Clifford Brown	Jenkins (GA) County Sheriff's Dept.	4/13/1919
Night Marshal Thomas Preston Stephens	Jenkins (GA) County Sheriff's Dept.	4/13/1919
Patrolman Adolph F. Butterman	Boston (MA) P.D.	5/1/1919
Patrolman Hugh C. Petrie	Cheyenne (WY) P.D.	6/7/1919
Sheriff Milton Harvey Stephens	Williamson (TN) County Sheriff's Dept.	6/27/1919
Sheriff Hendrix Rector	Greenville (SC) County Sheriff's Office	7/4/1919
Patrolman John Francis Young	Minneapolis (MN) P.D.	7/13/1919
Special Officer Jack Chelton Harris	Atchison, Topeka & Santa Fe RR Police (CA)	7/15/1919
Det. John Boss	New York (OH) Central Railroad Police	8/24/1919

Year/Total/Name	Agency	End of Watch
1919		
Det. George C. Klein	Denver (CO) P.D.	8/29/1919
Patrolman Louis Henry Hufnagel	Crafton (PA) Borough P.D.	9/8/1919
Patrolman John W. Edwards	New Castle (PA) PD	9/22/1919
Deputy Sheriff Otho H. Munger	Smith (KY) County Sheriff's Office	9/27/1919
Deputy Sheriff Edward Henry Foley	Sherburne (MN) County Sheriff's Office	9/28/1919
Game Protector John H. Woodruff	NY State Environmental Conser. (NY)	11/27/1919
Det. Lawrence J. Beers	Baltimore & Ohio Railroad Police (MA)	12/11/1919
1920		
Patrolman John Greer	Aberdeen (WA) P.D.	1/7/1920
Patrolman Henry Immen	New York (NY) P.D.	2/21/1920
Deputy City Marshal Green Wesley Rye	Plano (TX) P.D.	2/28/1920
Deputy J.T. Dixon	Wilkinson (GA) County Sheriff's Office	3/23/1920
Patrolman William J. Boyd, Jr.	Philadelphia (PA) PD	5/12/1920
Patrolman Frank S. Hallett	Minneapolis (MN) P.D.	8/25/1920
Patrolman William A. Moller	St. Louis Metro (MO) County Sheriff's Ofc.	10/16/1920
Patrolman Preston B. Anslyn	St. Louis Metro (MO) County Sheriff's Ofc.	10/16/1920
Patrolman George Nelson	Dunkirk (NY) P.D.	10/17/1920
Patrolman Claude Mitchell Earle	Monroe (LA) P.D.	11/9/1920
Agent Kirby Frans	U.S. Dept. of Treasury-IRS-Prohibition Unit	11/19/1920
Patrolman Roy O. Downing	Denver (CO) P.D.	12/2/1920
Special Officer Charles M. Daly	St. Louis Metro (MO) P.D.	12/10/1920
Agent James Francis McGuiness	U.S. Dept. of Treasury-IRS-Prohibition Unit	12/24/1920
Night Officer Ben Foret Ray	Sour Lake (TX) P.D.	12/26/1920
1921		
Det. Thomas Fletcher Thompson	Macon (GA) P.D.	1/2/1921
Patrolman Fred E. Buhland	South Bend (IN) P.D.	1/10/1921
Patrolman Thomas Hanna	San Francisco (CA) P.D.	1/23/1921
City Marshal Frank O. Real	Los Banos (CA) P.D.	1/30/1921
Patrolman William G. Pate	Columbus (GA) P.D.	2/5/1921
Chief of Police John J. Sturgus	Anchorage (AK) P.D.	2/20/1921
Patrolman Herbert J. Bischoff	Detroit (MI) P.D.	3/13/1921
Night Officer D. Frank Pincin	Mount Union (PA) Borough P.D.	5/31/1921
Capt. Harry Phoenix	El Paso (TX) P.D.	6/13/1921
Town Constable Mahlon Pascal Johnson	Waverly Town (WA) P.D.	6/14/1921
Patrolman Doc Lefler	Ashland (KY) P.D.	7/4/1921
Agent Charles Edward Howell	U.S. Dept. of Treasury-IRS-Prohibition Unit	7/17/1921
Deputy Sheriff Verner J. Yarborough	Fulton (GA) County Sheriff's Office	7/25/1921
Chief of Police Elmer Sundby	Eau Claire (WI) P.D.	7/26/1921
Patrolman Henry Frank Brown	Columbia (SC) P.D.	8/15/1921
Marshal Rueben T. Jones	Tarpon Springs (FL) P.D.	8/27/1921
Warden William Hoblitzell	New Jersey (NJ) Div. of Fish and Wildlife	9/17/1921
Det. John Olan Hall	Shreveport (LA) P.D.	10/20/1921
Deputy Sheriff John S. Evans	Clinch (GA) County Sheriff's Office	11/18/1921
Det. Samuel Slater	Grand Rapids (MI) P.D.	12/7/1921
Special Officer George Brandsma	Grand Rapids (MI) P.D.	12/7/1921
Patrolman Charles McGuire	Toledo (OH) P.D.	12/22/1921
Private Joseph Benjamin "Joe" Buchanan	Texas Rangers (TX)	12/26/1921
1922		
Policeman William Miles	Philadelphia (PA) P.D.	2/21/1922

Year/Total/Name	Agency	End of Watch
1922		
Patrolman Charles O. Legate	Seattle (WA) P.D.	3/17/1922
Patrolman Ernest H. Cassidy	Chicago (IL) P.D.	4/3/1922
Patrolman Blair McGovern	Glenolden (PA) Borough P.D.	5/10/1922
Patrolman Emory Farrington	Milton (MA) P.D.	6/8/1922
Agent Charles O. Sterner	U.S. Dept. of Treasury-IRS-Prohibition Unit	6/18/1922
Special Officer Alfred Allen Gifford	Chicago, Rock Island & Pacific RR Police (IL)	6/27/1922
Patrolman Ignatz Witkowski	Ford Village (MI) P.D.	7/4/1922
Agent Howell J. Lynch	U.S. Dept. of Treasury-IRS-Prohibition Unit	7/6/1922
Patrolman Bernard T. Cook	St. Louis (MO) Metro P.D.	7/7/1922
Inspector Robert Stuart Rumsey, Jr.	U.S. Dept. of Treasury-Customs Service	8/19/1922
Special Officer M.V. Torres	Texas & Pacific (TX) Railroad Police	9/6/1922
Inspector Jot Gunter Jones	U.S. Dept. of Treasury-Customs Service	10/1/1922
Colorado Ranger Edward P. Bell	Colorado (CO) Mounted Rangers	10/14/1922
Patrolman Richie Rose	Denver (CO) P.D.	10/31/1922
Patrolman Herbert Marlow	Dewey (OK) P.D.	11/11/1922
Game Warden Mertley E. Johnston	Maine Dept. of Inland Fisheries & Wildlife	11/14/1922
Game Warden David F. Brown	Maine Dept. of Inland Fisheries & Wildlife	11/14/1922
Chief of Police Hardy A. Revels	Lake City (FL) P.D.	11/20/1922
Officer William Whitfield	Indianapolis (IN) P.D.	11/27/1922
1923		
Deputy Constable Edward P. Neu	St. Louis (MO) County Sheriff's Dept.	4/3/1923
Deputy Sheriff William Burleson	Avery (NC) County Sheriff's Office	4/26/1923
Patrolman Frank E. Romanella	New York (NY) P.D.	7/26/1923
Patrolman Charles J. Reynolds	New York (NY) P.D.	7/26/1923
Patrolman John F. Creghan	Ridley (PA) Township P.D.	8/26/1923
Patrolman Joseph Mareno	Baton Rouge (LA) P.D.	9/18/1923
Patrolman Elmer E. Cobb	Boulder (CO) P.D.	11/19/1923
Deputy Sheriff James Farris Ball	McCreary (KY) County Sheriff's Office	12/14/1923
1924		
Patrolman William H. Anderson	St. Louis (MO) Metro P.D.	2/10/1924
Det. Charles George Nolan, Sr.	Grand Trunk (MI) Railroad Police	5/13/1924
Patrolman John Schmiegel	Saginaw (MI) P.D.	7/16/1924
Assistant Chief Perry Eugene Bostick	Ocala (FL) P.D.	10/20/1924
Patrolman Harry Borum	Terre Haute (IN) P.D.	11/23/1924
Patrolman Benjamin Frank Law	Covington (KY) P.D.	12/30/1924
1925		
Night Watch Officer John Gould	Oxford Village (MI) P.D.	2/13/1925
Patrolman Elmer M. Cox	Detroit (MI) P.D.	5/15/1925
Special Officer Allan F. Shoemaker	Chicago & Northwestern (IA) RR Police	5/17/1925
Constable Carl M. Bisbee	Nueces (TX) County Constable's Ofc. Pre. 1	7/25/1925
Deputy Constable R.R. Bledsoe	Nueces (TX) County Constable's Ofc. Pre. 1	7/25/1925
Patrolman Charles Lewis Cooper, Jr.	Pittsburgh (PA) P.D.	8/5/1925
Sheriff Richard Ellis	Scott (TN) County Sheriff's Dept.	8/13/1925
Patrolman David Sheehan	New York (NY) P.D.	8/22/1925
Patrolman Edward P. Fowler, Jr.	North Vernon (IN) P.D.	9/21/1925
Deputy Sheriff Charles C. Wortham	Shelby (TN) County Sheriff's Office	10/7/1925
Sgt. Daniel C. Chason	Fayetteville (NC) P.D.	10/22/1925
Patrolman James A. Henry	Chicago (IL) P.D.	11/27/1925
Patrolman James H. Carroll	Chicago (IL) P.D.	11/27/1925
Patrolman James H. Mateer	St. Louis (MO) Metro P.D.	12/17/1925
Special Agent Bert Zumwalt	Chicago & Alton Railroad Police (IL)	12/22/1925

Year/Total/Name	Agency	End of Watch
1930		
Agent Louis McClymonds Davies, Jr.	U.S. Dept. Treasury-IRS-Bureau-Prohibition	1/14/1930
Policeman Peter Muller, Jr.	Los Angeles (CA) P.D.	4/13/1930
Patrolman William J. Duncan	New York (NY) P.D.	5/17/1930
Patrolman George R. Neil	Chicago (IL) P.D.	5/19/1930
Special Agent Dale F. Kearney	U.S. Dept. Treasury-IRS-Bureau-Prohibition	7/6/1930
Patrolman Robert J. Card	Sterling (IL) P.D.	8/12/1930
Patrolman Michael Connolly	Portland (OR) P.D.	8/15/1930
Patrolman Louis Silva	Gallup (NM) P.D.	9/15/1930
Patrolman Walter Commins	Wyoming (OH) P.D.	9/16/1930
1931		
Deputy Sheriff Joseph A. Meyer	Galveston (TX) County Sheriff's Office	1/2/1931
Patrolman William Orma Sorrell	Cincinnati (OH) P.D.	3/24/1931
Det. William H. DeGive	New York (NY) P.D.	3/31/1931
Patrolman Edward O'Briest	Toledo (OH) P.D.	5/19/1931
Game Warden John L. Cox	Virginia Game & Inland Fisheries (VA)	6/28/1931
Patrolman Harry C. Beasley	Newark (OH) P.D.	7/2/1931
Inspector Charles Marcus Eldredge	Illinois Div. of Conservation-Div. of LE (IL)	7/4/1931
Night Marshal Virgil Paul Untied	Minburn (IA) P.D.	7/23/1931
Dep. Constable Francisco A. Cisneros	Willacy (TX) Constables Ofc. Precinct 2	7/26/1931
Constable William Franklin Haygood	Willacy (TX) Constables Ofc. Precinct 2	7/26/1931
Patrolman Charles D. Poole	Metropolitan (DC) P.D.	8/4/1931
Patrolman William J. Maguire	Pullman (WA) P.D.	8/21/1931
Patrolman Hugh Nichols	Nampa (ID) P.D.	10/5/1931
Chief of Police George Luckett	Depew (OK) P.D.	10/6/1931
Deputy Sheriff Robert Alexander Trice	El Paso (TX) County Sheriff's Office	11/18/1931
1932		
Deputy Sheriff Henry Isom Chandler	San Augustine (TX) County Sheriff's Office	1/11/1932
Policeman William J. Henderson	Philadelphia (PA) P.D.	2/28/1932
Officer Daniel A. Romberger	U.S. Dept. Treasury-Customs Service	4/25/1932
Inspector John Henry Heard	U.S. Dept. Treasury-Customs Service	5/2/1932
Cattle Inspector Joseph Calvin Dillman	Arizona (AZ) Livestock Sanitary Board	5/14/1932
Patrolman Clarence B. Campbell	New Castle (PA) P.D.	5/23/1932
Policeman Earl F. Sturtevant	Shannon (IL) P.D.	6/23/1932
Deputy Sheriff Louis Batista Chiara	Lander (NV) County Sheriff's Office	7/16/1932
Special Agent Norman G. Fowler	Union Pacific (NE) Railroad Police	8/29/1932
Det. Sgt. Porter Williams	Springfield (IL) P.D.	9/25/1932
Inspector Herff Alexander Carnes	U.S. Dept. Treasury-Customs Service	12/1/1932
1933		
City Marshal Albert H. Erdman	Longton (KS) P.D.	2/28/1933
Constable Stewart G. Coats	Forrest (MS) Constable's Office	3/23/1933
Patrolman Carl Strom	Sedro-Woolley (WA) P.D.	4/15/1933
Policeman Dave Reese	Jerome (AZ) P.D.	5/22/1933
Auxiliary Officer Louis John Schuetz	Lombard (IL) P.D.	7/30/1933
1934		
Sheriff Adolpho Rodrigues	Costilla (CO) County Sheriff's Office	1/1/1934
Deputy Sheriff Albert Pike Powell	Rogers (OK) County Sheriff's Office	2/4/1934
Sgt John S. Donlan	Seattle (WA) P.D.	5/20/1934

Year/Total/Name	Agency	End of Watch
1935		
Night Watchman Charles O. Riske	Moulton (TX) P.D.	3/2/1935
Patrolman Clifford Stang	Ann Arbor (MI) P.D.	3/21/1935
Special Agent Richard Kelly	Illinois Central (KY) Railroad Police	5/30/1935
Marshal George Coniff	Newport (WA) P.D.	9/14/1935
Marshal George Shocker	Emery (SD) P.D.	9/24/1935
Special Agent Omer Earl Davenport	Wabash (IL) Railroad Police	10/9/1935
Patrolman Clyde Appling	Northport (AL) P.D.	10/15/1935
1936		
Patrolman James I. Young	New York (NY) P.D.	2/12/1936
Sgt William P. Cullen	St. Louis (MO) Metro P.D.	3/2/1936
Deputy Sheriff Carlton Mason Stearns	Grays Harbor (WA) County Sheriff's Office	3/10/1936
Patrolman Joseph Ternansky	Cleveland (OH) P.D.	4/1/1936
Town Marshal Arnold Borson	Ghent (MN) P.D.	8/18/1936
Policeman Millard Williams	Tiptonville (TN) P.D.	9/24/1936
Policeman August Mayford	Alton (IL) P.D.	10/16/1936
1937		
Rural Policeman William Muldrow Strange	Sumter (SC) County Sheriff's Office	4/6/1937
Sheriff Lawrence I. Smoyer	Boone (NE) County Sheriff's Dept.	6/17/1937
Constable William Wathen	Boone (NE) County Sheriff's Dept.	10/3/1937
Constable Jesse P. Matthews	Panola (TX) Constable's Office Prec. 2	9/4/1937
Patrolman Edward P. Lynch	New York (NY) P.D.	12/7/1937
1938		
Chief of Police John Albert Rape	Huntersville (NC) P.D.	1/1/1938
Patrolman Anthony V. Tornatore	New York (NY) P.D.	1/6/1938
Constable Felix Valenzuela	Brewster (TX) County Constable's Ofc. 2	6/19/1938
Patrolman John A. Olson	Chicago (IL) P.D.	10/20/1938
Game Warden Dawson R. Murchison	Texas Game Fish, & Oyster Comm. (TX)	12/20/1938
1939		
Deputy Sheriff James D. Reddicks	Hardin (TX) County Sheriff's Dept.	6/30/1939
1940		
Detective Ferdinand Socha	New York (NY) P.D.	7/4/1940
Detective Joseph J. Lynch	New York (NY) P.D.	7/4/1940
Patrolman Charles H. Shaw	Nassau (NY) County P.D.	9/6/1940
Patrolman John A. Tibbs	Richmond (VA) P.D.	10/20/1940
1942		
Deputy Sheriff Charlie William M. Gaines	Lauderdale (TN) County Sheriff's Office	1/24/1942
Trooper James A. Long	Oklahoma (OK) P.D.	7/12/1942
Officer George Arnold Kemp	Thomasville (NC) P.D.	12/7/1942
1944		
Constable Lee Olen Jones	Cameron (TX) County Constable's Ofc. 4	5/21/1944
Lt. Keith Ellsworth	Charleston (SC) P.D.	10/6/1944
1945		
Chief of Police Edward Wiley Fox	Evarts (KY) P.D.	4/19/1945

Year/Total/Name	Agency	End of Watch
1947		
Inspector Clarence J. Trask, Sr.	U.S. Dept. Treasury-Customs Service	4/8/1947
Deputy Sheriff Warren Calhoun Guerry	Berkeley (SC) County Sheriff's Office	5/27/1947
Policeman Michael J. Dowd, Jr.	Somerville (MA) P.D.	6/12/1947
Sheriff Douglas Grant Manning	McCreary (KY) County Sheriff's Office	11/27/1947
Special Agent Harry Lloyd Ashley	Atchison, Topeka and Santa Fe RR (CA)	12/9/1947
Deputy Sheriff David Galloway	Letcher (KY) County Sheriff's Department	12/10/1947
Deputy Sheriff Willard Hall	Letcher (KY) County Sheriff's Department	12/10/1947
1948		
Private Robert B. Harris	Alexandria (VA) P.D.	9/11/1948
Wildlife Officer William I. Wright, Jr.	Wildlife Resources Commission (NC)	10/31/1948
1949		
Patrolman James S. Peters	Tulsa (OK) P.D.	4/14/1949
Deputy Sheriff Grover Dewey Kennedy	McCreary (KY) County Sheriff's Office	4/24/1949
Patrolman Morris D. Lopez	Tampa (FL) P.D.	7/9/1949
1951		
Patrolman Leroy Joseph LaFleur, Sr.	Miami (FL) P.D.	2/16/1951
Patrolman Alje M. Savela	Massachusetts State Police (MA)	8/31/1951
Patrolman William M. Carrico, Sr.	Carrollton (KY) P.D.	9/15/1951
Patrolman Clyde William Harrison	Kansas City (KS) P.D.	12/20/1951
Patrolman Peter G. Huber	Detroit (MI) P.D.	12/23/1951
1952		
Patrolman George J. Spearakos	Chicago (IL) P.D.	4/24/1952
Corrections Officer Filimon J. Ortiz	New Mexico Corrections Department (NM)	6/11/1952
Inspector Edwin H. Wheeler	U.S. Dept. Justice Immigration-Border Pat.	7/6/1952
1953		
Night Marshal Doyne Everett Lindsey	New Madrid (MO) P.D.	9/16/1953
Officer Richard S. Burchfield	Colorado Springs (CO) P.D.	11/26/1953
1954		
Policeman Frank W. Hardy	Seattle (WA) P.D.	3/12/1954
Sheriff Clarence Taylor	Owsley (KY) County Sheriff's Office	3/27/1954
Deputy Sheriff Robert Hensley	Owsley (KY) County Sheriff's Office	3/27/1954
Sheriff Hubbard Ferguson	Gallatin (KY) County Sheriff's Office	6/18/1954
1955		
Policeman Marvin Elton Wills	Fort Worth (TX) P.D.	12/25/1955
1957		
Officer Roger Lynn Winkelman	Cincinnati (OH) P.D.	11/1/1957
1958		
Deputy R.A. Bob Rogers	Polk (TN) County Sheriff's Department	3/8/1958
Chief Dep. James Louis Wright	Polk (TN) County Sheriff's Department	3/8/1958
Patrolman Emil A. Newberg	Pawtucket (RI) P.D.	6/30/1958
Private Frank Henderson Wall, Jr.	Augusta (GA) P.D.	11/18/1958
Officer Charles Bernoskie	Rahway (NJ) P.D.	11/28/1958
1959		
Officer Douglas Eugene Cantrill	Davis (CA) P.D.	9/7/1959
Sgt. Manuel Walker Trenary	Harrisonburg (VA) P.D.	10/8/1959
1960		
Constable William Austin "Bud" Boyatt	McCreary (KY) Constable's Office	12/7/1960

Year/Total/Name	Agency	End of Watch
1961		
Marshall William L. Meadows	Plainfield (IA) P.D.	1/23/1961
Patrolman Frederick Raymond Haller	San Leandro (CA) P.D.	4/20/1961
1962		
Trooper Charles Eugene Morris	Virginia State Police (VA)	3/2/1962
1963		
Officer Andrew R. Morales	Honolulu (HI) P.D.	12/16/1963
Officer Abraham E. Mahiko	Honolulu (HI) P.D.	12/16/1963
1964		
Det. Clarence D. Thompson	Terre Haute (IN) P.D.	3/8/1964
1965		
Deputy Sheriff O'Neal Moore	Washington (LA) Parish Sheriff's Office	6/2/1965
1967		
Policeman Louis R. Kuhn	Houston (TX) P.D.	5/17/1967
Det. Frederick W. Toto	Newark (NJ) P.D.	7/14/1967
Policeman Robert H. Keller	Huntington Park (CA) P.D.	10/5/1967
Patrolman Robert L. Tatman	Champaign (IL) P.D.	11/25/1967
Det. Gilbert M Silvia	Metropolitan (DC) P.D.	11/25/1967
Officer Walter F. Stathers	Miami-Dade (FL) P.D.	12/19/1967
1968		
Corrections Officer Donald Hiles	New Jersey Department of Corrections (NJ)	3/8/1968
Det. Robert Raymond Gonser	Michigan State Police (MI)	8/8/1968
1969		
Sgt. Julian Narvaez	Bernalillo (MN) County Sheriff's Dept.	3/26/1969
Policeman Rand J. Chandler	Camden (NJ) P.D.	9/2/1969
Agent Ronald Ernest Haskell	Nevada Div. Investigation & Narcotics (NV)	12/1/1969
1970		
Police Officer Frederick J. Cione, Jr.	Philadelphia (PA) P.D.	1/30/1970
Chief of Police Robert Hamrick	Rock Creek (OH) P.D.	3/20/1970
Officer Bernard M. Bennett	Sacramento (CA) P.D.	5/9/1970
Policeman Robert M Perry	Plainfield (NJ) P.D.	7/1/1970
Officer Ronald Tsukamoto	Berkeley (CA) P.D.	8/20/1970
Sgt. Carl Hiram Watson	Cordele (GA) P.D.	10/18/1970
1971		
Policeman Robert Bolden	New York (NY) P.D.	1/22/1971
Police Officer Leonard A. Christiansen	Riverside (CA) P.D.	4/2/1971
Police Officer Paul C. Teel	Riverside (CA) P.D.	4/2/1971
City Marshal Homer Edgell Fry	Mansfield (MO) P.D.	5/11/1971
Supervisor Samuel Anderson Pickels	Virginia Department of Corrections (VA)	7/23/1971
Policeman Ulysses Brown	Detroit (MI) P.D.	8/20/1971
Policeman Robert Rosenbloom	New Mexico (NM) State Police	11/8/1971
Trooper William Harrell Barrett	Kentucky State Police (KY)	12/19/1971
Policeman Larry Joel Kite	Mineral Wells (TX) P.D.	12/24/1971
1972		
Officer Rocco W. Laurie	New York (NY) P.D.	1/27/1972
Officer Gregory P. Foster	New York (NY) P.D.	1/27/1972
Officer William David Corn	DeKalb (GA) County P.D.	2/1/1972
Deputy Sheriff Lawrence Conley	Floyd (KY) County Sheriff's Office	4/12/1972

Year/Total/Name	Agency	End of Watch
1972		
Officer Phillip Cardillo	New York (NY) P.D.	4/14/1972
Policeman Robert L. Gallowitch	Chicago (IL) P.D.	5/24/1972
Officer Fred Early	Los Angeles (CA) P.D.	9/9/1972
Corrections Officer Jesus Sanchez	California Dept. of Corrections (CA)	10/6/1972
1973		
Patrolman Tommy Ray	Louisville (KY) P.D.	3/17/1973
Captain Larry Gene Beery	Kingman (AZ) P.D.	4/15/1973
Trooper Werner Foerster	New Jersey (NJ) State Police	5/2/1973
Officer William Vernon Welch	Fort Worth (TX) P.D.	5/21/1973
Patrolman Thomas Ray Carpenter	Colorado (CO) State Patrol	12/27/1973
1974		
Officer Michael Lee Edwards	Los Angeles (CA) P.D.	5/5/1974
Policeman Eugen Wallace Barge	College Park (GA) P.D.	11/7/1974
Patrolman William Thomas Cribb	Charleston (SC) County P.D.	11/15/1974
1975		
Night Marshal Carter Lee Curry	Doddsville (MS) P.D.	4/2/1975
Police Officer Franke Neal Lewis	Long Beach (CA) P.D.	12/13/1975
Detective Donald Robert Laabs	Manitou Springs (CO) P.D.	12/18/1975
1977		
Policeman John Whitoak Buckley	Arlington (VA) County P.D.	4/15/1977
Patrol Special Ofcr. Joseph W. Boswell	San Francisco (CA) P.D.	5/3/1977
Special Agent Larry E. Boles	Union Pacific (CO) Railroad Police	7/9/1977
Policeman Vito A. Chiaramonte	New York (NY) Housing Authority	9/26/1977
1978		
Sgt. Robert Jackson	Dothan (AL) P.D.	1/31/1978
Agent Jose Paz Gamez, Jr.	U.S. Dept. of Justice-Immigration-Border P.	4/21/1978
Sgt. Louis Henry Wagner, II	St. Tammany (LA) Parrish Sheriff's Office	6/3/1978
Police Officer Ronald E. Pope	Prichard (AL) P.D.	8/12/1978
Deputy Sheriff Juan Leo Ortiz	San Miguel (NM) County Sheriff's Dept.	9/17/1978
1979		
Deputy Constable Ricky Steven Lewis	Hidalgo (TX) County Constable's Ofc. P3	2/17/1979
1980		
Officer Alfred Morris Johnson, Jr.	Atlanta (GA) P.D.	2/16/1980
Deputy Sheriff Eugene N. Luther	Sacramento (CA) County Sheriff's Dept.	4/25/1980
Chief of Police Gregory B. Adams	Saxonburg (PA) Borough P.D.	12/4/1980
Corporal Robert G. Owen	Erie (PA) P.D.	12/28/1980
1981		
Police Officer Henry David McCall	Frostproof (FL) P.D.	3/5/1981
Patrolwoman Kathleen Garcia	Denver (CO) P.D.	3/28/1981
Officer Kenneth E. Bateman, Jr.	Darien (CT) P.D.	5/31/1981
1982		
Regional Admin. Rodolfo Felix Guillen, Jr.	Virginia (VA) Department of Corrections	6/14/1982
Officer Robert W. Yesucevitz	U.S. Gen. Services Admin. Fed. Prot. (MA)	7/20/1982
Sgt. Vincent Tyrone Tatum	Nevada (NV) Department of Corrections	9/2/1982
Officer William S. Hart	Hallandale (FL) P.D.	12/22/1982
1983		
Auxiliary Sgt Denis P. Foley	Will (IL) County Sheriff's Office	7/16/1983
Officer Lowell Clayton Tribble	Farmers Branch (TX) P.D.	8/27/1983

Year/Total/Name	Agency	End of Watch
1984		
Park Police Ofcr. Howard Shao Wai Huang	L.A. (CA) County Dept. of Parks & Rec.	3/11/1984
Det. Garland Lindwood Joyner, Jr	Portsmouth (VA) P.D.	3/18/1984
Deputy Sheriff Carnie F. Hopkins	Livingston (KY) County Sheriff's Dept.	9/9/1984
1985		
Chief of Police John William Mann	Trafford (AL) P.D.	5/20/1985
Officer Michael Erdahl	Washington State Dept. of Corr. (WA)	5/29/1985
1986		
Officer Kenneth Shawn McWethy	Albuquerque (NM) P.D.	2/1/1986
Patrol Officer Glenn R. Miles, Sr.	U.S. Dept. Of Treasury-Customs Service	2/21/1986
Chief of Police Murray W. Griffin	Belle Center (OH) P.D.	7/5/1986
1987		
Deputy Sheriff Charlie R. Anderson	Los Angeles (CA) Sheriff's Dept.	1/24/1987
Officer Kenneth Stanley Baldwin	Okaloosa (FL) County Airports P.D.	9/11/1987
1988		
Police Officer Jerry L. Hartless	San Diego (CA) P.D.	1/9/1988
Patrolman Stephen A. Sandlin	Mountainair (NM) P.D.	5/7/1988
Police Officer Ronald Hearn	U.S. Dept. Veterans Affairs Police Services	7/25/1988
Town Marshal Bobby R. Moore, Sr.	Fremont (IN) P.D.	7/26/1988
Lt. Thurman Earl Sharp	Marion (IN) County Sheriff's Dept.	12/15/1988
Trooper Johnny Montague Edrington	Kentucky (KY) State Police	12/21/1988
1989		
Police Officer Mark Anthony Williams	Knoxville (TN) P.D.	7/7/1989
1990		
Deputy Patrick Kelly Behan	Broward (FL) County Sheriff's Office	11/13/1990
Lieutenant Cecilia M. Cipriani-Benefiel	El Paso (CO) County Sheriff's Office	11/16/1990
1991		
Officer Eric King Wilson	Aberdeen (MS) P.D.	3/17/1991
1992		
Capt. James Rodriguez	New York Health & Hospital Police (NY)	3/26/1992
Officer William Gary Coffey	Poughkeepsie (NY) P.D.	5/20/1992
1993		
Master Officer Howard Ellsworth Dallies, Jr.	Garden Grove (CA) P.D.	3/9/1993
1995		
Patrol Deputy Wilburn Junior Agy	Liberty (TX) County Sheriff's Dept.	4/5/1995
Det. Lonnie C. Miller, Sr.	Jacksonville (FL) County Sheriff's Office	5/6/1995
1996		
Police Officer Brian Craig Roshong	Canton (OH) P.D.	7/20/1996
1997		
Chief of Police Bobby Spencer	Shannon (MS) P.D.	1/18/1997
1999		
Officer Davina Buff Jones	Bald Head Island (NC) P.D.	10/22/1999
Police Officer Kevin Brame	Dayton (OH) P.D.	11/1/1999
2002		
Officer Joseph Jerome Daniels	Birmingham (AL) P.D.	11/18/2002

Year/Total/Name	Agency	End of Watch
2006		
Police Officer Thomas T. Wood	*Maywood (IL) P.D.*	*10/23/2006*
Deputy Jeffrey Vaughn Mitchell	Sacramento (CA) County Sheriff's Dept.	*10/27/2006*
2007		
Officer Jose Vazquez	Chicago (IL) P.D.	2/12/2007
Corrections Officer Tyvon Whitford	Gainesville (FL) County Sheriff's Dept.	6/8/2007
Sgt. Christopher Reyka	Broward (FL) County Sheriff's Office	8/10/2007
2010		
Sgt Sean Drenth	Phoenix (AZ) P.D.	10/18/2010
2013		
Officer Jason Scott Ellis	Bardstown (KY) P.D.	5/25/2013
2017		
Det. Sean Matthew Suiter	Baltimore (Maryland) P.D.	11/16/2017
Agent Rogelio Martinez*	U.S. Dept. of Homeland Sec. Border Patrol	11/19/2017
Police Officer Donald O. Kimbrough+	Detroit (MI) P.D.	12/7/2017

*As *Unsolved* goes to the printers, Border Patrol Agent Martinez, accordingly to many law enforcement agencies, was killed while on duty. The investigation continues.
+Officer Kimbrough succumbed to complications from gunshot wounds suffered in 1972.

APPENDIX II

YEAR-BY-YEAR BREAKDOWN OF U.S. LAW ENFORCEMENT DEATHS COMPARED TO UNSOLVED LAW ENFORCEMENT HOMICIDES

Year-by-Year Breakdown of U.S. Law Enforcement Deaths Compared Unsolved Law Enforcement Homicides

Year	Deaths	Unsolved	Year	Deaths	Unsolved
1852	5	1	1897	48	3
1853	7	1	1898	72	9
1854	10	0	1899	65	6
1855	8	0	1900	70	4
1856	9	1	1901	84	10
1857	14	1	1902	89	1
1858	13	0	1903	89	10
1859	9	0	1904	84	1
1860	9	0	1905	74	8
1861	9	1	1906	87	5
1862	5	0	1907	98	15
1863	12	0	1908	126	21
1864	12	4	1909	90	8
1865	9	3	1910	105	7
1866	16	1	1911	132	16
1867	18	3	1912	108	14
1868	17	5	1913	121	12
1869	28	3	1914	118	9
1870	21	1	1915	138	17
1871	21	2	1916	164	9
1872	25	8	1917	173	19
1873	22	4	1918	173	8
1874	28	2	1919	218	20
1875	17	1	1920	202	15
1876	29	0	1921	245	23
1877	21	1	1922	244	20
1878	45	1	1923	223	8
1879	26	3	1924	263	6
1880	33	2	1925	250	15
1881	45	7	1926	241	7
1882	44	6	1927	272	10
1883	40	5	1928	253	15
1884	44	4	1929	268	14
1885	54	5	1930	307	9
1886	48	2	1931	265	15
1887	39	4	1932	277	11
1888	58	6	1933	227	5
1889	41	1	1934	243	3
1890	58	1	1935	222	7
1891	53	3	1936	198	7
1892	65	6	1937	191	5
1893	56	6	1938	191	5
1894	65	6	1939	123	1
1895	61	2	1940	134	4
1896	49	1	1941	143	0

Year-by-Year Breakdown of U.S. Law Enforcement Deaths Compared to Unsolved Law Enforcement Homicides

Year	Deaths	Unsolved	Year	Deaths	Unsolved
1942	125	3	1986	179	3
1943	87	0	1987	183	2
1944	93	2	1988	196	6
1945	114	1	1989	195	1
1946	140	0	1990	162	2
1947	128	7	1991	149	1
1948	139	2	1992	163	2
1949	107	3	1993	158	1
1950	116	0	1994	179	0
1951	137	5	1995	184	2
1952	119	3	1996	140	1
1953	120	2	1997	173	1
1954	137	4	1998	172	0
1955	121	1	1999	146	2
1956	108	0	2000	162	0
1957	120	1	2001	242	0
1958	113	5	2002	159	1
1959	110	2	2003	150	0
1960	130	1	2004	166	0
1961	141	2	2005	166	0
1962	143	1	2006	160	2
1963	137	2	2007	202	3
1964	151	1	2008	159	0
1965	139	1	2009	135	0
1966	162	0	2010	169	1
1967	194	6	2011	178	0
1968	193	2	2012	137	0
1969	195	3	2013	116	1
1970	223	6	2014	136	0
1971	248	9	2015	137	0
1972	228	8	2016	143	0
1973	276	5	2017	129	3
1974	280	3			
1975	240	3	Total	21,126	708
1976	202	0			
1977	196	4			
1978	215	5			
1979	217	1			
1980	207	4			
1981	203	3			
1982	195	4			
1983	193	2			
1984	185	3			
1985	176	2			

INDEX

Adams, Gregory B., 246
  Agway Supermarket, 246
  Beachem, Joseph, 249
  beaten and shot to death, 246-249
  FBI 10 Most Wanted List, 247, 248
  Saxonburg Borough (PA) PD., 246-249
Alabama, 299
  Birmingham PD., 297
  Mobile PD., 23
Alaska, 76
  Anchorage Police Department, 76-78
Allen, Joseph N., 34-35
  Brockman, Charles, 35
  Fort Collins (CO) PD., 76-78
  killed with a brick, 34
  The Jungle, 34, 35
Ambush of law enforcement ofcrs., xii, xiii, 52, 130, 206, 208, 213, 259, 323
Anderson, Charles R., 273-275
  Anderson, Beth, 273, 274
  Belisle, Trish, 275
  killed with a handgun, 274
  Los Angeles (CA) Sheriff's Dept., 273-275
  Mason, Roger, 274
Arizona, iv, 268
  Nogales PD., 4
  Phoenix PD., 316
Arizona Territory, 4
Assassination, 189, 190, 199, 220, 221, 222,

Baldwin, Kenneth Stanley, 271-272
  Gilbert, Larry, 272
  killed with handgun, run over with an automobile, 272
  Okaloosa County (FL) Airport PD., 271
  WEAR-TV, 272

Ball, Claude R., 26-27
  Calhoun County (WV), 26
  killed with a rifle, 26
  The Hur Herald, 27
  truancy, 26
  Weaver, Bob, 27
Bank robbery, 131, 157, 159
Barrett, William Harrell, 213-214
  Adams, Tim, 214
  Kentucky State Police, 213
  killed with a shotgun, 213
Bassett, Arthur H., 89-91
  ambushed, 90
  killed by a handgun, 90
  Rockford (IL) PD., 89
Behind the Badge Foundation, 156
Bell, Edward, P., Colorado Ranger, 81-82
  beaten to death, 82
  Colorado Law Enforcement Memorial, 82
  Harley-Davidson motorcycles, 81, 82
  Jennings, George, 81, 82
  Limon, Colorado, 81
Black Liberation Army, xii, 219, 220, 221
Black Lives Matter, 204
Black Panther Party, xi, 189, 191, 193, 208, 219
Bomb, x, 64, 74-75, 136-138, 219, 229, 303
Bootleggers, x, 81-83, 92, 100, 112, 114, 153
Bratton, William, iv
Brooks, David, 43-46
  Bradish, Avery, 45
  Central Station, 44
  Galloway, Alexander, 45
  killed with handgun, 44
  Los Angeles PD., 43
  University Station, 43, 45
Brown, Ulysses, 210-212
  Detroit (MI) PD., 210
  Hall, Renee, 211, 212
  killed by a handgun, 210

Burchfield, Richard S., 148-150
  Colorado Springs (CO) PD., 148
  killed with a handgun, 148
  McVay, Robert, 148-149
  Thanksgiving, 148

California, 41, 66, 67, 131, 201, 275
  Berkeley PD., 189
  Burbank Police PD., 273
  California Asian Peace Ofcrs. Assoc., 192
  Davis PD., 167
  El Segundo, PD., xvi
  Garden Grove PD., 281
  Long Beach PD., 236
  Los Angeles County, 259
  Los Angeles Dept. Parks & Rec. PD., 259
  Los Angeles PD., iv, vii, 43, 109, 215, 227
  Los Angeles Sheriff's Department, 273
  Manhattan Beach, xvi
  Plymouth, 300
  Riverside PD., 206
  Sacramento County Sheriff's Dept., 300
  San Francisco, 67, 191, 202, 220
  University of California
  Irvine Medical Center, 282
Cantrill, Douglas Eugene, 167-167
  Davis (CA) PD., 167
  killed by a handgun, 167
  Mentink, Victor, 167
  Southern Pacific Railroad, 167
Carpenter, Thomas, Ray, 224-226
  Campbell, Ian, 224
  Colorado State Patrol, 224
  Hettinger, Karl, 224
  kidnapped, 224-225
  killed with a handgun, 225
  Myers, James T., 226
  Onion Field, The, 224
Christiansen, Leonard A., 206-209
  also see Teel, Paul, 206
  ambush, 206-207

Black Panther Party, 208
Christiansen, Steve, 209
Communist Party of the United States, 208
  killed by a shotgun, 207
  Pentagon Papers, 208
  Riverside (CA) PD., 206
Civil Rights Movement, 172, 182, 185
Clark, Seymore L., 41-43
  Castleton, Melissa Ladene, 41
  killed with handgun, 40
  Murphy, John, 40, 41
  railroad, 41
  Smith, Robert Elbert, 41
  Weber County (UT) Sheriff's Dept., 41
Cione, Frederick J., 197-200
  assassination, 198
  Cione, Nick, 197, 199
  Gallagher, Charles, 199
  killed with a handgun, 198
  La Salle University, 199
  Philadelphia (PA) PD., 197
  Rizzo, Frank, 197
Colorado, 131, 225
  Broomfield district,
  Colorado Law Enforcement Memorial, 82
  Colorado Rangers, ix
  Colorado Springs PD., 148
  Colorado State Patrol, 224
  Denver PD., 250
  Fort Collins PD., 34
  Greeley, 201
  Limon, 81
  Loveland PD., 59
  St. James Catholic Church, 226
Connecticut, 204
  Connecticut National Guard, 20
  Connecticut Railway & Lighting Co., 20
  Waterbury PD., 20
Coniff, George, 118-124
  Bamonte, Tony, 120, 121, 122, 123
  Black, Elmer, 119, 120
  Giles, William M., 120

Unsolved, Cold-Case Homicides   352

Holmes, Darrell O., 120
Keogh, Pearl, 123
killed with a handgun, 119
Mangan, Dan, 120
Mother's Kitchen, 119, 121, 122, 123
  Newport (WA) PD., 118
  Ralstin, Clyde, 118, 119, 121, 123
  Sonnabend, Charles, 119, 120, 121
  Spokane PD., 118
  Spokane River, 121
  Washington Crime Laboratory, 122
Connolly, Michael Thomas, 112-114
  assault-drowning, 113
  Great Depression, 112
  Portland (ME) PD., 112
  Prohibition, 112
  rumrunners, 112, 113
Counterfeiting, 2
Cribb, William, T., 233-235
  Charleston County (SC) PD., 233
  Comen, Howie, 234, 235
  Cribb, Winifred, 234
  killed by handgun, 233
  robbery, 233
  Sam's Red & White Grocery store, 233
  Thompkins, Grover, 233
Cuba, 201, 202, 203, 204
  Havana, 203
Cunliffe, William Henry, 47-49
  killed with handgun, 48
  Royal Canadian Mounted Police, 47
  Seattle (WA) PD., 47

Dallies, Howard E. Jr., 281-284
  Garden Grove (CA) PD., 281
  killed with a handgun, 282
  motorcyclist, 281, 282
Daniels, Joseph J., 297-299
  Birmingham (AL) PD., 297
  Jacobs, Jody, 298
  killed with a handgun, 297
  Reno Chicken & Burgers, 297
  Roberts, Joe, 299
  Roper, A.C., 298

Dayton, Louis H., 98-101
  beaten to death, 98
  Clay County (IA) Sheriff's Office, 98
  Jensen, Emma, 98, 99, 100
  Spencer (IA), 98
Doxsie, Pitt M., 9-12
  Buchanan County Sheriff, 9
  Higbee, W.M., 11
  horse racing, 9
  Independence (IA), 9
  killed with a handgun, 10
  McClellan, Pitt, 11
  Pinkerton detective, 11
Drenth, Sean, T., 316-320
  Arizona State Capital, 316
  Colvin, Jon, 318
  DiMaio, Vincent, Dr., 318
  forensic psychiatrist, 318, 319
  killed with his own shotgun, 316, 317
  Lyon, Robert, Dr., 317
  pathologist, 317, 318, 319
  Pension Board, 318, 319
  Phoenix (AZ) PD., 316
  Rubin, Paul, *Phoenix New Times*, 318

Early, Fred H., 215-218
  Ashworth, Hollie, 217
  beaten and shot with a handgun, 216
  Bonnee, Michelle, 217
  Los Angeles City Council, 216
  Los Angeles (CA) PD., 215
  Medal of Valor, 217
  Parino, Roseanne, 217
  Reagan, Ronald, 216
  UCLA Medical Center, 216
Edwards, Michael, Lee, 227-232
  Coulter, Paul, 229
  DuPree, Daryn, 228, 231
  Edwards, Tobie, 227, 230, 231, 232
  Kilcoyne, Dennis, 229, 230
  killed with a handgun, 228
  Las Vegas (Nevada) Metro. Police, 229
  Long Beach, 227, 230

Los Angeles (CA) PD., 227
Los Angeles County Sheriff's Dept., 229
Los Angeles Police Academy, 227
Pearson, Bill, 230, 231
Sanchez, Rosemary, 229
Symbionese Liberation Army, 229
Ellis, Jason S., 321-324
Bardstown (KY) PD., 321
Ellis, Amy, 323
Exit 34, Bluegrass Parkway, 321, 322
Kentucky State Police, 323
killed by a shotgun, 322
Meadley, Michael, 323
Monroe, Chad, 322
police officer of the year, 321
Riley, Andrew, 323
Thompson, Jeremy, 323
Federal Bureau of Investigation, xvi, xvii, 149,158, 174, 230, 247, 248, 249, 255, 264, 269, 272
10 Most Wanted List, 247, 248
Ferguson, Hubbard "Hub," 151-154
bootleggers, 153
Carlton, U.P., 153
Chapman, Charlie, 154
Cleveland, Frank, 153
farming, 151
Gallatin County (KY) Sheriff's Dept., 151
Gallatin County News, 154
Gordon, Robert K., 153
Heilman, Harlan, 153
killed with a handgun, 153
Spencer, Earl, 154
Wheeler, Clarence, 152
Florida, 309
Broward County Sheriff's Office, 308
Coral Gables PD., 176
Eglin Air Force Base, 271
Jacksonville Sheriff's Office, 285
Miami-Dade (FL) PD., xvi, 312, 313
Okaloosa County Airport Police, 271
Panhandle, 271

Pompano Beach, 308
Foster, Gregory, P., 219-223
also see Laurie, Rocco, 219
Black Liberation Army (BLA), 219, 220, 221
Black Panthers, 219
killed with multiple handguns, 220
Mills, Jasper, 222
NYPD, 219

Gangs, 9, 115, 161, 323
Gangsters, 54, 81, 84
Garcia, Kathleen, viii, 250-253
Denver Police Department, 250
District 1 police station, 250
Garcia, Kathryn, 251
killed with a handgun, 250-251
Georgia, 165
Atlanta Police Department, 240
Augusta Police Department, 164
Gonser, Raymond, vi, 185-188
Civil Rights Movement, 185
Freeman, Tom, 186
killed by a rifle, 186
Knight, John, 186
Malcolm X, 185
Michigan State Police, 185
riots, 185
Good Government League, 162
Gould, John, "Jay," 83-85
bootleggers, 83
hijackers, 83
killed by a shotgun, 84
Malcolm, James, 84
Oxford Savings Bank, 84
Oxford Village (MI) PD., 83
Purple Gang, 83
Solwold, Michael, 84
Great Depression, 112, 115, 118, 126, 133
Griffin, Murray W., 266-270
Belle Center Village (OH) PD., 266
Griffin, Jody, 266, 267, 267, 269
killed with his own weapon, 267
Logan County Prosecutor's Office, 269

Logan County Sheriff's
Department, 267
  Mullet, Phyllis, 267, 269

Haggerty, Charles, 23-25
  Hodge, Roy, 24
  killed with handgun, 24
  Mobile (AL) PD., 23
Hamrick, Robert, 193-196
  beaten to death, 194-195
  Chapman, Dennis, 194, 195
  DeWine, Mike, 195
  Jefferson Village, 193
  Martin, Gary, 194
  Roaming Shores (OH) PD., 196
  Rock Creek (OH) PD., 193
  Rock Creek Gang, 193, 195
Hardy, Frank W., 155-160
  bank robbery, 155-157
  Behind the Badge Foundation, 156
  Chase, Vernon, 156-159
  killed by a handgun, 157
  Project Hardy, 160
  Royal Canadian Mounted Police, 159
  Seattle First National Bank, 155
  Seattle (WA) PD., 155
  Slessman, Howard, 156-159
  Vancouver (Canada) PD., 158
Harris, Henry Lee., 57-58
  killed with handgun, 57
  July 4th celebration, 57
  Seattle (WA) PD., 57
Hijacked aircraft, 203
Hobos/Transients, viii, 6, 28, 50, 114
Huang, Howard Shao Wai, 259-260
  Elliott, Charles, 260
  killed with an assault rifle, 259
  L.A. (CA) Dept. of Parks & Rec., 259
  Moore, Carl, 260
  Willowbrook, CA., 259

Illinois
  Alton Police Department, 125
  Champaign Police Department, 179
  Chicago Police Department, 146
  Edwardsville, 127
  Maywood Police Department, 303
  Monmouth, 7
  Rockford Police Department, 89
Indiana, 268
  Indianapolis PD., 79, 80, 92, 93, 94, 95, 96, 97
Industrial Workers of the World, 58,
Iowa, x, 7, 8, 52, 62, 86, 87, 116
  Alton Marshal's Office, 50, 51
  Clarinda, 33
  Clay County (Iowa) Sheriff's Ofc., 98
  Council Bluffs PD., 31
  Des Moines PD., 69
  Fruitland, 7
  Independence PD., 9, 11
  Iowa City PD., 86, 88
  Iowa State Bureau of Criminal Invest., 170
  Minburn Police Department, 115
  Muscatine PD., 6
  Plainfield Police Department, 169
  Polk County, 70
  Spencer, 98
  Washington, 100
  Waterloo PD., 36

John F. Kennedy Library, 254
Johnson, Alfred, Morris, Jr., 240-242
  Atlanta (GA) PD., 240
  Big Buy supermarket, 241
  killed with a handgun, 240-241
  Harris, Ponce, 240, 241, 242
  Slaton, Lewis, 242
  Velazquez, Vince, 242
Jones, Davina Buff, 292-296
  Bald Head Island (NC) PD., 292
  Brunswick County (NC) Sheriff's Dept., 292-293
  David, Jon, 295
  Gore, Rex, 294, 295
  Grasty, Karen, 294
  killed with her own handgun, 293

North Carolina Industrial
Commission, 294
  psychiatrist, 293
Joyner, Garland Linwood, 261-265
  case reopened, 262, 264
  Franklin, Billy, 263, 264
  Huntington, Robert, 264
  Joyner, Lillie, 263
  killed by gunfire, 261-263
  Portsmouth (VA) PD., 263, 264
  Warwick Swamp, 261, 264

K9, 176, 303, 321
Kaschmitter, Joseph, 50-52
  Alton (IA) Marshal's Office, 50
  hobos, 50-51
  killed with handgun, 51
  railroad, 50-51
Kemp, George Arnold, 142-145
  Davidson County Sheriff's Ofc., 143
  First National Bank, 142-144
  killed by assault, 143-144
  Loftin, W.C., 143
  North Carolina State Highway
Patrol, 143
  Thomasville (NC) PD., 142
  poker games, 142
  Pope, R.L., 143
Kentucky, 97, 151
  Bardstown Police Department, 321
  Gallatin County Sheriff's Dept., 151
  Kentucky State Police, 213, 214, 32
Kidnapped, xii, 127, 224, 225, 229
Kost, Lawrence E., 64-68
  automobile bandits, 66
  Cook, Frederick, 67, 70
  Kent, William B., 66
  killed with handgun, 65
  Los Angeles Police Department, 66
  Moline Drugstore, 64, 66
  San Francisco, 67
  Seattle Daily Times, 64
  Seattle (WA) PD., 64
  Smith, Lyle, 65
Ku Klux Klan, 172
Kuba, Louis R., 182-184

Bird, Ronnie, 183
Civil Rights Movement, 182
Houston (TX) PD., 182
killed by a sniper, 183
riot, 183
Short, Herman, 182
Texas Southern University, 182-183
Vietnam, 183

Laurie, Rocco W., 219-223
  also see Foster, Gregory, 219
  Black Liberation Army (BLA), xii,
219, 220, 221
  Black Panthers, 219
  killed with multiple handguns, 220
  Laurie, Adelaide, 222
  Metropolitan Police of St. Louis,
221
  Mills, Jasper, 221
  NYPD, 219, 220, 221, 222
Leeney, Edward M., 86-88
  Hargadine, Sam, 87
  killed during pursuit
  Iowa City (IA) PD., 86
Lewis, Franke, Neal, 236-239
  Gitschier, Denis, 236, 237, 238
  killed with a hand gun, 237
  Lewis, Linda, 237
  Long Beach (CA) PD., 236
Los Angeles Police Department, iv,
vii, 43, 109, 215, 227,
  Medal of Valor, 217
  SWAT, 229, 313
Los Angeles Police Protective League,
216
Louisiana, xvi,
  Louisiana Highway 21, 173
  Washington Parish Sheriff's Ofc.,
172
Luton, Edward, 102-104
  beaten to death, 103
  Hamilton (WA) Marshal's Office,
102
  Luton, Bessie, 103
  United States Constitution, 102
Lynch, Joseph J., 136-139

also see Socha, Ferdinand, 136
  killed by bomb, 138
  Morelock, Frederick, 137
  New York World's Fair, 136
  NYPD., 136
Maine, 112
  Portland Police Department, 112
Marine Corps, 160, 187, 240, 314
Massachusetts, 254
Mattern, George William, 69-71
  Des Moines (IA) PD., 69
  killed with handgun, 69
  Temp, the, 69, 70
Mayer, Charles "Karl," 16-19
  Gerver, Paul, 16
  killed with handguns, 16
  nitroglycerine, 16, 17
  Smith, Lafayette, 17
  stagecoach robbery, 18
  St. Paul (MN) PD., 16
Mayford, August, 125-127
  Alton (IL) PD., 125
  beaten and shot to death, 126
  Barkely, Claude, 126
  "door rattler," 126
  Edwardsville, Illinois, 127
  Faulstitch Cigar store, 126
  Uhle, J., 126
Meadows, William L., 169-171
  Buckman, Ernest, Mrs., 169, 170, 171
  burglary tools, 170
  Hartman Packing Plant, 169-170
  Iowa St. Bureau of Criminal Invest., 170
  killed by a rifle, 170
  nitroglycerin, 171
  Plainfield (IA) PD., 169
Mendelssohn, Paul, 20-22
  Connecticut National Guard, 20
  Connecticut Railway & Lighting Co., 20
  killed with handguns, 20-21
  New Haven County Sheriff's Dept., 21
  strikebreaking, 21

  trolley, 20-21
  Waterbury (CT) PD., 20
Mexico, 4, 5
Michigan,
  Detroit Police Department, 210
  Inkster, 185
  Michigan State Police, 185, 186, 187
  Oxford PD., 83
Miller, Lonnie C., 285-287
  Corey, Angela, 286
  Democratic Executive Committee, 285
  Jacksonville (FL) Sheriff's Office, 285
  killed with a handgun, 286
  National Council of Negro Women, 285
  Shah, Abdullah, 285-286
Miller, Paul, 95-97
  also see Schoen, Norman, 95
  Banks, John, 95-96
  Indianapolis (IN) PD., 95
  killed by a handgun, 95
  Schaller & Cole drugstore, 95
  Substation No 6, 95
Milwaukee (WI) Police Dept., second most-deadliest day in law enforcement, 72-75
  killed by a bomb were: Det. Frank Caswin,
  Det. Frederick Kaiser, Det. David J. O'Brien, Det. Charles Seehawer, Operator Edward Spindler,
  Det. Stephen Stecker, Det. Albert Templin, Station Keeper Henry Deckert,
  Det. Paul Weiler
Minnesota, 160
  Duluth, 275
  Fergus Falls, 58
  St. Paul PD., 16
Mississippi, 6, 173, 289
  Mississippi Bureau of Invest., 289
  Mississippi Highway Patrol, 290
  Shannon Police Department, 288
Missouri, 32

Kansas City PD., 53
Metropolitan Police of St. Louis
St. Louis, 2
Mitchell, Jeffrey V., 300-302
　Cosumnes River, 301
　McGuinness, John, 301
　Meiss and Dillard roads, 301
　Sacramento County (CA) Sheriff's Dept., 300
　shot with his own handgun, 300-301
　Turnbull, Tony, 301
Montana, 15, 76, 77, 119, 123
　Garrison, 13
　Livingston, 14
　Park County Sheriff's Office, 13
　Springdale, 13, 14
Moore, O'Neal, 172-175
　Bogalusa, Washington Parrish, 172, 174
　Civil Rights Movement, 172
　killed by a shotgun and rifle, 173
　Ku Klux Klan, 174
　Moore, Maevella, 174
　National States Rights Party, 174
　Rogers, David, 172, 173, 174
　Semitic Citizens Councils of America, 174
　Washington Parish (LA) Sheriff's Ofc., 172
Motorcycle, 81, 82, 86, 87, 105, 164, 243, 282
Muller, Peter Jr., 109-110
　bootleggers, 109, 110
　Georgia Street Station, 110
　killed with a handgun, 110
　Los Angeles PD., 109
　Tucker, Mildred, 110

National Committee to Combat Fascism, 190
National Law Enforcement
　Ofcrs. Memorial, Washington, D.C., vii, 24, 295, 328
National States Rights Party, 174
National Police Collectors Show, 146
Nebraska, 128, 131

Boone County Sheriff's Dept., 128
Nebraska State Patrol, 180
Neibert, Jacob, 6-8
New Mexico, 203
　Albuquerque, 201, 203
　Albuquerque International Airport, 203
　Bernalillo County Sheriff's Dept., 202
　Mountainair Police Department, 276
　New Mexico Attorney Gen. Ofc., 277
　New Mexico State Police, 201
　Torrance County Sheriff's Ofc., 278
New York, 54, 102, 204, 234
　British Pavilion, N.Y. World's Fair, 136
　East Village, 220
　Nassau County PD., 140
　New York PD., 136, 140, 219
　　Emergency Service Squad, 137
Nitroglycerin, 16, 17, 171
North Carolina, 142, 261, 264, 292, 293
　Bald Head Island PD., 292
　Davidson County Sheriff's Office, First National Bank, Thomasville, 142
　Gloucester, 263
　North Carolina Industrial Comm., 294
　State Highway Patrol, 143
　Thomasville Police Department, 142
North Dakota, 28
　Sanborn, 28
　Valley City PD., 28, 29

Officer Down Memorial Page, vii, 163, 187, 328
"Off the pig," 189
Ohio, 45, 70, 77, 151, 195, 268
　Belle Center Village PD., 266
　Cincinnati, 151, 153,
　Cincinnati Police Department, 1, 2
　Lima, 270

Logan County Sheriff's Dept., 267, 269
Rock Creek Police Department, 193
Owen, Robert, Glen, 243-245
  Bowers, Charles, 243
  Cambra, David, 243, 245
  Erie (PA) PD., 243
  killed with his own weapon, 243
Peace Officer Memorial Day, 166
Peak, Frank, 59-63
  English Ditch, ix, 59, 62
  killed with handgun, 61
  Loveland (Colorado) Police Department, 59
  Loveland Daily Herald, 60, 61
  Rosenburg, Alan, 60, 61, 62
Pennsylvania,
  Allison, 177
  Erie PD., 243
  Philadelphia Police Department, 197
  Saxonburg Borough PD., 246
Personius, Herman Myron, "Blackie," 28, 29, 30
  Burt, police chief, 28, 29
  killed with handgun, 29
  Moore, Dan, 29, 32
  vagrants, 28
  Valley City PD., 28
Pinkerton detective, 11
Prohibition related, x, 56, 81, 92, 98, 102, 105, 112,

Radical groups, 58, 193, 201
Raimo, Joseph, 53-56
  assassins, 53
  Black Hand mafia, 53, 54, 55, 56
  gangsters, 54
  Italians, 53
  Kansas City (MO) PD., 53
  killed with shotgun, 54
  Prohibition, 56
  Raimo, Frank, 55
Reddicks, James Duncan, 133-135
  Hardin County (TX) Sheriff's Dept., 133
  killed with a shotgun, 134

movie script, 133
Saratoga, 133
Third Degree, 134
traveling tent show, 133, 134
Republic of New Afrika, 202, 203
Research of a police unsolved homicide, 23
Reyka, Christopher, 308-315
  Broward County (FL) Sheriff's Ofc., 308
  Carlin, Christopher, 312, 313
  killed by handgun, 309
  Lamberti, Al, 309
  Miami-Dade SWAT, 313
  Miller, Michael, *Miami New Times*, 310
  Reyka, Autumn, 314
  Reyka, Sean, 314
  Riemer, Dan, 310
  Somohano, Jose, 312, 313
  Tundidor, Tomas, 313
  Walgreens, 308
  Wright, Jody, 313

Riots, 185, 190, 199
Rogers, R.A. "Bob," 161-163
  also see Wright, James, 161
  Copperhill, 161, 162
  Gibson, Carmel, 161, 162
  Good Government League, 162
  Greene, Emil, 162
  Gregory, Michele, 163
  killed by rifle, 162
  Lewis, W.A., 162, 163
  politically motivated killing, 161
  Polk County (TN) Sheriff's Dept., 161
  Turtletown Grill, 162
Rosenbloom, Robert, 201-205
  Albuquerque, 201, 203, 204
  Albuquerque International Airport, 203
  Arnold, Dennis, 201
  Barker, Larry, 204
  Black Lives Matter, 204
  Castro, Fidel, 203

Cuba, 202, 203, 204
DuBois, Chuck, 202
Holder, Eric, 203
Kerry, John, 203
killed with a handgun, 201
Martinez, Susana, 203
New Mexico State Police, 201, 203
Obama, Barack, 203
political asylum, 202, 203
radicals, 204
Republic of New Afrika, 202, 2032
Trans World Airlines, 203
Trump, Donald, 204
Royal Canadian Mounted Police, 47, 159,
Rumrunners, x, 112, 113

Sandlin, Stephen A., 276-280
  Carnation, James, 278, 279
  Carson, David, 276, 277
  Chung, Robert, 279
  Gillespie, Tom, 278
  killed with his own handgun, 276
  Mountainair (NM) PD., 276
  Torrance County Sheriff's Office, 278
Schoen, Norman L., 92-94
  Bootleggers, 92
  Indianapolis (IN) PD., 92
  killed by handgun, 92
Semitic Citizens Councils of America, 174
Shaw, Charles H., 140-141
  killed by a shotgun, 141
  Kirk, Robert, 140, 141
  Nassau County (NY) PD., 140
  observation arrest, 140
  Woodmere, 140
Shot (law enforcement officer) with own weapon, 76, 241, 251, 255, 267, 313
South Carolina, 233
  Charleston County PD., 233
  Columbia, xvii
  James Island, 233
Smeeman, Harry Valentine,

Ashland (Virginia) PD., 105, 107
Cross Brothers Grocery, 106
Morgan, Ashland, 106
prohibition, 105
Smeeman Award, 107
Smeeman, Mrs., 105
Smoyer, Lawrence I., 128-132
  also see, Wathen, William, 128
  Blankenship, George, 130
  Boone County (NE) Sheriff's Ofc., 128
  killed with a handgun, 129
  Noble, Leonard, 129
  Young family, 128
Socha, Ferdinand, 136-138
  also see Wathen, William 136
  killed by bomb, 138
  Morelock, Frederick, 137
  New York World's Fair, 136
  NYPD, 136
Spencer, Bobby, 288-291
  killed with rifle, 288
  McPherson, James, 288
  Mississippi Bureau of Investigation, (MBI), 289
  Mississippi Highway Patrol, 290
  Shannon (MS) PD., 288
  Trice, Carl, 288, 289
  Whitehead, Steve, 288, 289
Sperakos, George J., 146-147
  Chicago (IL) PD., 146
  Daniels, Dennis, 146
  killed with a handgun, 147
  Kozieniak, Stanley, 146-147
  robbery, 147
Stathers, Walter Franklin, 176-178
  Abrahams' house, 177
  Coral Gables (FL) PD., 176
  Droquett, Bertha, 176
  K9, 176
  killed by gunfire, 176
  Harley, Jim, 177
  prowler, 176, 177
  Smith, Greg, 176
Stoddard, Joseph, 1-3
  Cincinnati (OH) PD., 1

Unsolved, Cold-Case Homicides   360

first unsolved homicide, 1
  killed with a knife, 2
Sturgus, John, J., 76-78
  Anchorage (AK) PD., 76
  Baxter, Mrs., 77
  first police chief, 76
  killed with own weapon, 76
  liquor gang, 77
  McNutt, John, 76,77
  moonshiners, 77
Suicide murder controversy, xiii, xiv, 106, 168, 261, 262, 263, 264, 268, 276, 277, 292, 293, 294, 295, 316, 317, 318, 319,

Tatman, Robert Lawrence, 179-181
  Champaign (IL) PD., 179
  Champaign Police Historical Society, 180
  Jones, J.O., 179
  killed with his own weapon, 179
  Nebraska State Patrol, 180
  Ziegler, Zane, 180, 181
Teel, Paul, 206-209
  also see Christiansen, Leonard, 206
  ambush, 206-207
  Black Panther Party, 208
  Christiansen, Steve, 209
  Communist Party of the United States, 208
  killed by a shotgun, 207
  Pentagon Papers, 208
Tennessee, 161
  Copperhill, 161
  Polk County Sheriff's Department, 161
Texas,
  Dallas Police Department, 211, 212
  Farmers Branch PD., 256
  Hardin County Sheriff's Dept., 133
  Houston Police Department, 182
  Saratoga, 133
  Texas Rangers, 81
  Texas Southern University, 182
Third degree, 134
Train related, see Railroad

Tribble, Lowell Clayton, 256-258
  Bradfield, Jamille, 258
  Farmers Branch (TX) PD., 256
  killed with a handgun, 256
  Shaack, Sheila Tribble, 257
  Tribble, Frances, 256, 258
  Watkins, Craig, 257
Tsukamoto, Ronald Tsugio, 189-192
  Alameda County District Attorney's Ofc., 191
  assassination, 190
  Baker, Bruce, 190
  Berkeley (CA) PD., 189
  Black Panther Party, 189
  internment camp, 191
  killed with a hand gun, 190
  Lopes, Russ, 190, 191
  National Committee to Combat Fascism, 190

United States Constitution, 102
Untied, Virgil P., 115-117
  E.J. Shaw Grocery store, 115, 116
  Hagenstein, Lena, 115
  Hagenstein, William, 115
  killed by a shotgun, 116
  Minburn (IA) PD., 115
  pursuit, 116
  United, Jasper, 116
Utah, 41
  Uintah, 40
  Weber County Sheriff's Dept., 40

Vagrants, see hobos,
Vancouver (Canada) PD., 158
Vietnam War, 189, 222,
Virginia, 264
  Ashland Police Department, 105
  Portsmouth Police Department, 261
  Virginia State Bureau of Invest., 262

Wall, Frank Henderson, Jr., 164-166
  Augusta Chronicle, 164
  Augusta (GA) PD., 164
  Calhoun, Thad, 165
  Georgia Supreme Court, 165

killed with a handgun, 164
motorcycle, 164
Peace Officer Memorial Day, 166
Roundtree, Ricard, 165, 166
Sheehan's package store, 164
Washington, 77, 103, 156, 158
  Behind the Badge Foundation, 156
  Clear Lake, 171
  Everett, 77
  Hamilton Marshal's Office, 102
  Newport Police Department, 118
  Seattle PD., 17, 57, 64, 155
  Seattle First National Bank, 155
  Spokane PD., 118 119, 121, 122
  Washington Crime Laboratory, 122
Wathen, William, 128-132
  also see, Smoyer, Lawrence I, 128
  Blankenship, George, 130
  Boone County (NE) Sheriff's Ofc., 128
  killed with a handgun, 129
  Noble, Leonard, 129
  Young family, 128
West Virginia, 26
  Calhoun County, 26
Whitfield, William, 79-80
  killed with handgun, 79
  Indianapolis (IN) PD., 79
  unmarked grave, 80
Widman, Friedrich, 36-39
  gravestone, 38
  killed with handgun, 37
  Hartman, Tom, 37
  Leighton, E.A., 37
  Waterloo (IA) PD., 36
  Waterloo Reporter, 38
  Waterloo Police Protective Association, 38
  Wilson, Eunice, 38
Wilson, George W., 31-33
  Council Bluffs (IA) PD., 31
  Edmondson Memorial Hospital, 32
  killed with handgun, 31
  Richardson, W.H., 31, 32
Wisconsin, 72
  Milwaukee PD., 72-74

Wood, Thomas T., 303-307
  Chicago Magazine, 306
  killed with a handgun, 305
  Herguth, Robert, 305
  Maywood (IL) PD., 303
  Placko, Dane, 305
  Talley, Valdimir, 307
  West Suburban Major Crimes Task Force, WESTAF, 306
  Williams, Elvia, 306
  Wood, Helene, 303, 307
Wright, James Louis, 161-163
  also see, Rogers, R.A., 161
  Copperhill, 161, 162
  Gibson, Carmel, 161, 162
  Good Government League, 162
  Greene, Emil, 162
  Gregory, Michele, 163
  killed by rifle, 162
  Lewis, W.A., 162, 163
  politically motivated killing, 161
  Polk County (TN) Sheriff's Dept., 161
  Turtletown Grill, 162

Yesucevitz, Robert W., 254-255
  killed with own handgun, 254
  University of Massachusetts, 254
  U.S. General Services Admin. Federal Protection Service, 254
Young, George T., 13-15
  Beaver, E.V., 13
  Bellary, Frank, 13, 14
  Carney, 13, 14
  Garrison (MT), 13
  Logan (CO), 13
  Park County (MT) Sheriff's Ofc., 13
  posse, 15
  Railroad, 13, 14
  shot with handgun, 14
  Springdale (CO), 13, 14

UNSOLVED, COLD-CASE HOMICIDES

www.ingramcontent.com/pod-product-compliance
Lightning Source LLC
Chambersburg PA
CBHW070757020526
44118CB00036B/1808